GEORGE BUSH AND THE GUARDIANSHIP PRESIDENCY

George Bush and the Guardianship Presidency

David Mervin
Reader in Politics
University of Warwick

E
881
.M47
1996

 Published in Great Britain by
MACMILLAN PRESS LTD
Houndmills, Basingstoke, Hampshire RG21 6XS and London
Companies and representatives throughout the world

A catalogue record for this book is available from the British Library.

ISBN 0–333–61354–6 hardcover
ISBN 0–333–73865–9 paperback

Published in the United States of America by
ST. MARTIN'S PRESS, INC.,
Scholarly and Reference Division,
175 Fifth Avenue, New York, N.Y. 10010

ISBN 0–312–12961–0 clothbound
ISBN 0–312–21199–6 paperback

Library of Congress has cataloged the hardcover edition as follows
Mervin, David.
George Bush and the guardianship presidency / David Mervin.
p.   cm.
Includes bibliographical references (p.) and index.
ISBN 0–312–12961–0 (cloth)
1. United States—Politics and government—1989–1993.   2. Bush,
George, 1924–   .   I. Title.
E881.M47 1996
973.928'092—dc20   95–53273
                                                            CIP

© David Mervin 1996, 1998

This book is printed on paper suitable for recycling and made from fully managed and sustained forest sources.

10   9   8   7   6   5   4   3   2   1
07   06   05   04   03   02   01   00   99   98

Printed and bound in Great Britain by
Antony Rowe Ltd, Chippenham, Wiltshire

To Alice

Contents

Preface to the 1998 Reprint

At the conference on the Bush presidency held at Hofstra University in April 1997, doubt was cast on my contention that the physician's maxim of 'Do no harm' was central to an understanding of Bush's approach to governance (see pp. 34, 78 and 158). I should, perhaps, have supported my assertion more fully in the original hardback edition of this book, for the evidence is substantial. C. Boyden Gray, Counsel to the President, and one of those closest to George Bush, told me in an interview, 'President Bush's view about this is . . . the very first thing you do – and if you can't do this you ought not to be in government at all – is do no harm. It's sort of a first rule of a doctor, it's also the first rule of a public official. First, do no harm.' President Bush himself, in a speech in North Carolina on 15 November 1991, said 'Let me tell you what we won't do. The first rule of economic policy puts me in mind to (*sic*) the Hippocratic Oath: Do no harm.' Similarly, on 9 March 1992, the President, in speaking about welfare dependency, said 'The government's first duty is like that of the physician: Do no harm.'

DAVID MERVIN

Preface

This book is not, in any sense, a biography of George Bush; it is rather a narrowly focused study of his presidency. Considerations of relevance and the relatively few words available precluded dealing with many matters that others might find of interest in Bush's incumbency. For instance, my coverage of foreign policy issues is somewhat limited in scope and there is nothing here on Bush's alleged role in the Iran-Contra affair. Similarly, one of the great dramas of the period, Clarence Thomas's nomination to the US Supreme Court, receives only cursory mention.

My purposes in writing this book have been threefold. First, to scrutinize Bush's presidency on his own terms, to attempt, in other words, to understand how he saw his office and what he sought to achieve. Second, to consider how far Bush succeeded in meeting the monumental challenges that all presidents face in seeking to impose their priorities on what Richard Neustadt aptly characterizes as 'that maze of personalities and institutions and individuals called the government of the United States'. My third purpose has been to use the Bush example as a vehicle for a modest contribution to the study of the presidency in a more general sense.

Like other authors, I have had a lot of help. I am most grateful to the British Academy for their award of a research grant. I am indebted also to the University of Warwick for both additional financial assistance and the study leave necessary for the conduct of the research for this book.

Interviews with senior White House staff constitute the core of the research for this study. Not all my requests for interviews were successful, but most were and those that agreed to talk to me are listed on pages xiii–xiv. The kindness and cooperation I uniformly received from these people was extraordinary. They spoke frankly and at length about their experiences at the highest levels of the Bush Administration and, in so doing, contributed much to my understanding. In some cases they agreed to be interviewed more than once and others kindly met my convenience by coming to my hotel for the interviews.

Almost all of these conversations were taped and, in each case, they were conducted 'on background'. Accordingly, I agreed that I would not quote any interviewee in an identifiable way without checking with them first. This process led to some useful clarifications. It also caused me to remove one throwaway line while, in a handful of instances, sensitive comments have been made anonymous. It must be emphasized, however, that responsibility for the interpretation placed on these interviews rests with me alone.

The tapes and transcripts of these interviews are, at present, held by the Bush Presidential Materials Project, 701 University Drive East, Suite 300, College Station, Texas 77840–1899. These items are to be placed in the future Bush Presidential Library and are available to scholars under the conditions indicated in the previous paragraph.

This research also included conversations with a number of other authoritative sources including Louis Fisher of the Congressional Research Service; Jeff Eisenach of the Progress and Freedom Foundation; Terry Eastland of the Ethics and Public Policy Center; Charles Cooper, Assistant Attorney General in the Reagan Administration and Peter Liebold from the staff of Senator John Danforth of Missouri. I am most grateful for the additional help generously provided by these individuals.

My heartfelt thanks are also due to my friend of many years' standing, K. Larry Storrs of the Foreign Affairs Division of the Congressional Research Service at the Library of Congress. The hospitality, help and intellectual stimulation provided by Larry Storrs and his wife EJ made my visits to Washington infinitely more enjoyable and profitable than they would otherwise have been.

In developing my ideas on the Bush presidency I have had the benefit of advice and assistance from many quarters. These include my students at Warwick as well as a variety of friends and colleagues on both sides of the Atlantic. In particular, I was privileged to have the help of two distinguished American students of the presidency – Professor James Pfiffner of George Mason University and Professor Bert Rockman of the University of Pittsburgh. The former plied me with source material while also making most helpful comments on a number of chapters. Bert Rockman, meanwhile, read and commended on the entire manuscript. I am most grateful for all this generosity although, of course, the responsibility for any errors of fact or interpretation is entirely mine.

My appreciation is also due to Hayley Gilder, Secretary of the Department of Politics and International Studies, University of Warwick, for her skilful rendering of interview tapes into transcripts. Finally, and most important of all, I must thank my wife, Dr Kathleen McConnell Mervin, for all that she has contributed in so many different ways.

DAVID MERVIN

List of Interviewees

This research included interviews with the following:

Paul Bateman – Deputy Assistant to the President for Management and Director of the Office of Administration. Interview 15 November 1993.

David Q. Bates – Assistant to the President and Secretary to the Cabinet. Interview 17 November 1993.

Phillip D. Brady – Assistant to the President and Staff Secretary. Interview 15 November 1993.

Nicholas E. Calio – Assistant to the President for Legislative Affairs. Interview 19 November 1993.

Andrew H. Card, Jr. – Assistant to the President and Deputy to the Chief of Staff; subsequently Secretary of Transportation. Interview 15 November 1993.

James W. Cicconi – Assistant to the President and Deputy to the Chief of Staff (Staff Secretary). Interview 8 November 1993.

David F. Demarest, Jr. – Assistant to the President for Communications. Interview 12 November 1993.

C. Boyden Gray – Counsel to the President. Interviews 10 November 1993 and 21 March 1994.

Richard Haass – Special Assistant to the President for National Security Affairs. Interview 24 March 1994.

Edith E. Holiday – Assistant to the President and Secretary to the Cabinet. Interview 17 November 1993.

Constance Horner – Assistant to the President and Director of Presidential Personnel. Interview 10 November 1993.

Ronald C. Kaufman – Deputy Assistant to the President for Presidential Personnel and subsequently Deputy Assistant to the President for Political Affairs. Interview 19 November 1993.

John G. Keller, Jr. – Deputy Assistant to the President and Director of Presidential Advance. Interview 18 November 1993.

Bobbie G. Kilberg – Deputy Assistant to the President for Public Liaison. Interviews 19 November 1993 and 30 March 1994.

Charles E.M. Kolb – Deputy Assistant to the President for Domestic Policy. Interviews 12 November 1993 and 29 March 1994.

William Kristol – Chief of Staff to the Vice President. Interview 23 March 1994.

C. Gregg Petersmeyer – Assistant to the President and Director, Office of National Service. Interview 16 November 1993.

James P. Pinkerton – Deputy Assistant to the President for Policy Planning. Interview 8 November 1993.

Roger B. Porter – Assistant to the President for Economic and Domestic Policy. Interview 23 November 1993.

Edward M. Rogers, Jr. – Deputy Assistant to the President and Executive Assistant to the Chief of Staff. Interview 3 November 1993.

Gen. Brent Scowcroft, USAF (Ret.) – Assistant to the President for National Security Affairs. Interview 28 March 1994.

Katherine Super – Deputy Assistant to the President for Appointments and Scheduling. Interview 16 November 1993.

Gail Wilensky – Deputy Assistant to the President for Policy Development. Interview 14 November 1993.

Clayton Yeutter – Secretary of Agriculture, Chairman of the Republican National Committee and, finally, Counselor to the President for Domestic Policy. Interview 22 March 1994.

Introduction

George Bush, it is widely believed, was a failure in the White House. For some, his inability to gain re-election to a second term is sufficient evidence in itself of a less than successful presidency. Critics can also point to the shortage of significant legislation passed in Bush's name; his failure to address effectively a variety of domestic problems and the anaemic state of the economy at the conclusion of his four years in office. Even George Bush's ostensibly greatest triumph, victory in the Gulf War, has been subjected to savage criticism.[1] However, the calculation of success or failure in the White House is less straightforward than it sometimes seems.

The first thing to be said is that if Bush was a failure in office he hardly stands alone. Remarkably few presidents can be counted as successes, largely because the United States is an extraordinarily difficult country to govern. Governance is not easy anywhere, but the problems in America are especially formidable. They include an anti-authority, anti-leadership political culture; a Constitution that makes for a centrifugal rather than a centripetal distribution of power; an independent judiciary and an awesomely powerful legislative branch. The latter may well be controlled by the opposition, but even when it is not it is a chronically decentralized, individualistic and undisciplined body, full of members close to their constituents, beholden to interest groups, and generally unresponsive to the demands of party loyalty.

Elsewhere in the world, parties facilitate coherence and direction in a political system; they provide means whereby leaders can gain the agreement, the cooperation, or at least the acquiescence, of other leaders in that system. In the US, by contrast, parties are incapable of adequately fulfilling such functions. In the late twentieth century they lack the patronage resources they once commanded, they are largely bereft of serious programmatic commitments and are denied control of the processes whereby candidates are nominated. Parties have relatively little to offer presidents as they struggle to come to grips with the problems of governance.

1

A vast, amorphous federal bureaucracy presents another major area of difficulty for presidents attempting to impose their priorities on the policy-making machinery. The bureaucracy participates in both the formulation and the implementation of policy; however, it is a body led by political appointees whose loyalty to the White House may be questionable and staffed by career civil servants who often have their own agendas and are far less amenable to central direction than many of their counterparts elsewhere in the world.

Since the 1960s at least the media have provided further obstacles to the exercise of presidential power. Presidents now conduct public business and much of their private lives under the constant surveillance of television cameras. News broadcasts have supplanted parties, political meetings and peer group discussions as sources of voting cues for the electorate and television news executives have assumed agenda setting functions. Meanwhile journalists, from both the print and the electronic media, armed with First Amendment freedoms and energized by investigative zeal, have, in recent years, made governance even more difficult than it was in the past.

In addition to the constants mentioned above every chief executive must deal with a unique set of circumstantial variables. Even allowing for the weakness of American political parties a president with comfortable majorities in Congress stands a better chance of achieving his agenda than if the legislature is controlled by the opposition. Similarly, some presidents are elected with large popular vote totals while others fail to win even a majority of the votes cast, a variable that will affect the chances of success or failure in the White House. Furthermore, the combination of opportunities and constraints facing any given president will be dependent on the ethos of the time with president-led governmental action much more acceptable to the American people in some periods than in others.

These are some of the reasons for the modest levels of achievement of those who occupy the White House. They help to account for the fact, noted by John Kennedy, that while the president 'is rightly described as a man of extraordinary powers . . . he must wield those powers under extraordinary limitations . . . Every president must endure a gap between what he would like and what is possible.'[2] Any appraisals of presidents need to incorporate such considerations while, as far as possible, excluding the personal political preferences of the analyst.

The scholarly verdicts on the Bush presidency are not yet in, but it is difficult to believe that they will be favourable; he is most unlikely to perform well in any future presidential 'greatness' poll. While there are ample reasons for criticizing Bush's stewardship, some of which will be explored in this book, it should also be recognized that his conservative, non-activist, guardian approach doomed him from the start to an unsympathetic hearing in the academic community.

THE POLITICS OF ACADEME

There is plenty of hard evidence to support the allegation, often made by Republican politicians, that most academics in the relevant fields are liberals and/or Democrats.[3] For instance a fairly recent poll of the American professoriate found that 88 per cent of 'public affairs' faculty identified themselves as liberals while 12 per cent claimed to be 'middle of the road' and, remarkably, 0 per cent opted for the conservative label. In humanities departments, including history, 76 per cent were liberals, 9 per cent middle of the road and 15 per cent conservatives. Social science faculty, embracing, of course, political scientists, broke down as 72 per cent liberals, 14 per cent middle of the road and 14 per cent conservatives.[4] More specifically, a 1989 poll of members of the Presidency Research Group of the American Political Science Association found that 63.6 per cent identified as Democrats, 19.5 per cent as Republicans and 16 per cent as Independents. Of this same group of presidency specialists, 67.5 per cent voted for Walter Mondale in 1984 as against 23.9 per cent who cast their ballots for Ronald Reagan.[5]

These disparities in the academic community would, of course, be less important if we could be confident that scholars did not allow their personal ideological and partisan preferences to enter into their evaluations of presidents. Reason to doubt whether such restraint is in fact exercised was suggested by another poll among members of the APSA in 1984. This showed first that 76 per cent of American politics specialists were Democrats, but, more interestingly, also revealed that 96 per cent of those who identified as Democrats rated Ronald Reagan's 'overall performance in office' as only fair or poor, whereas 4 per cent adjudged it excellent or good. By contrast, of the Republican identifiers 71 per cent found Reagan's performance to be excellent or good, while 29 per cent deemed it to be poor or fair.[6] It is surely reasonable to conclude that such starkly different collective impressions are likely to have been driven by ideological and partisan considerations.

Historians it would seem are no less culpable in such matters. In the late 1980s, Robert K. Murray and Tim H. Blessing conducted a poll among American historians designed to incorporate President Reagan into earlier presidential 'greatness' rankings. At the end of this rather elaborate exercise involving 481 respondents out of 750 who were sent a detailed questionnaire, Reagan was ranked 28th out of 37 who have served in the White House. Out of six categories (Great, Near Great, Above Average, Below Average and Failure) Reagan was placed in the Below Average group between Zachary Taylor and John Tyler. According to this tabulation Reagan was inferior to chief executives such as Chester Arthur, Benjamin Harrison and William Howard Taft. Furthermore, leaving aside the rather special case of Richard Nixon, Reagan was effectively deemed to be the worst President of the United States in six decades.[7]

This is all rather odd for, irrespective of the merits of his policies and any doubts as to the quality of his intellect, Reagan appears to have been more successful than most modern presidents in imposing his priorities on the political system. His mastery of the process, in other words, despite some unfulfilled ambitions and a few serious set-backs, was, relatively speaking, quite impressive.[8] Murray and Blessing chose not to ask those polled either their political affiliation or what they took into account in making their evaluations, but, as I have argued elsewhere, further examination of their poll data suggests that those polled freely indulged their hostility to Reagan's policies in their evaluations of his presidency.[9]

It is also the case that much of the literature on the presidency is shot through with values and assumptions that lead inevitably to negative evaluations of Republican presidents.

Two figures dominate that literature – Franklin Roosevelt and Richard Neustadt. Most historians and political scientists have consistently and enthusiastically applauded Roosevelt's attempts to live up to Woodrow Wilson's maxim that a president 'should be as big a man as he can'. They have admired FDR's determination to make the presidency 'pre-eminently a place of moral leadership'; they have delighted in his vigorous expansion of the role of the federal government, applauded his commitment to social and economic reform and been impressed by his exceptional talents as a war leader. Roosevelt, according to William Leuchtenburg, enjoys demi-god status among historians and has cast a long shadow over his successors. 'From 1945 to the present, historians have unfailingly ranked him with Washington and Lincoln, and the men who succeeded him found one question inescapable: How did they measure up to FDR.'[10]

Among the political scientists there has been no more avid Roosevelt admirer than Richard Neustadt, the author of perhaps the most influential book on the presidency ever written. The status of *Presidential Power* as a classic work is undeniable – it has contributed much to our understanding of the politics of the presidency, yet it needs to be understood that it is a book heavily laden with liberal Democratic values. Throughout, Franklin Roosevelt's style of presidential leadership is presented as *the* model to which all who enter the White House should aspire, whereas President Eisenhower is portrayed almost as a figure of fun, a pathetic 'Roosevelt in reverse'.[11]

No doubt Neustadt's influence helps to account for Eisenhower's poor showing in early presidential greatness polls and it is worth noting that his ranking improved considerably when revisionists demonstrated that he was not really the indolent, passive chief executive of legend.[12] In other words, this later research showed that Eisenhower, in truth, had a sophisticated understanding of how power was exercised and led skilfully, if quietly, from behind the scenes, – he was not, after all, so totally removed from the Roosevelt model as everyone had thought. Nevertheless, Eisenhower is unlikely to climb the presidential rating tables very much higher given his conservative views and the liberal preferences of those making the evaluations.

THE ACTIVIST PRESUMPTION

Even if it is not a sufficient condition, for a modern president to enjoy the approbation of the scholarly community it seems that it is obligatory for him to be a chief executive in the liberal Democratic tradition best exemplified by FDR; a tradition which extends back to Woodrow Wilson and embraces Harry Truman, John Kennedy, Lyndon Johnson and, to some extent, Bill Clinton. For such presidents:

> 'government' appears as a vast reservoir of power which inspires them to dream of what use might be made of it. They have favourite projects, of various dimensions, which they sincerely believe are for the benefit of mankind, and to capture this source of power, if necessary to increase it, and to use it for imposing their favourite projects upon their fellows is what they understand as the adventure of governing men . . . the art of politics is to inflame and direct desire.[13]

This vision, shared by most students of the presidency, demands that chief executives be activists; success in the White House requires presidents who are architects of change; they are obliged to be doers and reformers. As Richard Rose has said, 'presidential scholars show a strong bias towards . . . activism', while Murray and Blessing observe that 'activeness' was an essential ingredient of presidential success for the historians they polled.[14] Similarly, Charles O. Jones in outlining 'the dominant perspective' used in evaluating the American political system notes that 'the good president, by this perspective, is one who makes government work, one who has a program and uses his resources to get it enacted. The good president is an activist; he sets the agenda.'[15]

Activism cannot sensibly be an end in itself. Not all legislation is conducive to the public good; some may arouse expectations that cannot be met and some would, no doubt, be better left off the statute book altogether. In discussing the merits of the veto, Alexander Hamilton alluded to conservatives, those who 'consider every institution calculated to restrain the excess of lawmaking, and to keep things in the same state in which they happen to be at any given period as much more likely to do good than harm.[16] In the same tradition, John C.

Calhoun said: 'There is often in the affairs of government more efficiency and wisdom in non action than in action.'[17] More recently, the conservative commentator Terry Eastland has suggested the liberal Democratic shibboleth 'Let's get the country moving again' is widely accepted in the United States today whereas 'it is considered impolite to ask exactly *where* . . . Presidents are expected to try to get it moving regardless of the facts of the situation ostensibly calling for movement or the government's competence to perform whatever is to be done or its authority to do so in the first place.'[18] As scholars rather than partisans, we are obliged to accept the legitimacy of a conservative tradition that embraces figures such as Calhoun, Calvin Coolidge, Eisenhower and Bush.

Activism is, of course, not restricted to liberal Democrats. Some Republican presidents nurture similar ambitions. They have come into office dissatisfied with the status quo and bent on bringing about change. Richard Nixon, for example, said: 'Seeking office by itself is not a worthwhile goal. What separates the men from the boys in politics is that the boys seek office to be somebody and the men seek office to *do* something . . . All the great leaders I have known have had goals greater than themselves. They sought high office not to be great but to do great things.'[19] In office, Nixon pursued a reform agenda, but was hardly an advocate of fundamental change. Ronald Reagan, by contrast, despite the impressions he sometimes conveyed of passivity, was, at heart, a radical conservative who aspired to bring about fundamental change, to reverse the thrust of the New Deal and its successor, the Great Society.

In evaluating Republican presidents like Nixon and Reagan it is not unreasonable to apply the same sort of criteria that might be used in measuring the success of similarly activist Democratic incumbents. Leaving aside any personal policy preferences we may entertain, and taking due account of the circumstantial variables appertaining during their time in office, we can legitimately ask of any such president: How far did they succeed in mastering the policy process to fulfil their ambitions for change? How many bills were passed into law in their name? How significant were those bills? Did they represent no more than minimal change, or did they really make a difference? Presidential success, it is assumed, can be calculated by some sort of 'scorecard'.[20]

GUARDIANSHIP

The problem with such 'scoreboard' calculations is that they include a presumption in favour of activism. They assume the desirability of change, whereas some presidents have no such aspirations; they 'come into office with a felt belief that success means holding the line against change in one way or another.'[21] Eisenhower and Bush clearly fall into this category. They were conservatives in the traditional sense of being largely content with things as they were. Such presidents are more-over, sceptical about what can be achieved by passing laws. Thus in an era when liberal Democrats were clamouring for the passage of laws as solutions to that most troubled of domestic problems, civil rights, Eisenhower took a different view. He was convinced that racial attitudes would not be altered by legislation: 'I do not believe that prejudices, even palpably unjustified prejudices will succumb to compulsion.'[22] George Bush, in campaigning for the Senate a few years later, similarly expressed his opposition to civil rights laws: 'I believe that the solution to this grave problem lies in the hearts and goodwill of all people and that sweeping federal legislation like the Civil Rights Act can never succeed.'[23]

Bush, like Eisenhower before him, was to become a guardian president. He was a conservator rather than an advocate of change. He sought to limit rather than to extend the reach of government and poured scorn on the social engineering of liberal Democratic presidents.[24] For the guardian governing is 'a specific and limited activity, namely the provision and custody of general rules of conduct, which are understood, not as plans for imposing substantive activities, but as instruments enabling people to pursue the activities of their own choice with the minimum frustration'.[25] Such thinking lay behind Bush's enthusiasm for free trade and deregulation and his reluctance to manage the economy. In domestic policy generally, he was guided by the physician's maxim of 'do no harm' and went out of his way to lower popular expectations of what could be accomplished by governmental action. In international affairs too, Bush as a guardian president was inclined to be cautious, anxious not to arouse hopes that could not be fulfilled while holding himself in readiness to deal with crises as they arose.

Guardian presidents like Bush do not present themselves to the electorate as expansive, omniscient leaders with solutions at hand to all manner of problems. It could be said of his administration as it was of Eisenhower's, that it was 'committed to conserving rather than creating, guarding rather than building.'[26] Presidents of this ilk harbour no grand schemes for reordering the world, and rather than embarking on crusades they are content to be reactive leaders, dealing with problems as they arise on a case-by-case basis. Such chief executives are likely to be short on charisma and flamboyance, to be disinclined to resort to rhetorical appeals and to specialize in working quietly behind the scenes. Such low-key notions of presidential leadership have little appeal to many scholars. Most academics are not taken by the implicit, or explicit, satisfaction with the status quo that such views appear to represent. Presidents, they believe should be dynamic, expansive leaders, alert to problems of injustice and deprivation and ready to harness the power of government for the public good. As far as possible, in other words, presidents should adopt Franklin Delano Roosevelt as their model.

EVALUATING PRESIDENTS ON THEIR OWN TERMS

The starting place for this study of George Bush's presidency is that he, like all presidents, is entitled to be judged on his own terms rather than on those favoured by his opponents, whether in the real world or in academe. As Richard Rose said in alluding to the hostility of scholars to President Reagan's policy objectives, he could reasonably 'ask political scientists to confine their judgement to how well he handled the political process'.[27] My scrutiny of Bush's incumbency will accordingly deal mainly with matters of process. That is to say, I am not at all concerned here with the desirability or wisdom of this president's policies with regard to the economy, abortion, civil rights, international affairs or anything else. My interest is rather in his competence, or effectiveness as a leader, on his capacity for statecraft, defined by Bert Rockman as his ability to 'steer the political system towards outcomes in accordance with [his] goals'.[28]

In studying any president, the legitimate questions to be asked include: What were his goals and how successful was he in overcoming the limitations on his powers to accomplish those objectives? What style of executive leadership did he adopt? How did he organize the White House? What techniques of management did he use and how well did he use them? How far did he succeed in getting the American people to follow where he chose to lead? What success did he enjoy in gaining the cooperation of Congress given the balance of party strength in the legislature? Was he able to bring the bureaucracy to order and to impose his priorities on the federal judiciary? Why was he more or less successful in fulfilling his agenda than other incumbents; how far was he the victim or the beneficiary of forces beyond his control?

These are the sort of questions that will be addressed in this book. What was Bush trying to achieve and how did he, in the words of John Kennedy cited earlier, seek to narrow, 'the gap between what he would like and what is possible'? In recent decades presidents have sought to escape these difficulties by drawing policy-making more and more into the White House and relying increasingly on their personal staff to help them fulfil their agendas. Unlike other appointees, White House staffers are men and women who have no other constituency but the president himself; they are hired and fired by him and are expected to devote all their energies to helping him achieve his goals. In contrast to cabinet and sub-cabinet members and senior bureaucrats, personal staff derive their authority from the president alone, and are much less likely to be torn by conflicting loyalties.

The president's personal aides, those who serve in the White House Office, have what John Hart identifies as three functions: coordination, gatekeeping and promotion.[29] Coordination is concerned with ensuring that policy-making and budgeting across the administration conforms with the president's wishes, gatekeeping refers to controlling access to the chief executive who would otherwise be swamped by a multitude of demands, while promotion involves the creation and maintenance of public support for him and his aims.

The White House Office of today has a staff of between three and four hundred.[30] There were 380 in the Bush White House and between 80 and 90 of these, at any one time, were senior or commissioned staff.[31] The most important members of this group were the 'staffers', the Assistants and Deputy Assistants to the President characterized by one of their number as people:

> who enjoyed truly remarkable power and discretion . . . who would sift through options papers long before a short list made its way into the Oval Office. They are the presidential gatekeepers who often determine whom he sees, where he'll speak and what he'll say; whether his cabinet will meet with him and when; what the topics will include; and what his major and minor foreign and domestic policy initiatives will entail.[32]

In the research for this book, I focused on this relatively small group of staff members at the heart of the Bush presidency. I interviewed approximately a third of those who served in these positions between 1989 and 1993, including 14 out of the 22 who, as Assistants to the President, were his most intimate advisers. Excluding the Office of the First Lady, there are 23 units within the White House Office. I interviewed senior staff from 14 of these units plus the Vice President's Chief of Staff. These interviews provided me with an invaluable set of windows through which I could view and better understand this presidency.

Rather than imposing any preconceptions on Bush's incumbency, I have endeavoured to scrutinize it from a White House perspective, giving voice, where possible, to some of those who worked closely with George Bush – men and women who were personal friends of the President, who admired him, who shared his views and were dedicated to doing what they could to fulfil his agenda.

Chapter 1 is devoted to some discussion of Bush's personality, his view of the world, his life experience, his political career prior to becoming President and his 'guardian' conceptions of presidential power. In the chapter that follows, I have outlined the strategies of leadership deployed by George Bush. As a preliminary to that discussion, I compare Reagan's 'outsider' mentality with Bush's 'insider' inclinations. I then discuss the emphasis in Bush's appointments policy on personal rather than ideological loyalty. Subsequent sections cover Bush's relations with Congress, his inadequacy in using his office as a bully pulpit, his relations with the press and his lack of ease before television cameras.

The organization of the presidency under Bush is the subject of Chapter 3. While most cabinet members were long-standing personal friends of the President, the Cabinet collectively met infrequently and usually only for mundane purposes. In common with other recent administrations major decisions under Bush were made in the executive mansion, by the President advised by senior White House staff. The legislative liaison and communications offices of the White House Office receive particular attention in this chapter; the tenure of John Sununu as Chief of Staff and that of his successor, Samuel Skinner, are also dealt with.

Chapter 4 begins by returning to the matter of statecraft; that which I argued earlier is the legitimate subject of atten-tion for political scientists. What was on Bush's agenda and how far he succeeded in meeting his objectives are the ques-tions at issue here. In discussing Bush's domestic policy achievements his staff repeatedly drew my attention to the Clean Air Act of 1990 and the Americans with Disabilities Act of the same year; for some of his staff, as for the President himself, his Points of Light programme was a major domestic policy initiative. These three accomplishments are the focus of discussion in this chapter.

As I suggested above 'scorecard' evaluations of presidents are inappropriate in the case of guardian presidents and this is pursued further in Chapter 5. *Congressional Quarterly* presidential success scores provide relevant evidence for assessing the performance of activist reforming presidents, but they are far less relevant in the case of conservative guardian presidents like Bush. Furthermore, preventing undesirable legislation from passing is central to the purpose of such pres-idents and the veto for them is an invaluable weapon. Bush's unusual degree of success in wielding the veto is not reflected in his low CQ scores. Such calculations also ignore the value of signing statements as a means of undermining the force of legislation, another stratagem available to guardian presi-dents that are covered in this chapter.

The failure of Congress in 1990 to pass a budget deal worked out between the administration and congressional leaders was a humiliating rebuff for Bush and a defining event for his presidency; this is the subject of Chapter 6. It begins with a consideration of the background to Bush's 'no new taxes' pledge and touches on the crucial role of Richard Darman, the Director of the Office of Management and Budget. While partly a result of the inherent tendencies towards ungovernability in the political system, the budget débâcle of 1990 also placed Bush's leadership in a poor light; demonstrating his lack of interest in domestic policy, as well as inadequacies in his organization of the White House and in his use of the bully pulpit.

Chapter 7 commences with a discussion of how foreign and national security matters were handled in the Bush administration and continues with a section on Central America. The United States troubled relationship with Nicaragua had bedevilled the executive branch's dealings with Congress in the Reagan years; James Baker, Bush's first Secretary of State, manoeuvred skilfully in 1989 to neutralize this source of contention between the President and Congress. Relations with Panama proved troublesome in that same year, but General Noriega soon provided an opportunity for swift and decisive military action that met with widespread approval within the United States. The second part of this chapter deals briefly with Bush's reactions to the momentous events taking place in Eastern Europe and the Soviet Union leading to the end of the Cold War.

If the budget crisis of 1990 provided one defining event for the Bush presidency the war in the Persian Gulf, the subject of Chapter 8, provided another. The former proved to be a leadership disaster, whereas the latter showed the President in an infinitely more favourable light. This is particularly the case if the analysis is concentrated primarily, as it is here, on the period between August 1990 and February 1991. Arguably, this crisis showed Bush at his best to set against the ineptitude of his leadership during the budget débâcle.

My final chapter allows me to pull together some conclusions while also touching on a number of important issues that could not be covered in any depth in the context of a relatively short study. Amongst these will be Bush's efforts to influence the federal judiciary, including his nomination of Clarence Thomas to the US Supreme Court. Consideration will also be given to the vagaries of Bush's civil rights policies, his handling of the abortion issue and the causes of his failure to gain re-election in 1992.

My interviews allowed me to draw on the experience and opinions of some of those at the very centre of the decision-making process. The insights provided by these key figures are important to an understanding of the Bush presidency, but, in my early chapters particularly, it may appear that I have presented this material somewhat uncritically. It seemed to me, however, that this was necessary in the interests of arriving ultimately at a suitably balanced appraisal that considered Bush on his own terms. Later parts of the book, most notably Chapters 6 and 9, are more critical.

1 The Making of a Guardian President

Presidents are entitled to be considered on their own terms rather than those of their political adversaries. It is necessary therefore to begin by recognizing that George Bush was a conservative and, as such, held views at odds with those that generally prevail in the academic community. When he was Vice President, Bush told the Ripon Society: 'I am a conservative. I voted along conservative lines when I was in Congress. I took conservative positions before assuming this job. I take conservative positions now.'[1] Some on the right of the Republican Party have questioned Bush's claim to the conservative label, but there is little doubt that he is a conservative in the broad sense of that term. He is, to use Michael Oakeshott's terminology, of a conservative 'disposition', tending to favour the status quo, to abjure crusades, to be deeply sceptical of innovation and to see the role of government in minimalist terms.[2]

Throughout his political career Bush rejected the liberal reformist nostrums associated with Franklin Roosevelt and his would-be emulators. In his autobiography Bush, in reflecting on his political philosophy in the 1950s, which by then 'had long been settled' said: 'I supported much of Harry Truman's foreign policy in the late 1940s. But I didn't like what he and the Democratic Party stood for in the way of big, centralized government – the attitude that "Washington knows best" and the policies and programs it produced. I considered myself a conservative Republican.'[3]

That early commitment to conservatism can be seen as arising from the influences Bush was exposed to during his youth, combined with his early experience in living and working in the very different environment provided by the oil fields of Texas. His beginnings were marked by wealth and privilege; born in Massachusetts, he was the second son of an investment banker who later became a United States Senator. His childhood was spent in Greenwich, Connecticut, in a house with three maids and a chauffeur to take him and his elder brother to preparatory school. After secondary education at an elite private school – Phillips Academy, known as Andover – Bush served with distinction as a bomber pilot during the Second World War, flying 58 combat missions and being awarded a Distinguished Flying Cross.[4] When the war ended Bush completed his education at Yale, another elite bastion; he majored in economics, earned a Phi Beta Kappa key and played a lot of sport.[5]

By his own admission, Bush evinced little interest in politics in the early years of his life. Nevertheless during this formative period he began to acquire values and attitudes that would later become politically relevant.[6] The dominant ethos was clearly one of conservatism tempered with the norms of *noblesse oblige*, and through the combined influences of family, church and school the young Bush absorbed the shibboleths of what one who shared the experience has characterized as an 'Eastern establishment creed'; this included maxims such as 'The meek shall inherit the earth.' 'Gentlemen don't ask people to vote for them,' 'Real men don't boast.' 'It's more blessed to give than to receive,' 'Public service is the purpose for entering politics.'[7]

George Bush's father, by all accounts a major influence on his thinking, personified this creed. Despite long hours as a businessman he devoted much of his time to voluntary and community work and impressed upon his children the obligation of the well born and privileged to enter public service. According to Bush himself, 'Our father had a powerful impact on the way we came to look at the world. Dad taught us about duty and service.'[8] Confirmation that the future President followed his father's teaching in such matters was offered later by Barbara Bush: 'Some people are motivated by money, some people by power and some people by public service. I put George in the latter category. He had no great ambitions to make a lot of money. I don't think you'd ever put George down as power mad. It's just public service.'[9]

After a long career in business, Prescott Bush became a candidate for the United States Senate at the age of 55, a decision which George Bush found not at all surprising, 'because I knew what motivated him. He'd made his mark in the business world. Now he felt he had a debt to pay.'[10] In the Senate, the elder Bush proved to be a congenial, dignified and diffident member of an institution that at that time was noted for its club-like atmosphere.[11] Close to Eisenhower, Prescott Bush was a moderate conservative with little interest in disturbing the status quo; he favoured civil rights and was troubled by Joe McCarthy's rampaging, but while 'he was respected widely and believed in principles, [he] left no substantive footprints.'[12]

The early influences on George Bush, in other words, were those of the Eastern establishment, of a patrician caste reared on hierarchical and elitist assumptions, largely content with things as they were and where any doubts that might arise from the existence of inequality and other societal ills could be assuaged by public service.[13] An emphasis on duty and service is consistent with that lack of vision that Bush was so often charged with. It involves no lust for change, but requires individuals to give something back in return for the advantages that have been bestowed upon them. They are obliged to serve, to offer their talents, their skills, and even their lives if necessary, to their country. As one of the most astute of Bush observers, David Hoffman, put it: 'Bush's vision of the country reflects the impact of a privileged childhood in which he was drilled with the importance of "giving back" to society some of the good fortune he inherited.'[14]

The conservatism that Bush grew up with was moderate, non-confrontational and relatively non-ideological, marked by civility, compassion and community. However, more than two decades of life and politics in Texas were to expose him to conservatism of a rather different stripe. After graduation from Yale in 1948 he and his wife set off for west Texas where he began work as a trainee in the oil industry. Two years later he struck out on his own and with a partner formed an independent oil company that traded in leases and royalties. These moves were less adventurous than they might seem. The trainee position was in a subsidiary of a company headed by 'a close family friend, [a] surrogate uncle and father confessor to all the Bush children.'[15] Furthermore, when Bush formed his own company, crucial investment support came from his uncle and from clients of his father's firm.[16] For all that, Bush was now subject to the intense anxieties of a high-risk, relentlessly competitive business where fortunes could be won and lost overnight. While cushioned from the dire financial losses facing others his business activities were certainly not without risk. 'No one really knows how much oil is underneath what land; mineral leases are complicated, and there's a lively market in them: Deciding where to drill, what equipment to use, whom to hire, how far to keep going – these are tricky judgments on which a lot of money is riding.'[17]

By declining in 1948 the readily available option of remaining in the cosy, structured environment of his youth and heading for Texas, Bush came under the influence of a different conservative tradition. He was brought into contact with the individualistic political culture of the Southwest where the role models were not the well born and the well connected but those who had made vast fortunes from inauspicious beginnings, a region where largely untrammelled capitalism was king and taxes, bureaucrats and all forms of government were despised. This was a part of the country where a neopopulist brand of conservatism flourished; it was harsher than its Eastern counterpart, more materialistic, marked by 'new money' rather than 'old money', less moderate and less compassionate and not tempered by genteel norms of duty and service.[18] After a decade in west Texas Bush moved eastwards and settled in Houston, eventually making it his political base. Houston is a town which 'conveys a sense of rugged individualism and laissez-faire; however diverse now, much of it remains very conservative. Can there, for example, be another major city anywhere that has no zoning? "Private property is sacred here," a local political figure explains. "People feel they should be free to do whatever they want with it." '[19]

This was the sort of conservatism that had Barry Goldwater as its standard bearer when Bush first ran for public office, and came into its own in 1980 with the election of Ronald Reagan to the White House. As will become clear when we examine his presidency, Bush remained primarily a product of his upbringing, but there is little doubt that his experience in Texas left a mark. When he sought election to the US Senate in 1964 Bush enthusiastically embraced Goldwater's agenda; he denounced the pending Civil Rights Act, attacked Martin Luther King, opposed Medicare and foreign aid and demanded that the United States leave the United Nations if the People's Republic of China was admitted. [20] Bush later disowned some of these views on the grounds that they were forced upon him by electoral considerations. Nevertheless his world view was, in part, shaped by the Texas phase of his career, adding influences that arguably contributed to some of the ambiguities in his thinking that were later to cause him difficulties.

THE MANNER OF THE MAN

Ingratiation, the ability to render oneself agreeable and likeable to others, is a major resource in a polity marked by an absence of ideology, insubstantial parties and an intense fragmentation of power.[21] Presidents like Franklin Roosevelt and Ronald Reagan exploited to the full their great capacity to be ingratiating – using it to develop productive relations with the press, with legislators and with the public at large.[22] When Reagan was in office, public opinion polls showed that many of those who disapproved of his policies nevertheless found him to be a likeable man.[23]

Despite poll rankings sometimes far in excess of anything Reagan achieved, Bush was never publicly liked in the same way. Particularly towards the end, Bush was seen in many quarters as a rather cold-blooded and uncaring patrician, out of touch with the needs and discontents of ordinary people. Senior members of Bush's staff argued that such negative perceptions of him and the invidious comparisons with his predecessor arose, in large part, from television induced distortions of reality. As the consummate television politician Reagan had managed to project an image of warmth and charm that obscured the reality of a rather cold and remote figure who had difficulty in remembering the names of members of his own Cabinet and was personally close to no one other than his wife.

According, to Bush's senior aides he is a far more admirable human being than media images conveyed while he was in office. We are assured that he was, in fact, a man of great warmth, kindness and sensitivity, who lacked pretension, was elaborately considerate as an employer and obsessively loyal to his friends. Thus James Cicconi, Staff Secretary and Deputy Chief of Staff, spoke with feeling of Bush's 'endearing qualities':

. . . a man who really didn't take himself too seriously, who was one of the most personable and kind people. Generous to a fault, really concerned with individuals and their problems. He took a very personal interest in everybody that worked in the building and how they were doing and how they were treated.[24]

Testimony to the unusual kindness and decency of the President and the First Lady was provided by John Keller, Director of Presidential Advance, who said '[They] are two of the most honorable, kind, honest people you would ever meet in your life.' When pressed Keller went on to say that while Bush might have some limitations as a leader, 'as a human being and a person I can't come up with any negatives for somebody like him, I just can't.'[25] Gregg Petersmeyer, Assistant to the President for National Service and a longstanding Bush protégé, spoke of his talent for dealing with people on a 'retail' basis in contrast to Reagan's undeniable strength in 'wholesale' politics: 'George Bush is the most admirable man that one will ever see in that office on a one to one basis. He has got a tremendous soft and warm heart. He hurts for people; feels for people.'[26]

Gail Wilensky, Deputy Assistant to the President for Policy Development, saw a difference between the public and the private man. The President was an 'incredibly nice man . . . a wonderful human being, unpretentious, funny. The woodenness that he sometimes portrayed in a crowd, speaking, is absolutely the opposite of what you see and feel when you meet the man . . . [he] just exudes personal warmth.'[27]

Contrary to the impressions of some of his critics Bush's intimates stressed his modesty and humility. Peggy Noonan referred to 'his diffidence and his determination. None of the great-man manner, self-deprecating, modest.'[28] One of those closest to him, C. Boyden Gray, Counsel to the President, suggested that Bush was given less credit than he deserved for his achievements while in the White House because of an inbred unwillingness to boast: 'He did all this, but because he was brought up by his mother never to talk about himself you know it just never came across.'[29]

Andrew Card who served in the White House as Deputy Chief of Staff and then in the Cabinet as Secretary of Transportation, said simply of Bush: 'He is a humble man.'[30] This view is endorsed by David Demarest, Assistant to the President for Communications, who, in illustrating the point, refers to his experience in going over speeches with the President while travelling on Air Force One: 'He would sometimes apologize for making changes in his speech . . . he cared about a researcher, or a speech writer not having their feelings hurt. He would say things like, "now don't tell him I really didn't like this, but I really don't like this page . . . I know they put a lot of effort into it." '[31]

That George Bush is personally a decent, civilized, even likeable human being seems beyond dispute.[32] These qualities allowed him to ingratiate himself with those with whom he came into contact and to make friends of them wherever possible. By assiduously cultivating personal relations throughout his career by telephone calls, thank you notes and Christmas cards Bush created a political resource of some consequence.[33] The value of that resource will become apparent in subsequent chapters when appointments, legislative relations and foreign policy are under consideration.

For Bush personal relationships were always far more important than political ideas. Some of the most devout Bush loyalists have remarked on his extravagant lack of interest in ideas. The President's eldest son, George W. Bush, told James Pinkerton who as Deputy Assistant to the President for Policy Planning, was responsible for injecting some ideas into the Bush White House: 'The problem with my old man is that he thinks you can solve problems one at a time, with good character, good judgment, a good team, and all that stuff. Jebby [his brother] and I understand that you need ideas, principles – based on belief.'[34]

Gregg Petersmeyer, almost as close to Bush as to be a surrogate son, commented very similarly. As he saw it the President worked very hard in dealing with individual decisions as they came down the conveyor belt towards him, but he was disinclined to step back and say:

'What is it of all these things on the conveyor belt that I
think is the most important to define and project?' . . . he's
not contemplative. He doesn't sit back and say there really
are three things I care about. He's a man of action. He'd
much prefer to go play tennis or write a note to somebody.
. . . [He's not] interested in ideas for ideas' sake. I think he's
interested in the application of ideas and people and
leadership to certain situations.'[35]

Bush's lack of interest in ideas touches on a charge that was
to haunt him throughout his presidency, his perceived lack
of 'vision.' Unlike Reagan he was not driven by any desire
to change the world, he was broadly satisfied with things
as they were and saw no need for a blueprint or a master
plan of reform. Leadership demanded honour, integrity,
a sense of public service and experience. There was no
'need for an overarching vision. Rather, he believes he
possesses the right training and the intuitive sense to
make correct decisions as problems come his way. He is
the embodiment of pragmatism: self confident about
his ability to find solutions without holding to a master
blueprint.' [36]
When asked late in his presidency why Americans should
re-elect him Bush gave an answer that had little to do with
ideas or issues: 'I've tried to serve with a sense of decency. I
think people look at that. I think we have tried to look at
family values. We try to live them. We talk about my caring,
and I do. And I think those things come through . . . I think
[the American people] say, Hey, these times have been rough,
but the President's doing his best, and I disagree with him on
this or that, but he's a good man.' As Richard Brookhiser noted,
Reagan confronted by the same question would have
mentioned two issues: 'cut taxes, fight the evil empire', and
Clinton would have referred to a multitude of issues, whereas
Bush 'ultimately answers it with himself'.[37] If we are to consider
Bush on his own terms, however, his answer makes sense. It
was a logical response for a president who saw no need for
change and on numerous occasions vaunted American society
and the political system. Such circumstances required not
visionaries, but honourable, decent and experienced leaders,
qualities which Bush could claim to possess.

RELEVANT EXPERIENCE ?

In campaigning for the presidency George Bush made much of his curriculum vitae, exuberantly proclaiming on occasion, 'Ready from day one to be a great president.'[38] On the face of it, Bush certainly did appear to be far better qualified for service in the White House than some recent incumbents. Jimmy Carter, for instance, had undeniably been a man of high intelligence, but his prior experience as Governor of Georgia, a relatively small state with a part-time legislature overwhelmingly controlled by the Democrats, was less than suitable preparation for the rigours of executive leadership in Washington. Furthermore, Carter's campaign as an outsider, fiercely critical of Congress and its procedures, ensured that his relationship with the legislature would be a difficult one.

President Reagan also campaigned as an outsider in 1980. He had gone into politics after a long career in the entertainment industry and this was followed by two terms as the governor of one of the largest and most important states. However, Reagan's knowledge in the principal area of responsibility for a chief executive of that era – foreign affairs – was derisively inadequate. In contrast to his two predecessors, Bush entered the White House with what one source referred to as 'the best vitae in American public life' while another went so far as to say that he had 'the best résumé [and] the best experience' of any modern president.[39]

When Bush sought the presidency in 1988 he undoubtedly had behind him a long and varied record in national politics. He had made his electoral debut 24 years before when he unsuccessfully sought a seat in the United States Senate; he was elected to the United States House of Representatives in 1966 and served for two terms. After another abortive attempt to reach the Senate he was appointed, by President Nixon at the end of 1970, to the position of US Ambassador to the United Nations. At the beginning of 1973 Bush became Chairman of the Republican National Committee. Briefly considered in 1974 as a possible nominee to be Gerald Ford's Vice President, George Bush instead became head of the US Public Liaison Office in the People's Republic of China. In 1976 President Ford appointed him Director of the Central Intelligence Agency where he served for slightly less than a year. After losing the contest for the Republican nomination to the presidency in 1980 to Ronald Reagan, Bush was chosen by the latter as his running mate and served as Vice President from 1981 until 1989.

Closer scrutiny of Bush's record in public life prior to 1989 however, raises questions about just how well qualified he was for the presidency. Service in the national legislature is undeniably a useful experience for a future chief legislator, but Bush's congressional career was relatively short and came to an end 18 years before he entered the White House. Whilst in Congress he compiled a conservative voting record while being careful to maintain cordial relations with his oppponents. He was neither confrontational nor controversial, quickly slipping into the congenial, deferential and cooperative mode required by the norms of the institution.[40] 'Above all, he was a pragmatist more attuned to the interpersonal dynamics of politics than devoted to ideology.'[41]

It is reasonable to assume that Bush's four years in Congress gave him some understanding of the convoluted mechanisms whereby that body conducts its business; it will also have helped him later to comprehend better the motivations of legislators. Nevertheless most of those who had served with him in the House had left by the time he became President; his service had been too brief for him to acquire a position of real influence and being of a conservative disposition he had been disinclined to put together a consequential legislative record.[42]

As United States Ambassador to the United Nations Bush began to acquire the foreign policy expertise that was to become one of his greatest strengths. It was, however, a modest beginning, based more on establishing potentially useful personal relationships with fellow diplomats than on any real participation in the making of American foreign policy. Whilst Bush was at the UN, Henry Kissinger, the National Security Adviser, blocked direct access to President Nixon in the foreign policy area and the Ambassador suffered humiliation on the key issue that came to the fore during his tour of duty – the controversy over the seating of communist China.[43]

Unaware of the secret diplomacy then being conducted with China by Nixon, Kissinger and Secretary of State William Rogers, Bush worked hard in an unsuccessful effort to ensure that Taiwan at least retained a seat in the General Assembly on the admission of the People's Republic. This had been US policy previously and Bush beavered away innocent of the fact that the hope of seating Taiwan had been abandoned months previously by those really responsible for the making of foreign policy in the Nixon Administration.[44]

George Bush's foreign policy role was not noticeably greater during the Ford Administration. When he became head of the United States liaison operation in Beijing it was made clear to him that his duties were very limited. Henry Kissinger 'explained that Bush was to be little more than a listening scout for the US. He was not there to implement policy Initiatives would be handled by Washington, meaning Kissinger himself.'[45] In a biography heavily favourable to Bush his China period is referred to as a 'sabbatical' and as an 'exotic interlude'; his presence in Beijing was 'insignificant. He was playing in Kissinger's sandbox. Bush did the backslapping and tailwagging as a mere public relations man while Kissinger came and went on his high-level, substantive dealings with the Chinese power wielders.'[46]

As Ford's Director of the Central Intelligence Agency, Bush won plaudits for helping to restore the morale of an institution that had recently been battered with severe criticism. He energetically courted the media and repeatedly testified on Capitol Hill, but his work at the Agency was almost entirely concerned with public relations and image-making rather than matters of substance. And even at the CIA the ever-present Henry Kissinger continued to prevent Bush from becoming more involved in policy matters by denying him access to intelligence material of the highest classification coming into the State Department.[47]

Two terms as Reagan's Vice President provided the most impressive entry on Bush's résumé when he ran for the presidency in 1988. Much has been made of the insignificance of the vice presidency in the past. Franklin Roosevelt's first Vice President, John Nance Garner, famously declared the office to be 'not worth a bucket of warm spit'.[48] In similar vein Thomas Marshall, who held the position under Woodrow Wilson, observed that the vice president 'is like a man in a cataleptic state: he cannot speak; he cannot move; he suffers no pain; and yet he is perfectly conscious of everything that is going on about him.'[49] In the modern era Lyndon Johnson was bitterly frustrated as Kennedy's Vice President; Hubert Humphrey suffered similarly in the Johnson White House and Spiro Agnew had difficulty in even getting to see President Nixon and was used primarily as a political hatchet man.[50]

In recent decades it would seem that vice presidents have fared rather better; they have been given offices in the White House, have acquired sizeable personal staffs and been asked to take on important responsibilities.[51] Thus Bush assumed the chairmanship of a number of presidential task forces designed to coordinate the implementation of policies extending across several agencies. One of these, the Task Force on Regulatory Relief, gave Bush a role of some significance in furthering deregulation, a central plank of Reagan's economic policy. Bush also chaired the South Florida Task Force, concerned with combating the drug trade and was appointed chairman of the Terrorism Task Force.[52]

In addition, President Reagan made considerable use of his Vice President for foreign policy purposes. By the spring of 1987 Bush, in his capacity as Vice President, had travelled to no less than 73 countries; in many cases these visits were for funerals or other ceremonial purposes, but more than a few had a substantive purpose.[53] It is claimed, for instance, that Bush played an important part in persuading European governments to accept Pershing and cruise missiles, an essential preliminary for one of President Reagan's principal foreign policy achievements, the INF treaty.[54] It is also the case that George Bush met with the President on a weekly basis and in 1985 Reagan went so far as to say: 'I don't think there's ever been a vice president that has been as much involved at the highest level in our policy-making and our decisions than George, or that has been a better vice president than he has. He's been the best.'[55]

It is evident that vice presidents now enjoy much higher profiles than before and regularly accept major assignments. Nevertheless there is ample reason to question the value of service as vice president as preparation for the presidency. Despite the changes of recent years, vice presidents are still destined to remain presidential acolytes and errand boys. Abject loyalty to the President is an essential requirement of the job; those who take it on, in other words, are obliged to sacrifice their independence and self-respect. If they should be foolish enough to display a mind of their own, to dissent from the president's policies, either openly or though leaks, they will quickly find themselves isolated, denied influence in the making of decisions and in grave danger of losing their claim to the succession. Arthur Schlesinger Jnr, who favours abolition of the office, has remarked with his usual pungency: 'Under most Presidents, the Vice Presidency is much less a making than a maiming experience' leading not to 'education but emasculation'; a position that constantly demands 'sedulous loyalty, deference, self-effacement and self-abasement'.[56]

Few vice presidents have met these requirements more meticulously than George Bush. When selected as Reagan's running mate, despite having, among other things, assailed Reaganomics as 'voodoo' economics in the primaries, Bush immediately told his staff: 'We're now a wholly owned subsidiary and we're going to behave like one.'[57] Subsequently, those who attended meetings at the highest level in the Reagan White House reported that the Vice President hardly ever expressed an opinion and was always elaborately deferential to the President.[58] Bush, however, remained unrepentant, shrugging off gibes that he was a 'lapdog' or that he had 'placed his manhood in a blind trust,' insisting that 'in our family loyalty is not a character flaw.'[59]

Bush's resolute unwillingness to be seen as in any way less than completely loyal to President Reagan was reinforced by his delicate relationship with conservatives in his party. Right-wing Republicans had long doubted his conservative credentials and his presidential ambitions demanded that he should be careful not to alienate a vital element of the coalition required for his election in 1988. In the long run, however, Bush's obsessive unwillingness to put any light between himself and Ronald Reagan had seriously adverse consequences. It contributed to what were ultimately profoundly damaging perceptions of him as a political 'wimp', as a man lacking in beliefs and convictions.

The indignities that are heaped upon vice presidents make service in that office, in some ways, an unsatisfactory preparation for the desperately difficult problems of leadership that presidents must grapple with. Nevertheless, Bush's eight years in the post had some value given the importance that foreign policy assumed during his presidency. His overseas missions on Reagan's behalf had improved his understanding of the issues and his meetings with world leaders facilitated the personal diplomacy that, a few years later, was to become a hallmark of his own conduct of foreign policy.

Overall, however, Bush's pre-presidential political experience was of limited relevance. He had held a range of national offices, but none of them were in the fullest sense leadership positions. In each case he was not a principal decision-maker, policy-making was not his responsibility, he was, at best, a number two carrying out the mandates of others. None of this had prepared him for the monumental challenges that every president faces; he had no real experience of wrestling with Congress, the bureaucracy, interest groups and public opinion in order to fulfil an agenda. He came to the presidency, according to David Hoffman, 'having prepared extensively in the sense of watching and absorbing, but also with scant experience in actually wielding great power, in pushing others to reach his goals, in mastering the fine art of political leadership.'[60] To put it another way, George Bush's training in statecraft was far less sufficient than he and others suggested.[61]

A GUARDIAN IN THE WHITE HOUSE

As I indicated at the beginning, those who become presidents are entitled to be considered in the light of how they see their role and how successful they are in achieving their goals. One problem with this line of analysis in the case of George Bush lies in the widespread suspicion that he did not really have goals; many, even within his own party, have accused him of having no clear sense of where he wanted to lead the country, of being without convictions or beliefs, of wanting office not to achieve lofty purposes, but merely for the 'honor of it all'.[62] Shortly before Bush was elected President, George Will, an influential conservative critic, wrote:

> Sure he has a purpose: he wants to be president. But he seems to want that only because it is the next rung up, and climbing the ladder of public life is his life. This is an old axiom: Some people seek office to be something; others seek office to do something. Bush is one of the former. In this, the contrast with Ronald Reagan is complete.[63]

While not without some validity this indictment requires further consideration. The comparison with Ronald Reagan is, for instance, somewhat invidious. A clear-cut, pre-conceived, radical agenda was, without doubt, one of Reagan's strengths yet, in that regard, he was unusual. Presidents typically take up office without a clear sense of what they intend to do. Even great achievers like Franklin Roosevelt could be said to have lacked 'vision', to have become president without a master plan or blueprint. As Theodore Lowi argues, 'no one knew Roosevelt's specific positions and plans until after he became president in 1933,' and much the same could be said of Kennedy, Nixon, Carter and Clinton.[64] Critics in the media and on the right of his party like Will constantly berated Bush for his failure to work to a 'roadmap' in the way that Reagan had done ignoring the fact that his non-ideological, case-by-case, reactive, problem-solving style was more attuned to the American political tradition.

Comments by George Bush in 1988 provide some understanding of how he saw his role and what he hoped to achieve in office. Unlike Reagan in 1981 he had no desire to lead a crusade. 'We don't need to remake society,' he said as his campaign got under way. 'We don't need radical new directions.'[65] This not only reflected Bush's cautious conservative instincts, it was also appropriate for a candidate who had been a loyal Vice President and now sought to ride into office on the back of a popular incumbent widely perceived to have been largely successful in office.

In his speech accepting his party's nomination at the Republican convention Bush spelled out his responsibility to build on the foundations laid by Reagan, saying: 'I am your candidate because the most important work of my life is to complete the mission we started in 1980. And how, and how do we complete it? We build on it.' Bush went on to glory in the successes of Reaganomics before recognizing that: 'Things aren't perfect in this country. There are people who haven't tasted the fruits of the expansion . . . farmers . . . urban children . . . the homeless.' But the key to the solution of these problems lay in economic growth which would be secured 'by maintaining our commitment to free and fair trade, by keeping government spending down, and by keeping taxes down.'

The latter crucial article of the Reaganite faith was enshrined in the famous pledge 'Read my lips: No new taxes,' while other goals specified by candidate Bush included '30 in 8' – thirty million jobs in eight years, 'first-rate' schools for every American child, a 'drug-free America', laws designed to ensure that the 'disabled are included in the mainstream', and environmental legislation. In foreign policy he would continue with the present administration's policy of 'peace through strength' coupled with further work towards disarmament.

Having indicated his determination to carry the Reagan revolution forward Bush added an emphasis of his own, deploring the recent emergence of materialism, complaining of greed, graft, corruption and self-centredness and declaring 'I want a kinder and gentler nation', a theme that he took up again at his inauguration, asking:

> Have we changed as a nation even in our time? Are we enthralled with material things, less appreciative of the nobility of work and sacrifice? My friends, we are not the sum of our possessions. They are not the measure of our lives. In our hearts we know what matters. We cannot hope only to leave our children a bigger car, a bigger bank account. We must hope to give them a sense of what it means to be a loyal friend, a loving parent, a citizen who leaves his home, his neighborhood, and town better than he found it.

In line with these echoes from his upbringing, the new President also used his inaugural address to reiterate his belief that many social problems were best taken care of, not by the expenditure of public money, but by voluntary service – sentiments that gave rise to the establishment of the Points of Light Movement, a development much derided elsewhere, but, for Bush, a particularly important part of his programme.[66]

It is evidently not the case that Bush had no agenda. He saw no need for fundamental change and inclined to the view prevalent in the Eisenhower administration 'that the less the government did, the more the people would progress and prosper.'[67] Nevertheless, Bush did have goals and, as we have seen, in accepting the nomination he advanced a number of specific proposals designed to consolidate the achievements of the previous administration while also smoothing off some of the rougher edges.[68] It was not a programme likely to meet with the approval of his political opponents and even within the Bush Administration there were those who found it thin, insubstantial and insufficiently activist.[69] William Kristol, the Vice President's Chief of Staff, confirmed that there was a group within the White House including himself, Dan Quayle and Jack Kemp, Secretary for Housing and Urban Development, that chafed under Bush's passivity and advocated 'an activist, conservative agenda, à la Reagan, or, in some respects, more à la Thatcher.'[70]

Bush's approach to the presidency can be contrasted with some of the alternatives. Liberal Democrats, among whom most political scientists are to be found, have required presidents to be activists, innovators and reformers. They have been expected to take up office armed with creative ideas and legislative proposals designed to relieve American society of its many ailments. Presidents, it is assumed, cannot sit on the sidelines while so many citizens suffer from inequality, poverty, illiteracy, drug abuse, disease and other forms of distress.

Vigorous leadership from the White House to deal with these and other problems has been an imperative for liberal Democrats. They have encouraged presidents not to be too finicky about the Constitution, an instrument, as they see it, that needs to be interpreted creatively, stretched, if necessary, to accommodate desirable extensions of the reach of government, for the power of government in the right hands could be a potent force for good. It followed that the president's principal role was that of chief legislator, for by formulating and passing laws governments could provide the muscle and the money required to improve the conditions of life for the American people. The number of bills passed in the name of the president was a crucial measure of his success in office. Presidents, in short, should be like FDR or Lyndon Johnson, they should, above all else, be activists and innovators in the White House.[71]

Conservatives, on the other hand, tend to despise big government and remain sceptical as to what can be achieved by passing laws. This has not, however, prevented some Republican presidents from becoming innovators or advocates of substantial change. Theodore Roosevelt provides a good example and Richard Nixon can be similarly categorized. The latter's heroes were 'Teddy Roosevelt . . . a man of action who could think and Woodrow Wilson . . . a man of thought who could act.'[72] As we saw in the previous chapter, Nixon distinguished between 'men' and 'boys' in the White House. The latter sought office for the sake of it while the former wanted to make use of the power they acquired.[73] As President, Nixon was one of the 'men'; he was innovative in international affairs and an activist in domestic policy, vigorous in pursuit of a full agenda including major items such as welfare reform, government reorganization, the introduction of a 'new' federalism and the establishment of the Environmental Protection Agency.

In domestic policy, Ronald Reagan was even more of an innovator than Nixon had been. He came into office profoundly dissatisfied with the status quo and bent on fundamental change. Notwithstanding a notoriously disengaged operating style, Reagan was not content to leave things largely as they were. Unlike say Eisenhower and Ford, he was not prepared broadly to accept the assumptions of the New Deal and the Great Society. By comparison Reagan had high ambitions; he embarked on a frontal assault against, what he saw as, a high taxation, big spending, big government system. Reagan, in other words, was attempting to alter the terms of the political debate and was, in that sense, an innovator.

George Bush lacked both the opportunity and the inclination to be an innovator and proved instead to be a guardian in the White House. By definition guardians, who guard, protect or preserve, are largely satisfied with the status quo, even though they may recognize a need for marginal change. This was Bush's position in 1988. At the Republican convention he argued that, in general, all was well in America, even if there were a few imperfections in need of attention. Three years later Bush still persisted with this line of argument vaunting the 'greatness' of America's 'free enterprise system [that] lets one person's fortune become everyone's gain,' and going on to say 'no system of development has nurtured virtue as completely and rigorously as ours, and we've become the most egalitarian system in history and one of the most harmonious.' Such problems as there were, could be largely left to the 'common decency' of the American people, in other words philanthropic effort and volunteer activity.[74] This satisfaction with the existing state of things extended to the political system; Bush retained an unwavering faith in American political institutions, asserting: 'I believe in the integrity of the process. I believe our institutions can still work.'[75]

Guardian presidents are unlikely to be flamboyant, charismatic leaders. They are disinclined to be visionaries and they do not come armed with an ideology, or a master plan. Leadership for them is not about crusading, nor is it about working to a blueprint, it is about problem-solving on a case-by-case basis. As Bush began his campaign for the presidency he said: 'I am a practical man. I like what's real. I'm not much for the airy and the abstract. I like what works. I am not a mystic, and I do not yearn to lead a crusade.'[76] At his inauguration the President contrasted his approach with that of other, more ambitious, leaders when he said: 'Some see leadership as high drama, and the sound of trumpets calling. And sometimes it is that. But I see history as a book with many pages – and each day we fill a page with acts of hopefulness and meaning.'[77] This was to see executive leadership, as other guardian presidents have done, as a quiet, low-key, largely behind-the-scenes activity with an emphasis on prudence and caution.[78]

This is not likely to satisfy Bush's many critics who demand to know why he wanted to be president in the first place if he had no plan and no ambitions to change the world. Was this not proof that he just wanted to be president for the sake of it? This is to misunderstand how a guardian president sees his role. He takes the view that the United States needs at the helm, not a visionary or an ideologue, but a qualified and competent leader able to deal with problems and crises as they occur. As Ed Rogers, a senior member of the White House staff, saw it, Bush's ambition to be president arose from the conviction that he was especially well qualified to meet the demands of the office. He believed, 'I will effectively handle whatever comes my way, I will handle it better than anyone else . . . I am the best equipped person through experience, temperament, beliefs, philosphy and upbringing. I am the best person to handle the challenges that are presented by the presidency.'[79]

The guardian president is also deeply sceptical of the power of government to correct the ills of society, a view which Bush has consistently held. When he ran for the Senate in 1964 he cast doubt on the pending Civil Rights bill, arguing, like Eisenhower, that progress in race relations would only come about through moral suasion: 'I believe that the solution to this grave problem lies in the hearts and goodwill of all people and that sweeping federal legislation like the Civil Rights Act can never fully succeed.'[80] Nearly three decades later Bush's doubts as to the possible gains from government action remained, he was a president, 'grounded in the belief that government has only limited power, to fix the economy, revive the cities, change the cycle of poverty or radically attack social ills.'[81]

Guardian presidents such as Bush do not share the dreams of hyperactive chief executives like Lyndon Johnson, with their infinite faith in what government can accomplish given the will and the right sort of leadership. After Johnson's election in his own right, the first session of the 89th Congress saw the passage of 84 out of 87 major measures proposed by the President and, before he left office, there were close to 500 social programmes in place providing 'for everything from flood control to birth control to rat control' and much else besides.[82]

None of this impressed Bush who was to condemn Johnson's Great Society for its failure to eradicate social problems, for being a 'crusade [that] backfired'.[83] He wrote off such schemes in his inaugural address. 'The old solution, the old way, was to think that public money alone could end [social] problems. But we have learned that that is not so.' Rather than throwing money at the ills of society it was necessary to draw on 'the goodness and the courage of the American people', to engage the talents of the elderly and the energy of the young in community service, to return to timeless notions of 'duty, sacrifice, commitment, and a patriotism that finds its expression in taking part and pitching in.'[84]

Guardians not only question the positive value of government action, but are concerned that such action, far from improving the situation, may make matters worse. In defence of that position Bush took to invoking the Hippocratic Oath, saying on one occasion in reference to urban problems: 'The government's first duty is like that of the physician:Do no harm.'[85] That same caution was to be found in Bush's approach to foreign policy. He told Brent Scowcroft, his Assistant for

National Security, shortly after taking office: 'I want to do something important [in foreign policy], but I want to proceed prudently. I don't want to do anything dumb.'[86]

In 1990, Bush was criticized for his cautious reaction to the efforts of the Baltic states in trying to break free from the Soviet Union, and responded: 'I don't want to do something that would inadvertently set back the progress that has been made in Eastern Europe.' The President went on to express his concern about the possibility of backlash by elements hostile to Gorbachev if the US went too far in its support of the Baltics. He continued: 'I love the old expression of Yogi Berra's. You say, "What happened to the Mets, Yogi?" He said, "Well, we made the wrong mistakes." I expect in this job I'll make plenty of mistakes, but I don't want to make the wrong mistakes.'[87]

The crisis for the Bush presidency brought about by the slide of the American economy into recession provoked similarly circumspect responses. In October 1991, the President resisted advice that the economy should be stimulated by a tax cut saying: 'What I don't want to do is to make the situation worse.' Later in a speech in Rome Bush said: 'You notice when tax cuts were proposed, long term interest rates shot through the roof. I have a responsibility to see that I don't make proposals that will set back the economy.'[88] Once again Bush had shown that 'Do no harm' was the leitmotif of his Administration. Unlike Kennedy, Johnson, Nixon or Clinton, Bush disdained intervention in the economy. apparently believing that given time the recession would correct itself, the business cycle would turn again. Bobbie Kilberg, Deputy Assistant to the President for Public Liaison reported Bush as saying, 'massive intervention does not make sense, but this economy is going through changes which are fairly fundamental, it has got to restructure itself.'[89]

Other sources have drawn attention to the President's tendency to talk about the economy in weather terms, alluding to the recession as a 'thunderstorm' and as a 'hurricane' in the devastation that it caused. According to one who heard these remarks they were 'a sign of the true Bush on the economy . . . There is nothing a president can do about it but take cover and live through it and wait for the sunshine.'[90] Such views were, of course, anathema to liberal activists and to some in

Bush's own party, but the President believed, according to his Staff Secretary 'that:

> . . . recessions happen; that they are the result of business cycles. That government action can perhaps help to even them out to some degree – maybe take out the lowest of the low. But, by and large, these are business cycles that do change in time. And the thing we need to do is to keep consistent economic policies that foster a good climate for business so that the economy can come back.[91]

As a guardian in the White House Bush also believed that he had a responsibility to prevent others in government from doing harm and it was in that spirit that he wielded the veto regularly and, as we shall see, successfully. In addition, Bush assumed the role of guardian to the Constitution, believing that since Vietnam and Watergate, Congress and the media had become excessively assertive at the expense of the presidency.[92] This had been most notably the case in the realm of foreign policy where, as will become clear in later chapters, Bush consistently and aggressively fought to preserve presidential prerogatives.

Yet if Bush battled tenaciously in defence of his constitutional position in foreign policy, his apparent passivity in domestic affairs was to become a source of recrimination central to his defeat in 1992. His Democratic critics castigated him for his laissez-faire attitude towards the economy and interpreted his disdain for grandiose schemes of social reform as the insensitive responses of a patrician, personally untouched and unmoved by the concerns of ordinary people. His political enemies in the media and Congress denounced him as a do nothing president prepared to sit on his hands in the face of recession and deep-rooted social problems.

Even within his own party, Bush's inaction in domestic policy provoked intense criticism. Right-wing Republicans were no less opposed to big government than the President, but that did not, in their view, justify making the presidency a centre of inaction in domestic policy. In 1991, Jack Kemp, Secretary for Housing and Urban Development in Bush's Cabinet, obliquely criticized the President when he said: 'The White House is the epicenter of national policy. There are problems of poverty and despair and economic decline in many people's neighborhoods which the president has both a moral and political obligation to address.'[93] Like others on the right of the Republican Party, Kemp believed there were conservative answers to pressing urban problems such as welfare dependency, unemployment, drug abuse, education and crime, but, as his comment implied, translation of those ideas into goverment policy required real leadership from the White House.[94]

As we have seen, conservative Republicans also lambasted Bush for not being more like Ronald Reagan. For not having a vision of where he wanted to take the country, for lacking a blueprint, or master plan, for appearing to have so few settled beliefs, or convictions, for being so irredeemably pragmatic. In this analysis however, I am not concerned with the wisdom or otherwise of George Bush's policy preferences. I am examining his incumbency in the light of how he saw his role, what he was trying to achieve, and the methods he used in attempting to reach those goals. The latter will be considered in the next chapter.

2 Strategies of Leadership

Guardian presidents have only limited agendas. Sceptical of what can be achieved by governmental action they are inclined to be passive rather than activist in office. Nevertheless, like all presidents, they are engaged in a constant struggle to impose their preferences and priorities on the notoriously intractable American political system. In grappling with these daunting problems different presidents deploy varying strategies and techniques and the purpose of this chapter is to review George Bush's utilization of some of these approaches. Accordingly, I will touch on his appointments policy, his legislative relations, his reluctance to make use of the bully pulpit, his relationship with the press and his lack of comfort with television. First, however, it will be useful to compare and contrast the fundamentals of Bush's style of presidential leadership with those of his predecessor.

AN INSIDER IN THE WHITE HOUSE

Reagan was, of course, a conviction politician with an ideological edge to his conservatism. He arrived in Washington, moreover, as a quintessential outsider, as a chief executive who, despite a veneer of charm and geniality, regarded bureaucrats and legislators as the enemy, as political adversaries to be overcome using whatever means were necessary.

For Reagan and his senior advisers, gaining control of the federal government demanded a hard-headed approach to appointments; if career bureaucrats were to be brought into line they had to be supervised and directed by carefully selected presidential appointees. To obtain one of these positions it was not enough to be an enthusiatic campaign worker, a competent administrator, or a good Republican; most important of all, appointees had to be fully committed to the ideas and progammes that Ronald Reagan had advocated in campaigning for the presidency.[1]

Congress meanwhile was best regarded as a hotbed of ruthless opponents, unremittingly hostile to all that Reagan hoped to achieve. For a few years the Senate under Republican control was reasonably responsive to the popular will, but 'the House [was] a different matter, with recent incumbent reelection rates of 98 percent or better [and Democratic control] ever since 1954. The lower chamber, part of the permanent government syndrome, frequently combined with other elements of the establishment in attempting to thwart the Reagan program.'[2] To overcome such resistance Reagan had no inhibitions about going over the heads of members of Congress to appeal to their constituents. During the epic struggle over the budget in 1981 Reagan's exceptional communications skills were complemented by his staff launching grassroots lobbying blitzes in selected congressional constituencies, where voters and key campaign contributors were induced to pressurize pivotal legislators.[3]

The Reaganites, it is clear, were more than willing to play hard-ball with Congress and the President's mastery of television was a major resource in that regard. Moreover, not only was Reagan an effortless performer before television cameras, he was also content to devote most of his efforts to being the front man of his administration. That is to say, provided that the broad principles he stood for were being respected, he was pleased to leave to his staff the details of policy formulation and implementation while he concentrated on promotion and salesmanship.

It was Reagan's ideology and his outsider status that lay behind his confrontational style and his demands for fundamental change. Bush had no interest in changing the world and came from a totally different background. He sought the presidency out of a conviction that he was especially well qualified to address problems as they arose; he had been brought up to revere public service and had himself held a range of government jobs. At the beginning of his 1988 campaign, he said:

> I do not hate government. I'm proud of my long experience in government. I've met some of the best people in the world doing the people's business in the Congress and in the agencies. A government that serves the people effectively and economically, and that remembers the people are its master, is a good and needed thing.[4]

Similarly, shortly after taking office, Bush spoke to an audience of high-ranking career civil servants in the federal government. The President told these senior Washington bureaucrats: 'You are one of the most important groups I will ever speak to. What we really have in common is that each of us is here to serve the American people. Each of is here because of a belief in public service as the highest and noblest calling.'[5] These were sentiments wholly unpalatable to good Reaganites who despised bureaucrats and all they stood for and took very seriously their leader's maxim: 'Government is not the solution to our problem; government is the problem.' For Bush, by contrast, those who worked in government were not enemies, they were people he knew, who shared his values and his commitment to public service – they were people he could do business with.

APPOINTMENTS

While Bush respected career officials in the federal government in a way that Reagan did not, he nevertheless understood how important the appointment process was as a principal means whereby presidents gain control of the executive branch. In the modern age, 'The personnel resources at the president's disposal are considerable: 600 top-level cabinet and White House appointments, 700 non-career Senior Executive Service (SES) appointments, and 1,700 Schedule C appointments, along with many other honorary and commission appointments.'[6] Bush recognized that he would need good loyalists, not only in the White House and his Cabinet, but also throughout the federal bureaucracy to monitor and lead government departments.

As James Pfiffner has observed: 'The major criterion for all new Presidents in their appointments is loyalty, but loyalty comes in many guises: partisan, personal, ideological.'[7] Party loyalty is, at best, a weak reed in the American context, and ideology, while highly relevant in the case of Reagan, could hardly serve for a distinctly non-ideological president like Bush. The single most important criterion for appointment in the Bush administration was, at the outset at least, longstanding personal loyalty to George Bush. No one better personified this quality than Chase Untermeyer, the first Assistant for Presidential Personnel. He had been associated with Bush since his student days; first as a campaign worker when Bush ran for Congress in the 1960s, and then as an intern on Congressman Bush's staff. After serving in the Texas House of Representatives 1977–81, Untermeyer became Vice President Bush's Executive Assistant. He was then Assistant Secretary to the Navy in Reagan's second term, before, in early 1988, being appointed by the Republican National Committee to prepare for the transition to a possible Bush presidency. After the 1988 election, Untermeyer took charge of personnel recruitment for the incoming administration.

In staffing his Administration Bush was able to draw on the many personal relationships he had developed over the years. According to Constance Horner, Untermeyer's eventual successor, the President 'knew probably more Americans than any other human being has ever known, and he knew them with a kind of conscious attention . . . He spent time cultivating thousands of personal relations.'[8] For years Bush and his wife meticulously attended to friends and colleagues, carefully keeping in touch with those they had met in Texas, at the UN, in Washington and abroad; these relationships were kept alive by thank you notes, telephone calls and a Christmas card list that, according to one source, was 30,000 strong by 1986.[9] By drawing people into his circle in this way and holding them there, Bush put together a valuable leadership resource. Fiercely loyal himself, he could expect that loyalty to be reciprocated and, in the right circumstances, it could be a substitute for party or ideology.

As the Bush administration began to take shape the *New York Times* reported one anonymous friend of the President as saying: 'Loyalty is his ideology, his vision.' The article went on: 'Republicans agree that if ideology was the the most important quality in the Reagan appointments, the loyalty factor shaped the Bush team. Mr Bush has stocked his Administration with old friends from similar affluent Ivy League backgrounds . . . [he] prefers to appoint people he knows and with whom he is comfortable.'[10]

In explaining why the Bush White House was so relatively harmonious at the beginning, at least, Untermeyer said that people were appointed who came from the same background as the President, sharing 'a basic consensus that what matters is public service, plain and straight dealing, and the essential issues that propel American life, such as family, military service, and hard work in the private sector . . . Many of them have worked on Bush campaigns going back to Texas days or the late 1970s. They are a part of the President, if you will.'[11] This comment refers to White House staff, but given the size of the President's circle of friends it was possible also to place large numbers of them among the rank and file political appointees in government agencies. Some cabinet secretaries particularly close to the President like James Baker, Nicholas Brady and Robert Mosbacher could be allowed largely to select their own subordinates, but tighter control was needed in other departments.[12]

One of those responsible for such matters, Ronald Kaufman, Deputy Assistant to the President for Presidential Personnel, saw his responsibility as follows. In selecting 140 or so political appointees for, say, the Department of Health and Human Services, he was obliged to ensure that those appointed would move the army of bureaucrats in that department in the right direction. 'It is very important that people the President trusts and knows best, who understand best where [he] wants to move his country philosophically and policy wise, get those jobs . . . Just because a guy's got a great résumé it doesn't necessarily mean he can motivate that army [in] the direction that the President wants him to.'[13] Despite Kaufman's references to philosophy and policy it is clear that, at the beginning, personal loyalty to George Bush was the dominant criterion for appointment in contrast to the ideological loyalty demanded of those who sought posts in the Reagan Administration. 'The Reagan folk had opinions; they were more concerned with things like abortion [and] deep philosophical questions . . . That was their litmus test. My litmus test was more of [personal] loyalty.'[14]

By his own admission fanatically loyal to Bush himself, Kaufman stressed the vital importance of personnel to the process of governing and spoke of lecturing Senate Republicans on the need for state and regional appointees unreservedly loyal to the President. According to Kaufman, the venerable Republican Senator Strom Thurmond welcomed him to a lunch by saying: 'Ron, thanks for coming, we are here to discuss our appointments for regional jobs.' Kaufman responded, 'With all due respect they are not your regional appointments, they are George Bush's appointments. Let me just tell you . . . these are George Bush's important foot soldiers, to make sure he gets re-elected by carrying through his policies in the region.'[15]

In making appointments at the beginning the Bush Administration was also at pains to recruit more women. Furthermore, as part of his effort to differentiate himself from Reagan, the new president was anxious to appoint from ethnic minorities and laid stress on the need for ethical soundness among appointees.[16]

It is interesting to note, however, that later in his administration Bush appeared to have second thoughts about his appointments policy, downplaying his emphasis on personal loyalty and replacing it with a concern for policy orientation. Untermeyer eventually left the White House to be replaced by Constance Horner and Kaufman moved sideways to become Deputy Assistant to the President for Political Affairs. Horner, a Reagan Democrat, assumed responsibility for appointments in 1991, believing that she had been selected by Bush to change course:

> I think he wanted me to introduce a policy orientation to a greater extent than had been [the case] at the beginning of his administration. I had a reputation as being a heavily policy orientated conservative and I think I was selected because going into an election year the President believed that he was vulnerable for lack of policy rigor in his appointments. I think he was occasionally distressed to discover that some issue he had a history of being committed to was not being well served through some of his appointments.[17]

Ultimately, it seems, as the 1992 election approached, Bush and his advisers came around to the view that personal loyalty was not enough in making appointments. They had become increasingly aware of the disaffection of the far right of the Republican Party, a development that eventually culminated in Patrick Buchanan's challenge for the nomination.

LEGISLATIVE RELATIONS

The success or failure of a president, however limited his agenda, is greatly dependent on his relationship with Congress. Despite Reagan's laid-back, wisecracking geniality in meetings with congressional leaders, his Administration had adopted an aggressively confrontational approach. By comparison Bush's objective situation and his instincts were quite different. He had neither the desire, nor a mandate, for radical change; both Houses of the legislature were under Democratic control and he entered the White House as a former congressman and Washington insider who gloried in having more friends in public life than anyone else.

As he took up the reins of office, Bush went out of his way to give the impression that he wanted a more civilized and less confrontational relationship with Congress – one that stressed conciliation, compromise and bipartisanship. At his inaugural ceremony the President made gestures designed to prepare the ground for executive–legislative harmony. He effusively hailed Dan Rostenkowski, the Chairman of the mighty House Ways and Means Committee, with a 'Hi Danny' and ostentatiously greeted other long-serving Democratic friends such as Senator Daniel Inouye of Hawaii and Representative Jack Brooks of Texas.[18] And then, during his address, the President turned to the Democratic leadership and said:

> To my friends – and yes, I do mean friends – in the loyal opposition – and yes, I mean loyal – I put out my hand. I'm putting out my hand to you, Mr Speaker. I'm putting out my hand to you Mr Majority Leader . . . The American people want action. They didn't send us here to bicker. They asked us to rise above the merely partisan.

Once again Bush used words that Ronald Reagan would never have uttered, but he evidently was hoping to overcome the problems of divided government by adopting a 'kinder, gentler' style of legislative leadership.

In furtherance of this strategy Bush, as usual, drew on personal relationships, allegiances that 'have always been much more important to Bush than political ideas, policy preferences

or any abstract intellectual concern'.[19] Arising from his own
service in the institution, he already numbered senior members
of Congress among his friends and he now worked to supple-
ment and strengthen these links. Members of Congress,
accompanied by a few carefully selected constituents, were
invited to the White House; some legislators were given
guided tours of the family quarters by the President himself
who also took to appearing regularly on Capitol Hill to socialize
with old friends, playing racquetball with Representative Sonny
Montgomery and lunching with Representative John
Hammerschmidt.[20] The potential benefits to be obtained from
such activity were spelled out by one congressman. 'He builds
personal bridges, and that makes the margin of consideration
for him broader,' said Representative Charles (Chip) Pashayan
Jr, Republican of California. 'It's harder for someone who has
some personal affinity with George Bush to deny him when
he makes a request.'[21]

The determination of Bush, at the beginning of his presidency, to work with rather than to go to war with Congress
was evident from an exchange in December 1988 between the
President-elect and Wayne Valis. The latter had been responsible for liaison with business groups in the Reagan
Administration and, in that role, had played a large part in
generating the telephone blitz that had made possible Reagan's
dazzling triumphs in 1981 in getting Congress to agree tax
and budget cuts.[22] Now flanked by some 'trade association
heavies' Valis explained the value of mobilizing business
interests at the grass roots as a way of applying pressure on
individual members of Congress only to have Bush respond:
'We are not going to do it that way Wayne.'[23] Reflecting on
this incident later Valis said: 'We were stopped in our tracks.
It was unilateral disarmament in the face of George Mitchell
and company'.[24]

The beginning of a new era in legislative relations was
announced by Bobbie Kilberg, Deputy Assistant to the President
for Public Liaison. 'This is a very different White House,' she
remembered telling a gathering of business executives. 'George
Bush does not believe in confrontation. He believes in the art
of the possible, he believes in conciliation, he believes in
consensus and he believes in civility. He would not be comfortable with a public liaison office mounting massive grassroots

campaigns.' Other presidents had used threats and reprisals against members of the legislature, whereas Bush 'does not like the thought of going over the heads of his friends in the Congress.'[25]

It was not just strong-arm tactics that Bush objected to, as Kilberg was to find out in an incident involving one of the President's closest friends in Congress, Representative 'Sonny' Montgomery, Democrat of Mississippi, who joined the House in 1966 when Bush himself was first elected to that body. An abiding memory for Kilberg from her time in the White House is of being upbraided by a testy President for having the temerity to encourage interest group representatives to telephone Montgomery. The President surrounded by agents moving down a corridor in the White House stopped on seeing Kilberg and said, 'Come here. Did you have a whole bunch of [people] call up Sonny Montgomery?' 'Well yes, I did.' 'Why did you do that?' 'Well we need that vote sir.' Bush responded: 'He's a friend of mine. Don't you do that [again] without asking me.' Later, as Kilberg noted, the President shed such inhibitions; eventually 'he began to clearly see that you just had to beat members of the Congress over the head,' but for the moment he adamantly refused to make use of what had been one of Reagan's most potent weapons.[26]

The contrast between Reagan the outsider and Bush the insider was neatly drawn by William Kristol '[Bush] really was a creature of Washington and didn't like the idea of populist pressure on Congress or on the executive branch. Reagan was the opposite. '[He] always understood himself to be, whatever the self-deception and whatever the limitations, basically a populist spokesman for the people against the establishment'.[27]

We must be careful, however, not to make too much of Bush's conciliatory approach to Congress, for there were occasions when he was prepared to play hard-ball with legislators. As will be made clear later, Bush under the influence of his tough-minded Counsel, C. Boyden Gray, made repeated use both of signing statements and vetoes to shape public policy and to defend his prerogatives against congressional encroachment.[28]

THE BULLY PULPIT

Another strength of the Reagan Administration had been the President's ability to deliver speeches that caught the attention of the media and the nation and pressured Congress into cooperation. Bush, by contrast, was always disinclined to use his office as a bully pulpit. As will become apparent in subsequent chapters, this was a major flaw for, in the modern age, skill at 'going public' has become an essential requirement of presidential leadership, indispensable not only to campaigning, but to governance.[29] Bush's reluctance to mount the bully pulpit was a matter of aptitude and inclination. Even the sturdiest of Bush loyalists readily concede that he lacked the exceptional talent for communication possessed by his predecessor. 'Reagan could go to the American public with his own great personal communication skills and really make the Congress squirm, often forcing them into altering their positions. Bush didn't have that ability.'[30]

For Reagan, moreover, making telling speeches was a priority, whereas Bush saw his role in a different light. He insisted on being a 'hands-on' chief executive rather than a salesman, or a mere mouthpiece for his administration. C. Boyden Gray argued that Bush could deliver effective speeches, but chose not to expend effort in that way. 'He could on occasion give a good speech . . . like the acceptance speech in 1988, the acceptance speech of 1984 as Vice President . . . He has the capacity to do it . . . [but] for one reason or another he didn't want to do it.'[31] Gregg Petersmeyer believed that the President took the view that 'He wasn't supposed to be making speeches . . . he was supposed to be making decisions.'[32] According to another senior aide Bush had 'a visceral antipathy to public communication . . . he thought poorly of it, he thought it was cheap.'[33] James Cicconi explained that the President tended 'to distrust the power of rhetoric'. On occasion, such as the crisis created by the invasion of Kuwait, he could be articulate and compelling, but, in general, he took the view that 'leadership consists of doing the right things, making the correct decisions, making the tough calls and being willing to be held accountable to those standards.'[34]

Some Bush loyalists contend that he was less effective than Reagan as a communicator because of his greater awareness of the complexity of issues. Reagan's simplistic stances made for good sound bites and could be readily comprehended by the public, whereas Bush's recognition of the many variables was detrimental to good speechmaking and conveyed a wishy-washy image of a man without convictions.[35]

One staff member commented on Reagan's propensity to see political questions in black and white terms, while Bush 'saw the grey, saw the complexity of issues.'[36] Similarly, Kilberg suggested that Bush took the view that it was necessary to:

> . . . lower the rhetoric . . . [while] recognizing the complexity of life today in the domestic arena . . . [Some people] saw things in black and white; [they] thought everything was going to hell in a hand basket and wanted simple solutions to complex problems. [They] wanted people to rhetorically tell them what they wanted to hear and make them feel better. George Bush wasn't going to do that; that was pandering of the sort that he did not believe in.[37]

For conservatives particularly, deregulation was one of the great issues during the Reagan-Bush years and Clayton Yeutter agreed that Bush's more sophisticated position led to communication problems. Like others on the right of his party Reagan favoured deregulation almost without qualification, whereas Bush's position was more complicated. While generally enthusiastic about deregulation, he accepted that: 'there are times when regulation is appropriate.' This 'was a very sound rational reasonable position, but sometimes . . . [such] positions get you into trouble . . . [suggesting a] weak . . . ambivalent . . . or nebulous position.'[38] The fact that Bush had to deal with issues that were less clear-cut than they had been during Reagan's time was conceded by the conservative William Kristol: 'To apply some of these conservative principles to areas like health care and welfare or whatever is more complicated than simply cutting taxes or building SDI. Managing the break up of the Soviet empire, in some respects, is more complicated.'[39]

By 1992 the onset of recession had become the most pressing issue in domestic politics and David Demarest, head of the White House communications operation, gave some insights into the President's agonizing over how that issue should be addressed. Bush apparently believed that the state of the economy faced him with two choices. On the one hand he could engage in 'a lot of empathetic rhetoric', stressing his concern for those who were suffering from economic distress and leaving aside the fact that the economy, despite its present difficulties, was fundamentally sound. Suitably 'empathetic' speeches were compiled, but Bush worried that if he spoke in those terms people would conclude 'that the President thinks that things are really bad' and the effect of this would be 'to drive this economy further into the ground.' On the other hand, if he gave upbeat speeches emphasizing the underlying strength of the economy this would only seem to confirm the claims of the press and the pundits that the President was out of touch. Given these two choices Bush went 'right down the middle. He said: 'I know there are people out of work, I know that people are hurting, I know that there are a lot of families out there that are struggling to make ends meet, but I also know that this economy is not as bad as people are portraying it.' As Demarest pointed out this was 'a muddled message from a communicator . . . and therefore doesn't get through.'[40]

As a communications specialist Demarest also provided an interesting riposte to those on the right of Bush's party who have pilloried the President for his failure to use his office as a bully pulpit. 'Speeches get coverage when they do one of two things,' Demarest noted, 'when they attack or . . . if you announce a new program.' However, 'a new program means new dollars. You are in a budget deficit [and] you are not going to be announcing many new dollar items.' Furthermore, conservatives, in particular, 'wouldn't have wanted us to announce new spending programs. What they wanted us to do was to attack Congress, over and over and over again.' The problem with that strategy was that 'George Bush doesn't believe that gets you where you want to go.' He takes the view that given the low regard in which 'the American people hold politicians these days that will just come across as more noise; as people not being able to solve anything in Washington.'[41]

Finally, it can be said in defence of Bush's failure to make use of the bully pulpit that the circumstances under which he held office were not conducive to the use of rhetoric. Great oratory may be appropriate for presidents who see themselves as agents of change, but that was not Bush's mission. 'We are entering,' Peggy Noonan said, 'an anti-rhetorical age.

There seems to be a rhythm to such things. FDR's great oratory was followed by that of the more prosaic Truman.'[42] Like the latter, Bush came into office with a mandate in domestic affairs to maintain the course set by his predecessor; similarly, on the international scene, it fell to him to preside over a fraught period of change – arguably in neither arena was tub-thumping rhetoric called for.

THE FOURTH ESTATE

If a president is to fulfil his objectives a good relationship with the various forms of media is crucial. Those who work in the print and electronic media influence public opinion by their selection of news and their criticisms of those in government. They also play a major role in setting the public policy agenda. Presidents constantly at odds with the media will face grave difficulty in governing, as many have discovered. Ronald Reagan's innate friendliness, his self-deprecating humour and his easy charm initially served him well in his dealings with journalists. However, he later became increasingly inaccessible to the press. Relatively few press conferences were held and those that did take place were elaborately stage-managed and rather stilted affairs. Otherwise members of the White House press corps found that they were largely restricted to shouting questions at a hearing-impaired President as he made his way to and from a loudly clattering heiicopter.

George Bush came into office intent on creating a healthier relationship with the press. As he had done with Congress, he held out the hand of friendship to journalists seeking to draw them into a mutually beneficial relationship with him. The President informed his press secretary Marlin Fitzwater that 'he wanted to get to know a lot of reporters on a personal level, he would like to have a more informal relationship with them.'[43]

In pursuit of this strategy Bush met with journalists far more frequently than 'the Great Communicator' had ever done. In the first year of his presidency he appeared at 32 press conferences as against the 47 that Reagan held over a period of eight years.[44] The new President also met constantly with journalists on an impromptu basis, inviting them to dinner in the White House and watching movies with them.[45] In other words, Bush began his presidency by carefully courting the media, with Fitzwater frankly explaining: 'George Bush recognizes the press's need to get information and its value to him as a leader of the country. You tell the press what you are doing and you tell them why and you hope to do it in such a way that they understand and support'.[46] It is evident that by making himself accessible, drawing journalists into his network of personal relationships and speaking frankly to them, Bush hoped in the early days of his presidency to neutralize potential media hostility and to enhance thereby his governing capability.

At the beginning, Bush's attempts to get the press on his side appeared to pay off; his 'relations with the White House press corps were good.'[47] In the long run however, his strategy proved to be much less successful, with several of his most senior staff ultimately complaining bitterly about his treatment at the hands of the press. When asked in 1993 whether the press had been more antagonistic to Bush than other presidents John Keller said, 'Oh God yes, God yes. I mean, it was so blatant at some points during the [1992] campaign.'[48] C. Boyden Gray, one of those closest to the President, said simply: 'The press, they are adversaries, they are the enemy, so I guess you have to expect them to [act like] the enemy.'[49] David Demarest was more measured, but thought that the press was always harder on Republicans than Democrats.[50] The media were 'extremely harsh on Bush' according to Gail Wilensky, who added that press hostility 'was much worse than for Reagan' mainly because he was suspected of selling out to the right.[51]

GOVERNING WITHOUT TELEVISION

Since the 1950s the place of television in American politics has assumed gargantuan proportions. It has become the primary vehicle of political communication, monopolizing elections, supplanting parties and driving newspapers to the wall. Television executives nowadays are able to assume agenda setting functions and, in the right hands, as Ronald Reagan demonstrated, television can be an awesomely potent instrument of government. George Bush's attempt to govern without television, or at least to downsize its role, has been given less attention than it deserves. The possibility that such an attempt would be made was aired by Peggy Noonan: 'Some president is going to put TV in its place. Someday a smart man or woman will come in and say I don't exist to feed that thing. Get it back in its cage. I have a country to govern. It will be an interesting presidency. (It may be Bush's.)'[52]

After years of complaining of being manipulated by Reagan's image-makers, television reporters in early 1989 discovered that the new administration had a different approach. There was to be no equivalent of Michael Deaver to take charge of Bush's image; there would not be a theme of the week and presidential trips would not be tailored to meet the requirements of nightly television news broadcasts. Lesley Stahl of CBS News recalled that the Reagan White House was obsessive about 'making the evening news. They set their clock by Dan Rather's schedule', whereas the Bush staff had different priorities: 'This White House doesn't care if the President gets on the evening news or not.'[53] This was confirmed six months later by research done by the Center for Media and Public Affairs. In monitoring the television network coverage of the first 100 days of three presidents it was established that there were 336 items about Bush, 790 about Reagan and 906 about Carter.[54]

In part these differences reflect the contrasting agendas that Carter, Reagan and Bush brought to the White House. The first two were outsiders challenging the old regime; they stood for change, for confrontation and conflict, all of which made them eminently newsworthy. Bush's emphasis on continuity, conciliation and compromise on the other hand, did not make for riveting television news items. Beyond that Bush was never able to conceal his distaste for image-making, for packaging, for the public relations aspects of a president's role. His final legislative liaison chief, Nick Calio, spoke of Bush's unwillingness to 'communicate through sound bites or by creating perception. He had a specific aversion to that.'[55]

Bush's resistance to all forms of handling and lack of amenability to direction for image purposes was noted by his Director of Advance John Keller, who observed that if Ronald Reagan was told 'to walk straight and walk left, he would walk straight and walk left, [but] George Bush wouldn't do that. He would not take instruction that literally.' Advance staff who had worked for Reagan would throw out ideas and would have to be diplomatically told, 'That's a great idea but this guy's not Ronald Reagan. He won't do that, you can't tell him to do that. He will look at you like you have got something growing out of your head.' In Keller's view Bush's disdain for image-making was a mark of his integrity; he resisted packaging out of 'not wanting to lie to the American people, not wanting to mislead them . . . he was almost too honest for his own good to be a president, or to be a politician in these times.'[56] On the other hand, while Bush may have been averse to packaging for governing purposes, he showed no such reluctance when campaigning for office in 1988.[57]

The lack of enthusiam for image-making was also a matter of Bush's style. As we have seen, unlike his predecessor, he believed that his primary function was governing rather than salesmanship. As one distinguished Bush watcher, David Hoffman, put it, the President 'views the communications part of his job with more than a little suspicion. It does not seem to him a natural way to advance his goals, which he would rather push with private diplomacy and politicking. He devotes himself to personal relationships and is uncomfortable with the impersonal nature of the mass media.'[58]

It was presumably the President's lack of comfort with television that accounts for the relatively few occasions when he gave prime time addresses to the nation. By late November 1981 Reagan had given seven such addresses while Bush gave only two during the comparable period. One devout Bush loyalist, Bobbie Kilberg, conceded that delivering speeches from the Oval Office for the benefit of television was not his forte: 'He couldn't talk to a box.' He was far better talking off the cuff in situations where he could make eye contact with his audience. Under these conditions he was, according to Kilberg among others, very impressive, whether talking one on one, to an audience of two thousand in an auditorium, or at an informal press conference: 'He could communicate. He was extraordinary in sessions in the Roosevelt Room around the table.' In contrast to his predecessor, 'he could discuss any issue in depth, answering the secondary and tertiary questions, in addition to the primary question, and knowing precisely what he was talking about.'[59]

The difficulties posed by television for Bush went beyond his discomfort with the camera when making speeches. Relatively few Americans would see much of those speeches anyway and their perceptions of the President were heavily dependent on the images he conveyed as he went about his duties, as all modern presidents do, under the constant surveillance of television cameras. Even walking across the White House lawn to a waiting helicopter is a source of images, either favourable or unfavourable. Such occasions were effortlessly handled by an instinctive, highly trained and experienced performer like Reagan, but Bush was a different matter, lacking the instinct and the training. This was highlighted by Richard Ben Cramer, with some literary licence, in comparing the two men when Bush was Vice President:

> You watch Reagan do something public, anything, like walk across the lawn to his chopper: every movement is perfect. There he goes . . . with his big western walk, shoulders back, hands swinging easy at his sides, the grin raised to perfect angle, then one hand aloft in a long wave . . . and every instant is a perfect picture. It doesn't even matter if they're screaming questions at him. At any one millisecond, as the shutter clicks, the President is perfect: relaxed, balanced, smiling, smooth.
>
> Now watch Bush make for his chopper: hey, he knows that agent! – not part of his detail, but he met him on the last trip to Houston, got a kid who wants to go to West Point, wrote a letter for him. So Bush twists around and waves to the agent – lets him know he's seen him, bends his head back to Bar to tell her, that's Keith, the *agent* remember? 'MR VICE PRESIDENT? MR VICE PRESIDENT?' a photographer is yelling, and it's Fred, the *Life* guy, who was on the trip to Cleveland last week, so while he's talking to Bar, and pointing to the agent, he makes a face to Fred, to let him know he doesn't have to shout. He *knows* him see. Fred's a friend! And there's Steely waiting at the chopper stairs, Jack Steel! Known him for – God! Twenty-five years? And so he's got to goose Steely, let him know he's glad to see him, and he's making a face at Bar about the way the

photographers are shouting, and he twists around to see if the agent has seen him, oughta ask him, but the engine's so loud, and the wind's whipping his hair in his face, which he's screwing up to yell, as he pauses – gotta ask him – trying to balance, crouching in the engine wind, one foot up on the stairs: 'Hey! How's your *son*? . . . YOUR SON? . . .' And at any one moment, as the shutter clicks, Bush looks like a dork.[60]

The inability of Bush to cope with the various demands of television was partly a matter of personality. From his birth he appears to have been bereft of histrionic talent; his sister 'affirms that George has never been an actor in any sense. He plays it straight whatever it is. What you see is what you get.'[61] Others close to Bush have confirmed that he is a rather transparent man, singularly lacking in the guile and the art of dissembling so necessary in both the theatre and politics. His father was a singer of note, but none of that talent surfaced in his second son, who lacked both the ability to project himself and the sense of timing that singing requires.[62]

There were other personality characteristics that placed Bush at a disadvantage on television. As Duffy and Goodgame suggest he was too frenetic and too 'hot' for a medium best suited to cool relaxed performers in the mould of John Kennedy and Ronald Reagan. And while Bush's wondrously fractured syntax may have been charming and unexceptional in private conversation it did nothing to enhance his image on television.[63]

We may reasonably assume that the inadequacies of George Bush when confronted with a television camera were also related to his upbringing. Given the chronic weakness of party in the United States, electoral politics requires candidates willing to sell themselves to the voters as individuals. To use a distinctively American word, those who seek public office are obliged to grandstand, defined in Webster's as 'to act or conduct oneself with a view to impressing onlookers.' However, Bush had been brought up in a household where such behaviour was unacceptable. His mother, according to his wife Barbara, an even more important influence on the future President than his father, taught her children that any form of braggadocio was to be avoided. Dorothy Bush continued with such admonitions even when her children were mature adults, rebuking her son for referring to his war record in a campaign speech.[64] In his autobiography Bush describes an incident where his mother chastised him after reading news reports of his speeches: 'You're talking about yourself too much George.' He explained that the voters were entitled to hear about his qualifications leading his mother to concede reluctantly, 'Well I understand that, but try to restrain yourself.'[65] It seems that by temperament and upbringing, George Bush lacked the exhibitionist tendencies that American politics requires in the television age.

Furthermore, his guardian style of presidential leadership did not make for good television pictures. As we have seen, that style involves a low-key, non-flamboyant approach to leadership which emphasizes behind-the-scenes, problem-solving, rather than high-flown rhetoric. Rhetorical flourishes and guardianship do not sit well together whereas rhetoric or 'leadership as high drama and the sound of trumpets calling' delights media moguls as Reagan and his image-makers knew only too well. Guardians and conservatives moreover are reluctant to inflate public expectations; they are constantly on guard against any tendency to delude the people into thinking that government can do more than is really feasible. Bush's aides took the view that the overexposure of their man on television was likely to give just such an impression. 'It's not honest,' said Fitzwater the White House press secretary. 'The president of the United States cannot solve every problem from warts to AIDS.'[66]

CONCLUSIONS

The strategies of leadership deployed by George Bush were, quite obviously, far removed from those used by Ronald Reagan. Reagan stood outside the system, denouncing its inadequacies and aggressively demanding fundamental change. Such an approach could hardly be expected from Bush given his establishment roots, his contentment, broadly speaking, with things as they were and his long record of service in a range of public offices. Rather than villifying the bureaucracy, castigating the national legislature or striving to manipulate the media, Bush held out his hand, hoping to circumvent such obstacles through personal relationships. This president, furthermore, had neither the aptitude nor the inclination to use his office as a bully pulpit. He declined, in other words, to make use of a strategy that all modern presidents with activist ambitions have deemed essential. Similarly, Bush had a powerful aversion to all forms of image-making and strove to govern without television. The question of how far these strategies were either well-conceived or successful in their application will be addressed more fully elsewhere in this book.

3 Organizing the Presidency

It is self-evident that the presidency is a collective rather than an individual institution. Media pundits and academic commentators may use terminology such as 'the age of Roosevelt', 'the Johnson years' and 'the Reagan era', but these are simplistic labels concealing the truth that every modern president is utterly dependent on a large White House staff. A suitably skilled and effective staff is essential if a president is to stand any chance of carrying his 'choices through that maze of personalities and institutions called the government of the United States'.[1]

In wrestling with the acute problems of governance in the United States presidents not only have staff, they are also given the opportunity to place political appointees into leadership positions in the executive branch. However, the loyalty of such appointees to the president and his agenda is by no means guaranteed. From Cabinet members on down, political appointees are subject to conflicting pressures. They are brought within the ambit of career civil servants, they are influenced by pressure groups and they may be intimidated by congressional committees. Political appointees, in other words, cannot be relied upon to do the president's bidding. While appointed by him they are not answerable to him alone and there is always a danger that they will 'go native' in the department to which they are assigned.[2]

Presidential staff, while not immune to the possibility of divided loyalties, are less vulnerable to external pressures and are, accordingly, less likely to pursue agendas other than the president's. On the other hand, the fact that virtually all presidential staff are hired and fired at the discretion of the chief executive alone has consequences for democracy. Holding those who make policy acccountable to the people is one of the hallmarks of a democratic polity, whereas the proximity of White House staff to the president and his dependence on them creates a situation where vast power may reside in the hands of non-elected officials.

These concerns were brought into sharp relief by the Watergate crisis when the American public became aware of the marginalization of Richard Nixon's Cabinet and the major roles assumed by presidential aides such as H.R. Haldeman and John Ehrlichman, senior White House staff who, by definition, were subject neither to election nor to Senate confirmation, and were answerable only to the President.

THE CABINET

The election of Jimmy Carter in 1976 was partly attributable to Watergate and at the beginning of his term the new President insisted, with typical hyperbole, that 'there will never be an instance while I am President when the members of the White House staff dominate or act in a superior position to the members of our Cabinet.'[3] As John Hart has shown, however, Carter failed to live up to his promise, with the Cabinet in his Administration proving to be no less prone to domination by White House staff than it had been in previous presidencies.[4]

The relegation of the Cabinet to a secondary role in policy-making has long been a feature of the American national government. Franklin Roosevelt made scant use of his Cabinet and the same can be said of Truman, Kennedy and Johnson. Eisenhower's formalistic approach to governance led him to make more use of Cabinet meetings, yet even he did not come remotely close to the cabinet government model associated with parliamentary systems. Whilst Cabinet meetings were held regularly, Eisenhower was not disposed to place the Cabinet at the forefront of policy-making; it 'served more as a sounding board than as a policy-considering body.'[5] The possibility of making a reality of cabinet government was floated during the Reagan transition, but when faced with the realities of government his Administration proved to be 'one of the most staff directed and centralized presidencies of the modern era.'[6] Under Reagan the full Cabinet met rarely and delegated extensively to a system of cabinet councils while the really important policy decisions were taken within the White House.

George Bush's long experience in government may account for his showing little inclination to overstate the possibilities of cabinet government when running for the presidency in 1988.[7] During his Administration meetings of the Cabinet took place 'about once every four to six weeks' and these were, according to David Bates, the first Cabinet Secretary, briefing sessions rather than policy-making exercises.[8] This was confirmed by Bates' successor Edie Holiday: 'For the most part [Cabinet meetings] were opportunities for information exchange and not working policy development meetings. They were opportunities for the President to hear what was on the mind of the Cabinet . . . and for the Cabinet to share key issues that they were working on.' At times of crisis, such as the budget imbroglio of 1990 and the Gulf War, Cabinet meetings assumed a somewhat greater importance. Thus during the War, 'there were still information exchange meetings, but it was a time of war and so there was a very active and aggressive interest on the President's part in having members of his Cabinet understand what [the Administration] was trying to do and what was happening [while also providing them] with an opportunity for input.'[9] Vice President Quayle describes Bush Cabinet meetings as 'stilted, boring affairs. Instead of creative ferment and the clash of ideas, there were droning reports – Carla Hills would give one about trade, and then Baker would give one, and Darman another, and so on. The truth is, Cabinet meetings are an anachronism.'[10]

Following the precedent set by the previous administration cabinet councils for domestic policy were established parallel to the statutorily required National Security Council. An Economic Policy Council was set up, chaired in the President's absence by the Secretary of the Treasury, while the Attorney General became chairman of the Domestic Policy Council. These councils facilitated 'broad inter-agency policy-making' with the Domestic Policy Council, for instance, providing a forum for the development of a drugs strategy, an issue of concern not only to the Office of National Drug Control Policy, but also to the Department of Health and Human Services, the Department of Justice, the Treasury and the State Department. The Clean Air Act, one of Bush's most important legislative accomplishments, went through the Domestic Policy Council, and the Economic Policy Council 'resolved all trade matters and trade policy decisions for recommendation to the President.'[11]

While these cabinet councils were undoubtedly valuable arenas for the consideration of complicated policy detail, there is little reason to suppose that the really momentous issues of policy were dealt with at that level. One observer noted that the Bush White House regularly bypassed 'the cabinet council system in resolving key issues', while another, Burt Solomon, reported that a senior Bush aide had said that 'the most important issues are "rarely" entrusted to Cabinet councils.'[12]

It is clear that the workings of the Bush Administration, like almost all others, were far removed from cabinet government; Cabinet meetings were infrequent and were usually used for briefing and information exchange purposes. Cabinet councils played a part, but did not make the decisions on the major policy questions. Nevertheless, there is a sense in which George Bush can be said to have 'made more effective use of his Cabinet than had most of his recent predecessors.'[13] While the Cabinet as a collectivity may have meant little, some individual members in the early months were believed to carry weight to an unusual degree.[14]

In May 1989 concern among senior presidential staff at Cabinet members announcing major decisions without informing the White House began appearing in the press. One such incident was the announcement by Veteran Affairs Secretary, Edward Derwinski, that his department would not be appealing against a federal judge's ruling on Agent Orange, the controversial defoliant used in Vietnam. Without consulting the President, Derwinski thereby reversed a decade of government policy on the issue. In a newspaper article discussing this affair an Administration official was quoted as remarking that the White House was 'reactive to its own Cabinet members. Bush's own style is kind of reactive not to lay down priorities for these guys. The President wants leadership to come from the Cabinet. He regards White House staff as facilitating information, not really shaping policy. So he's letting the Cabinet do their own thing.' Major players in the Cabinet were identified as James Baker, Secretary of State; Jack Kemp, Secretary of Housing and Urban Development; Defense Secretary, Richard Cheney; Secretary of Commerce, Robert Mosbacher; and Transportation Secretary, Samuel Skinner. Nicholas Brady, Secretary of the Treasury, was characterized as 'unassertive' but his close friendship with the President 'provides him with special access.'[15]

David Hoffman and Ann Devroy of the *Washington Post* wrote in a similar vein a few months later, observing 'For now, Bush is not inclined to impose discipline on his brood, associates say. Particularly in domestic policy, Cabinet members say they feel Bush has given them wide latitude, as long as they do not stray from his overall goals.'[16] The 'For now' at the beginning of this quotation was particularly apt for by 1990, power, in domestic policy, was shifting sharply away from the Cabinet and becoming narrowly concentrated in the hands of the most senior of senior White House staff, most notably John Sununu, the Chief of Staff, and Richard Darman, the Director of the Office of Management and Budget. It was inevitable that such movement would occur as Stephen Hess explained a few months into the Bush Presidency: 'Whatever power Bush's Cabinet wields now is the most it is likely to get. For during any Administration's course, White House impatience with bureaucratic inertia and Secretaries' tendency to reflect their agencies outlook ensures that power will "drift" into the White House. At best, Bush has only slowed the inevitable.'[17]

The extent to which this shift occurred was, however, limited somewhat by George Bush's leadership style. As we have seen, an essential feature of Bush's approach to leadership was his emphasis on personal relationships and his Cabinet was made up almost entirely of people whom the President knew well personally – it was indeed 'A Gathering of Friends.'[18] Senior members of the Cabinet included longstanding and close friends such as James Baker, Nicholas Brady and Robert Mosbacher. Others had served alongside Bush in previous administrations. Carla Hills, who became US Trade Representative, had been Secretary of Housing and Urban Development in the Ford Administration. Richard Thornburgh, the Attorney General, was first appointed to the post by President Reagan. Similarly, William Webster had been Director of the FBI and Director of the Central Intelligence Agency in the Reagan Administration before reappointment to the latter position by Bush. Elizabeth Dole, the Secretary of Labor, had been a senior member of Reagan's White House staff before becoming his Secretary of Transportation. Bush's

first Secretary of Agriculture, Clayton Yeutter, had served in
the Nixon and Ford Administrations and had been a Cabinet
officer as US Trade Representative during Reagan's second
term. Richard Darman had been an Assistant to President
Reagan and then Deputy Secretary at the Department of the
Treasury. Richard Cheney, Secretary of Defense, had been
Ford's Chief of Staff. Edward Derwinski held junior office in
the Reagan Administration and had been in the US House of
Representatives when Bush was a congressman.

Given the close personal ties between Bush and his Cabinet
and his method of operating there was little chance of his
allowing White House staff to wall him off from cabinet secretaries in the way that H.R. Haldeman and Donald Regan had
done with regard to Richard Nixon and Ronald Reagan. This
was, after all, the man who almost made a fetish of keeping
in touch with friends and acquaintances; as one of his senior
staff remarked, 'Bush saw everybody he wanted to see. He
was not an isolatable [*sic*] figure.'[19] Edie Holiday, who became
Cabinet Secretary in June 1990, explained in some detail the
mechanisms whereby Bush maintained contact with members
of his Cabinet. Ms Holiday and her staff acted as a two-way
conduit between Bush and the executive agencies. They looked
after the President's interests by keeping abreast of initiatives
and 'big surprises' emanating from government departments
while also acting as an advocate for Cabinet officers in the White
House. The latter need arose 'when their policies were being
discussed or heard, or if they wanted to come and see the
President.' Alternatively, 'if they thought something was
happening against their wishes', it was the Cabinet Secretary's
duty to say, 'no you can't do this without talking to Secretary
X because he or she has a very real interest in this issue . . .
[We were] eyes and ears for the Cabinet in the White House
and eyes and ears for the President in the Cabinet.'[20]

As in all administrations Cabinet members from time to
time felt cut off from the President and became convinced
'that some decision had been made where the President had
been misled or had not heard their side of the story.'
Nevertheless, Ms Holiday insisted, 'our President was accessible to any Cabinet member on any issue within a certain
time . . . there were times when he couldn't get to a Cabinet
member because of pressing business, but we maintained

channels of communication.' There was nothing to prevent a Cabinet officer from 'picking up the phone and calling the President, or the President picking up the phone and calling the Cabinet members . . . [this was done] quite frequently; the President encouraged that.' It was also possible for Cabinet members to send written communications to the President on Fridays with the understanding that they would be transmitted directly to him rather than being filtered through the White House staffing process. In short, according to his Cabinet Secretary, President Bush 'worked very hard to maintain separate channels of communication with his Cabinet'.[21]

For all that, as will become apparent later, there is little question but that Cabinet members took second place to White House staff principals when major policy decisions were being made, most notably in domestic policy. Such tendencies may cause alarm among academic purists, but they were eminently justifiable according to Andrew Card who served both in the White House and the Cabinet – for the first three years of the Bush Administration he was Deputy Chief of Staff and then became Secretary of Transportation. Card had no doubt that it was:

> . . . up to the White House to give direction to Cabinet agencies. There were Cabinet members who were not able to pursue their own agenda, but it wasn't their job to pursue their own agenda, it was to pursue President Bush's agenda . . . The White House role in directing the Cabinet is entirely appropriate; the Cabinet is not a management structure, it is a body designed to discuss policy priorities and then manage the bureaucracy.[22]

Vigorous support for Card's position was provided by James Pinkerton, Deputy Assistant to the President for Policy Planning, an 'ideas man' or the closest in the Bush White House to an intellectual in residence. Pinkerton was scornful of anything like cabinet government for the United States. Cabinet members, he insisted:

> . . . are the slaves of their own constituencies . . . They are seemingly incapable of producing any policy that doesn't reflect the institutional bias of their department. So to talk about cabinet government means you are talking about the

education department doing what the education lobby wants it to do; the same with agriculture and so on down the list. That's not leadership, that's some sort of academic senate . . . where everybody gasses away and nothing happens.

Pulling major decisions into the White House was essential in Pinkerton's view; he also thought the problem of accountability could be taken care of by getting rid of the president at the next election if his White House dominated administration should be found wanting.[23]

THE WHITE HOUSE OFFICE

According to the *US Government Manual*:

The White House Office serves the President in the performance of the many activities incident to his immediate office. The staff of the President facilitates and maintains communication with the Congress, the individual members of Congress, the heads of executive agencies, the press and other information media, and the general public. The various Assistants to the President are personal aides and assist the President in such matters as he may direct.[24]

The White House Office is the 'command centre' of the modern presidency; it exists to advance the president's agenda and it is here where major policies are formulated.[25] In the latter regard, Nicholas Calio and James Cicconi echoed the sentiments expressed above by Andrew Card and James Pinkerton. For example, Calio indicated that while policy on relatively minor matters might be formulated at the departmental level the really important decisions were made in the White House. 'Policy making on marine mammals might go on at the Commerce Department . . . but policy making on tax and budget matters is generally pulled within the White House. The Treasury Department has a major role and the Office of Management and Budget does, but the work center and the point of entry is generally at the White House.'[26]

James Cicconi saw the dominance of White House staff in the policy-making process as an inevitable outcome of the emergence of the modern presidency: 'It was part of the evolution of the presidency into an institution which the American people looked to more, [asking it] to provide leadership in a variety of areas that were traditionally left more to cabinet departments . . . There is no doubt that there is a lot of involvement and even a degree of interference by policy people in the White House with what the agencies do.' This could be justified, Cicconi argued, on three grounds: first, 'there was a tendency for agencies to become the captives of the bureaucracy;' second, 'for any major initiative to succeed the involvement of the President and the White House was vitally important,' and third, 'virtually all major policy initiatives these days had inter-agency ramifications [whereas this was not] necessarily true 20 or 30 years ago.'[27]

As these and other witnesses have confirmed cabinet government in the United States is unworkable and presidents are greatly dependent on the assistance provided by their closest aides. 'It is the White House staff on whom modern presidents rely to coordinate the development of their important policies, to control the flow of sensitive information, to keep a close watch on Cabinet responses and to manage crisis actions.'[28] In broad outlines the nature of the White House staff operation remains the same from one presidency to another, but differences of emphasis and structure occur reflecting the contrasting personalities and leadership styles of different chief executives.

There were 23 units in the Bush White House Office ranging from the Office of the Chief of Staff to the Office of the First Lady. [29] The research for this book was based on interviews with a number of those responsible for these various operations. Included amongst these were the offices of the Chief of Staff, the Staff Secretary, National Security Affairs, the President's Counsel, Communications, Public Liaison, Legislative Affairs, Management and Administration, Economic and Domestic policy, National Service, Advance, Appointments and Scheduling, Political Affairs, the Cabinet Secretary and Presidential Personnel. The functions of several of these units have already been touched upon and this will occur again in subsequent chapters. For instance, it will become apparent later that the President's Counsel was an especially significant office in the Bush White House. The Office of National Service was particularly important to Bush and its functions are discussed in Chapter 4. Brent Scowcroft, the Assistant for

National Security Affairs, was, unquestionably, a major player in the Bush White House and his role is discussed in Chapters 7 and 8. In the present chapter I will focus initially on Bush's first Chief of Staff before some further consideration of legislative liaison. I will also discuss Communications and Public Liaison and conclude with the tenure of Samuel Skinner as Bush's second Chief of Staff.

CHIEF OF STAFF I – JOHN SUNUNU

John Sununu, Bush's Chief of Staff for the first three years of his presidency, has been heavily criticized by both journalists and academics. According to *The Economist*: 'Mr Sununu's time as George Bush's tyrannical chief of staff was . . . disastrous,' while Bert Rockman, a senior presidential scholar, when asked to compare Sununu with predecessors in the post said:'I think he is one of the worst. He is clumsy as hell and has no political instinct or sense. He is tied to the fringe of the Republican Party and has kept Bush focused on that fringe while the economy and other issues have brought the president into trouble with the electorate.'[30]

In some respects Sununu was an unlikely candidate for the Chief of Staff position. Bush tended to surround himself with people much like himself, whereas Sununu was clearly not in that category. A Lebanese-Greek American, born in Cuba, and a former professor of engineering, Sununu had made his political reputation as an abrasive Governor of New Hampshire. The link with Bush dated back to the 1988 primary season when the Vice President was beaten into third place in the Iowa caucuses and looked likely to lose in New Hampshire. In desperation, Bush turned to Sununu who commanded an effective state organization and was able to provide the advice and direction needed for Bush to win the New Hampshire primary convincingly. As a reward for these efforts, crucial to Bush's elevation to the White House, Sununu was appointed Chief of Staff.[31]

Some support for the generally negative perceptions of Sununu's tenure in the post has been provided by middle level staff. Kristin Taylor, Director of Media Relations, was bemused by the Chief of Staff's use of obscene language, his apparently constant state of rage and his gratuitous alienation of presidential friend and foe alike. As she saw it, in the end, 'what was originally conceived to be the perfect political balance – the good cop/bad cop dynamic duo of George Bush and John Sununu – actually turned out to be much too much bad, not quite enough of the good.'[32] Charles Kolb, who from March 1990 was Deputy Assistant to the President for Domestic Policy, remarks on Sununu's intolerance of opposition from any quarter, whether in the White House itself, the media or Congress. The Chief of Staff had a 'penchant for belittling those who disagreed with him' and his domineering style stood as an obstacle to policy innovation. 'People kept their mouths shut to avoid being yelled at.' John Keller avoided Sununu wherever possible, declining to expose himself to being screamed at: 'Sununu was a great screamer. He'd have these tantrums that were just ludicrous.'[33]

Some of Sununu's more senior White House colleagues took a more charitable view of his conduct. C. Boyden Gray, the President's Counsel and close friend, was a major figure in the White House and something of a Sununu rival who clashed with him on occasion. Nevertheless, Gray was adamant, 'I had a very good relationship with Sununu. You always got into arguments with him because he was an intellect of the highest order. He knew what he thought and he knew what he was doing and when you got into arguments with him they were fierce . . . but he never bore any grudges and if he got mad or impatient with your point of view it would last for 30 seconds and then be gone.'[34]

Andrew Card, the Deputy Chief of Staff, was an old hand who had served in the Reagan White House and observed several chiefs of staff in action. In his view Sununu was 'outstanding' in the role, second only to James Baker. He combined high intelligence with good political sense, brought necessary discipline to the White House and the Cabinet while complementing the President's management style. 'He was extremely valuable in forming a constructive relationship with Congress on the Clean Air Act and the Americans with Disabilities Act, two of the premier issues in the Bush Administration.' Sununu's command of the detail of legislation was exceptional and he 'was very tough in driving policy from concept to reality'. It was only when his personal problems intruded that his value to the President was lost.[35]

The perspective of one of those principally responsible for legislative liaison was provided by Nicholas Calio. Personally, he got on 'extremely well' with Sununu and was impressed by his accessibility to people like himself. Calio acknowledged that the Chief of Staff's abrasive style sometimes made for difficulties in congressional relations, but added,: 'When he got involved in an issue he would come up [to Capitol Hill] and deal with the members and talk to the members and do what had to be done. Overall he had a productive relationship with Congress.'[36]

The first Staff Secretary, James Cicconi, was full of praise for Sununu's leadership in the early part of the Bush presidency. During that period the White House was a 'fairly collegial place [which] functioned pretty well. A smooth running staff operation was put in place and the President's major priorities from the campaign were dealt with.' The Chief of Staff could be abrasive, but he also had a sense of humour and was endearingly unpretentious. All this seemed to change however, with the abortive budget agreement of 1990. From then on Sununu and his collaborator in the budget negotiations, Richard Darman, the Director of OMB, became excessively 'defensive and critical of others. This criticism was aired openly, particularly by Darman, and as a result senior staff meetings became rather awkward affairs'.[37]

A number of those who observed Sununu at close range obviously do not altogether confirm the intensely negative impressions of his stewardship that have appeared in the press and the academic literature. While by no means uncritical, these witnesses recognize that there were advantages to the Chief of Staff's modus operandi and see that some of the charges made against him are less than fully sustainable.

One of the complaints against Sununu was that he made himself a gatekeeper in the Bush White House comparable to Donald Regan, Reagan's second Chief of Staff, who came close to controlling all forms of access to the President.[38] There was, however, little chance of this happening to the same extent given Bush's hands-on approach and his emphasis on personal relationships. As I noted earlier, it was not easy to isolate Bush; it was an essential part of his nature to keep channels open and active and he communicated with whoever he chose, whenever he was inclined to do so.[39] Nevertheless by 1990 complaints began surfacing in the press from Republican leaders about the President becoming 'too isolated and too dependent on his chief of staff'.[40]

The conservative Republican, Representative Vin Weber of Minnesota, had remarked on this tendency earlier in the year. He argued that Sununu 'really does dominate the decision-making process at the White House totally.' In what is obviously a reference to the pre-Regan, Reagan White House, Weber said that in the previous administration:

> You'd ask, 'how do I influence the decision on this issue?' and it would be 'you need Jim Baker,' and on issue X, it would be 'see if you can get his friend Ed Meese to talk to the President," or on something else, it would be, "enlist Cap Weinberger." When you ask how to influence decision-making in the Bush White House, it's always the same answer: Sununu.'[41]

Weber was concerned with decision-making rather than access and presumably he had domestic policy particularly in mind. The dominance of Sununu in that arena was made possible by the President's well known lack of interest in domestic matters. There was never any chance of Bush being isolated and allowing anyone else to take control of the making of foreign and national security policy, whereas his conservative, guardian posture with regard to domestic affairs created a vacuum that Sununu, and his ally Darman, moved to fill.

As Bush himself recognized, his style of leadership required a hard-nosed chief of staff.[42] If the President was to be conciliatory and accommodating towards powerful adversaries such as Congress, the media and interest groups, he needed someone to run the White House who would be tough, uncompromising and even brutal on occasion. A head man was wanted who would bring order to a large staff and would ensure that decisions were made. This person would give direction to the Administration and would fulfil the vital function of making certain that White House officials and Cabinet members were working for the fulfilment of the President's agenda rather than some other order of priorities.

It made good tactical sense for Bush to appoint someone like Sununu to head his staff for, as Andrew Card saw, he complemented the President's more genteel, kinder, gentler approach.[43] It made it possible for Bush to make agreeable statesmanlike noises on key issues, confident that whatever he said would be offset by his belligerent Chief of Staff. One press commentator compared Bush and Sununu to a wrestling team where one played off against the other: 'Gentleman George and Snarlin' Sununu. Bush may call himself the "environmental President" and the "education President," but he has Sununu to make sure this rhetoric stays relatively cheap.'[44]

Sununu was also valuable to Bush as a 'lightning rod', in that he deflected odium for unpopular decisions that would otherwise fall on the President and undermine his standing with the public.[45] It is also particularly useful for conservative, guardian presidents such as Eisenhower and Bush, instinctively sceptical of what can be achieved by passing laws or spending public money, to have on their staff prominent naysayers, senior aides who can help them in resisting populist pressures – Sherman Adams performed that function for Eisenhower and Sununu recognized that he was expected to do much the same for Bush: 'I know it means I'm going to be perceived as the guy who has to say no, and the president as the guy who . . . might say yes. There hasn't been any planning in the roles; it's just something I understood when I took the job – that end of the stick would be mine.'[46]

Another role assumed by Sununu was that of the link between the Administration and conservative Republicans. Those on the right of the party had longstanding doubts about the President's conservative credentials and for a while at least Sununu appeared to provide some reassurance to an essential element of the coalition that had elected Bush. As a devout Catholic he was in a position to help keep the President in line on abortion and he was also influential on scientific and technological matters. Some of Sununu's colleagues doubted the strength of his conservative convictions beyond his abhorrence of abortion, but in any case his credibility with the right was eventually to be badly eroded by the 1990 budget deal.[47]

The ultimate *raison d'être* of a president's chief of staff is to assist the chief executive in the infinitely problematical endeavour of fulfilling his agenda and there is plenty of evidence that Sununu took that responsibility very seriously indeed. Strenuously denying that he did anything that did not meet with the President's approval the Chief of Staff said:

> There is a fundamental premise that everyone in this city minimizes and that is I'm no freelancer. I meet with the president dozens of times during the day . . . [he] knows I'm following his agenda. What other people may look at is the result not being what they would have liked [but] the aspect of our relationship that is critical is that I know enough about the president to do exactly what he wants done. Exactly what he wants done.[48]

Confirmation of Sununu's unstinting devotion to Bush's objectives was offered by Ed Rogers, his Executive Assistant. He observed that Sununu is a man who approaches nothing half heartedly; he becomes 'totally consumed and absorbed' by what he becomes involved with. Accordingly, in the White House, he became 'a true Bush believer, a Bush zealot . . . we used to say around the White House, if Bush had a runny nose, Sununu had double pneumonia. If Bush kind of grimaced and didn't want to see somebody, Sununu would make them an enemy and make them an enemy for the rest of his life!'[49] Similarly James Pinkerton believed the Chief of Staff was obsessively dedicated to the cause of serving Bush and willing to use for that purpose his 'own self as the battering ram against all comers'.[50]

The Chief of Staff not only rigorously pursued the President's agenda, he also ran the White House in a manner that faithfully reflected the reactive, non-ideological, guardianship style of the President. As one former staffer commented: 'This is a White House consumed with day-to-day tactics, much like the president is. At the morning staff meetings, all you heard is what's up, what's going on, what do we have to react to today. It's not how do we want to approach the next week, the next several weeks.'[51] The absence of a grand plan, or of weekly sub-themes in the manner of the Reagan White House, was, of course, consistent with the President's preferences. At one stage Rogers complained to the Chief of Staff about the Administration's lack of an overall strategy – dealing with everything on an ad hoc basis, he said, 'is killing us.' Sununu was clearly unmoved. 'Look, you want a strategy, my strategy is to maintain maximum flexibility so that I can take advantage of opportunities as they arise.'[52] This was, of course, the very essence of the style adopted by George Bush.

As we have seen, Sununu's aggressive, abrasive style had value as a counter to the President's more congenial posture. Some of those close to Bush doubted whether his kid glove approach in dealing with a deeply partisan Congress was appropriate.[53] Arguably, a legislature firmly under the control of the opposition warranted grim resolution and tough talking from the Chief of Staff. Moreover, interest groups and the media are enormously potent forces in American politics that need to be vigorously resisted if the chief executive is to keep control of the policy process. Having said that, Sununu undoubtedly overplayed his hand on innumerable occasions, arrogantly and sometimes brutally laying into friend and foe in a manner often damaging to the cause he was so dedicated to, the advancement of the President's agenda.

Notwithstanding Calio's defence discussed above and the problems of divided government, there is little doubt that Sununu's extravagant belligerence towards Congress was often a serious liability. Every president has to work with Congress and there is little to be gained from treating the legislature with undiluted contempt. Democratic Senator Timothy Wirth of Colorado was offended by the Chief of Staff's 'condescending attitude' towards many of those on Capitol Hill. 'He has no respect for the intellectual capacity of any of us. He comes up here with that kind of attitude, and our attitude is, who elected you? He in no way acknowledges that there are smart people in Congress too.'[54]

During the 1990 budget negotiations with congressional leaders, Sununu and his ally Richard Darman outraged legislators by their boorishness and studied rudeness. Finally, the very senior Democratic Senator Robert Byrd of West Virginia could stand it no longer and said:

> I have had 30 years in the US Senate, and I have participated in many such summits and I have never in my life observed such outrageous conduct as that displayed by the representatives of the President of the United States. Your conduct is arrogant. It is rude. It is intolerant. I know the President of the United States. I respect him, and I know

that if he knew of your outrageous conduct in these meetings that he would not tolerate it.[55]

Byrd, like Wirth, was a Democrat, but Sununu was hardly
any less savage in his dealings with leading Republicans in
Congress. In the early months of the Bush Administration it
was reported in the press that Sununu had taken exception
to comments made by Representative Robert Michel of Illinois,
the House Republican leader and had 'dressed Mr Michel
down in terms that many in the House found insulting.'[56]
Representative Mickey Edwards of Oklahoma, the Chairman
of the House Republican Policy Committee found himself in
a telephone shouting match with the Chief of Staff over presidential prerogatives in foreign policy. Edwards reported that
Sununu had hung up on him three times as he tried to enlighten
him on the contents of the bill in question.[57] After the
infamous 1990 budget deal was made public Republican
Senator Trent Lott of Mississippi made some critical comments
on television; when the Chief of Staff was asked to react to
Lott's remarks he said: 'Senator Lott has become an insignificant figure in this process.' Subsequently, Lott made clear his
anger at the calculated insult while drawing attention to the
foolishness of Sununu's behaviour given his position as the
spokesman for a minority president. 'I'm going to be here for
sure for four years and two months and maybe longer. There
are only 45 Republicans over here, and one day they are
going to need my vote.' When asked about the possibility of
reconciliation Lott said: 'He is going to have to crawl over
here and beg for it . . . He just stuck the wrong pig.'[58]

The leaders of powerful interest groups normally regarded
as the natural allies of Republican presidents were also not
immune to humiliating tongue lashings from President Bush's
principal aide. Richard Lesher, the President of the US
Chambers of Commerce, aroused Sununu's wrath by having
the temerity to support Senator Daniel Moynihan's proposal
to cut the payroll tax for Social Security. Contacting Lesher
by phone, Sununu indicated his displeasure by announcing
'I'm going to chain-saw your balls off.'[59] Similarly, in 1991,
Bobbie Kilberg made arrangements for a White House meeting
with leaders of the American Medical Association to discuss
the highly sensitive health care issue. Sununu believed the

AMA had purposely misled the White House about its position and then made public statements detrimental to the Administration's stance. At the meeting the Chief of Staff's behaviour was so abusive and insulting as to cause consternation among his own staff. More importantly, it provoked bitter resentment in the AMA delegation, and as a result, Kilberg recalled, 'for months they wouldn't work publicly with any of us.' The AMA leaders also speedily made sure that this unseemly verbal brawl received maximum publicity. 'It was all over the tabloids in five minutes. They left and went out to the steps where the press were waiting and proceeded to say that Sununu had insulted them and that they were leaving.'[60]

As Bush's Chief of Staff, John Sununu was not the unmitigated disaster often suggested, but he was, at best, a mixed blessing. The President needed a tough-minded zealot in the White House to complement his own more decorous style. The good cop/bad cop routine had its uses, as did the Sununu link with the right. Sununu clearly did possess considerable administrative skill; with him at the helm the White House did function reasonably efficiently – decisions were made and the President's agenda, such as it was, was broadly implemented. Nevertheless, for all the Chief of Staff's famous intellect and hard-headedness, he could also be remarkably naive.

One of the keenest and closest observers of Sununu, Ed Rogers, commented on his inability to understand the lasting damage caused by his abrasive behaviour. He seemed to think 'that he could insult somebody and humiliate them at 2 o'clock, share a friendly encounter with them at 4 and everything would be OK.' As we have seen, this may have worked with some equally formidable figures such a C.Boyden Gray, but it was ill-advised as a general strategy. Rogers also found it strange that, unlike most people, Sununu was prone to be much harsher in his treatment of total strangers than he was in dealing with those close to him. 'A freshman congressman would come in, or someone he'd never met before representing the AMA or whatever and he would soak them, really chewing them out from the time they set foot in the office . . . strangers didn't get that sort of deferential, formal, listening, smiling and nodding that goes on here in Washington.'

Another of Rogers' shrewd observations may help to explain

the enigma of John Sununu – an exceptionally intelligent and able politician who seemed unable to grasp how counter productive gratuitous insults and crass behaviour could be. 'Sununu felt no pain,' Rogers explained. 'Pain is a helpful mechanism in that it lets you know that you are involved in behaviour that is bad for you. You put your hand on the stove and it burns you and you know you should move your hand, or else your hand will be consumed by fire . . . He felt no pain and you have to, to some degree, to be a good chief of staff.'[61] This is to suggest that Sununu lacked basic sensitivity: that he was insensitive to the outrage and resentment that he generated and oblivious to the harm that it could do to him and the man that he served. In the early part of Bush's presidency this mattered less, but when the going got rough in 1991 with the onset of recession and the steep decline in the President's popularity, the adverse consequences of Sununu's behaviour became more apparent. It was now, with the 1992 election rapidly bearing down on him, that the President needed allies. He needed the support of the sort of people in Congress, the media and the interest groups that Sununu so delighted in offending. It was George Bush's increasing awareness of this, plus the concerns about Sununu abusing his public office for private purposes, that led finally to his departure from the White House.[62]

After the Chief of Staff, Assistants to the President are the principal members of his staff and it is not without significance that the Bush Administration began with 13 assistants compared with the 22 in the last year of Reagan's presidency and 20 in the first year of Clinton's. As an unambitious, conservative, guardian president with a limited agenda, an aversion to image-making and a distaste for florid speech- making, Bush had less need of an extensive staff. In particular, it is not surprising that the legislative liaison and communications operations in his White House were smaller and less highly regarded than they had been in the Reagan years.

LEGISLATIVE LIAISON

Frederick McClure, Bush's first Assistant for Legislative Affairs, was a low-profile, former Senate aide with a substantially smaller, less-well paid and inexperienced staff when compared to Reagan's.[63] Furthermore, it became clear at an early stage that legislative liaison was firmly under the control of John Sununu, the Chief of Staff, who assumed the chairmanship of a legislative strategy group within the White House.[64]

Members of Congress soon became convinced that McClure was 'out of the loop', that he was not privy to decision-making at the highest level and that he was not invested with the authority to speak on the President's behalf.[65] The weakness of the congressional relations section of the White House Office became glaringly apparent during the abortive and very damaging struggle to secure the nomination of former Senator John Tower of Texas as Secretary of Defense. The rejection of the Tower nomination on the floor of the Senate by a vote of 47–53 was only the ninth such rejection of a Cabinet nominee and the first since 1959.[66]

Evidence of the subordination of legislative liaison to the Chief of Staff (and on this occasion to the Director of the Office of Management and Budget) was provided during the budget crisis of 1990. Nicholas Calio, at that point Deputy Assistant to the President for Legislative Affairs in the House, had a special responsibility for tax issues. However, the first he knew of the President's crucial abandonment of his 'no new taxes' pledge was when he was faxed a copy of the five-line statement already released by Marlin Fitzwater, the Press Secretary. As Calio ruefully observed, Bush's reneging on his most important election promise caused uproar among House Republicans and drastically 'undermined party unity'. The lack of any forewarning to legislative liaison staff made their job immeasurably more difficult. 'We had no time to warn anybody on the Hill. [An essential requirement in] legislative affairs because it can ease whatever kind of obstacles are created later.'[67]

Staff responsible for maintaining good congressional relations might have also regretted the statement that Sununu made on 9 November 1990 to a group of conservatives. Rather than conceding that the budget deal was a disaster for the Administration the Chief of Staff claimed that it was a triumph that provided for restrictions on future spending and would, therefore, act as a restraint on those who lusted after big government. As Sununu saw it, the President would now be able to use his veto more, focusing on 'preventing things from taking place. Let me suggest the following,' he went on. 'There's not another single piece of legislation that needs to be passed in the next two years for this president. In fact, if Congress wants to come together, adjourn, and leave it's all right with us. We don't need them.'[68]

At first sight this was a distinctly imprudent statement, demoralizing to legislative liaison staff and gifting valuable ammunition to the President's political enemies. Indeed, in the coming months, the liberal media and Democratic spokesmen repeatedly seized on Sununu's remark as evidence of the Administration's barren and callous approach to the recession and other problems. It should be remembered, however, that Sununu spoke for a guardian president; for a chief executive who had no time for the activist, reforming model so beloved of liberal Democrats and political scientists. As we saw in Chapter 1, Bush had always doubted the efficacy of government action as a means for curing social ills and regularly invoked the physician's maxim of 'do no harm' as a first rule for public policy-makers.[69]

Nicholas Calio, who eventually replaced McClure as Bush's overall chief of legislative liaison, understood and agreed with the President's reasoning:

> There were many things, in our view, that Congress involved itself in, that government involved itself in, that really [they] shouldn't – micro-managing markets, micro-managing foreign policy. And a lot of the stuff Congress did wasn't any good. Our job was to stop things getting done; it was more defensive than offensive . . . Congress is constantly casting around for legislation on all sorts of issues; it doesn't always help, it doesn't always make things better, in many cases it makes things worse.[70]

Calio's guardian president boss could hardly have expressed his position more clearly himself.

David Demarest, Assistant to the President for Communications, put a slightly different gloss on Sununu's infamous remark. In indicating that it would be just fine with the Administration if Congress left immediately and passed no legislation for the next two years Sununu was, according to Demarest, saying:

The answers to America's problems are not in Congress . . . the answers are in the communities, the answers are in the states, the answers are in your own backyard. When you ask John Q. Public what is going to rebuild his neighborhood, or what's going to get drugs out of his school, they are going to say the family, the schools, their teachers, their ministers, their churches. Congress is going to be about fiftieth on the list.[71]

As Demarest saw all too clearly, Sununu's statement had disastrous political consequences and it undoubtedly contributed to Bush's defeat in 1992; nevertheless it did coincide with the President's world view and his conservative, guardian notions of governance. It is important to bear this in mind if we are to consider Bush's presidency on his own terms rather than those of his political adversaries.

COMMUNICATIONS

Demarest, on his appointment as Director of Communications in the Bush White House, was surprised to discover how wide his responsibilites would be and how few staff he would have to aid him in meeting those obligations. Unusually, he had no longstanding connection with Bush prior to his service as Communications Director, or principal 'spin doctor', in the 1988 campaign. Demarest's White House responsibilities were to be much wider; he was now placed in charge of speech-writing, public liaison and integovernmental affairs. Public liaison staff facilitate two-way relationships betwen the president and interest groups and make possible the building of coalitions in support of his policies. The intergovernmental affairs office, on the other hand, is responsible for communication between the chief executive and state and local governments.[72] In the previous Administration, there had been separate Assistants to the President for public liaison and intergovernmental affairs. Furthermore, 'while Ronald Reagan had roughly 60 or so people to fulfil these functions, I would have 25 to do all that, and that took me by surprise.'[73]

Critics of the Bush presidency have made much of the downsizing of the communications operation that had existed during the Reagan years and have been much taken by allegations that speech-writers were less well paid and were denied White House Mess privileges.[74] A different perspective on these matters is offered by Demarest. The fact that he had wider responsibilities and fewer staff led the press to assume that the President 'wasn't interested in speeches and wasn't interested in the kind of grassroots efforts in building coalitions that Ronald Reagan was interested in. I don't think that in reality it meant that at all.' It was simply the case that the new regime wanted to create new structures within the White House and as 'mine was one of the biggest staffs to start with it got a disproportionate hit in terms of trying to staff these other functions.'

As to the claims about pay and mess privileges for speech-writers, seen by some as deeply symptomatic of a devaluing of such activity, Demarest pungently remarked: 'It was a crock, it was an absolute crock.' Far from not being allowed to employ speech writers at more than $40 000, as Podhoretz claimed, he had hired speech-writers at $60 000 and the matter of mess privileges was without significance. To eat in the White House Mess it was necessary to hold a commission, that is to say to be either an Assistant to the President, a Deputy Assistant to the President or a Special Assistant to the President. Some Reagan speech-writers had held commissions, but it was decided that this would not happen in the Bush White House. 'Because they didn't get commissions they didn't get Mess privileges, but I never took this as any kind of targeting at the speech-writers, of devaluing their function and ironically, none of the people that became speech-writers for Bush ever had a commission.'[75]

PUBLIC LIAISON

The Office of Public Liaison had been an essential element in the Reagan White House. By carefully cultivating the leaders of a myriad of sympathetic interest groups, those who worked in public liaison were able to mobilize support in the country on behalf of the President's policies.[76] As Bobbie Kilberg made clear, George Bush was deeply sceptical of public liaison activity for two reasons. First, as noted in the previous chapter, as a former member of Congress himself, he had a fastidious aversion to going over the heads of legislators. Second, he believed that the office had become altogether too big under Reagan:

> . . . with some staff members promoting their own agendas and becoming captives of their constituencies; representing the interests of those constituencies to the White House rather than the interests of the White House to the constituencies. Bush realized that it had to be a two-way street, but he felt that an imbalance had occurred in the later Reagan years. What the President wanted was a very lean, small shop that focussed on his priorities and that was an integral part of the communications apparatus reporting directly to the Assistant to the President for Communications.

Bush was determined to avoid a recurrence of what had happened in the Reagan White House, where public liaison had been 'a free standing operation headed by an Assistant to the President and viewed as a separate office representing all those pesky interest groups that were going to make life difficult for [the Administration].'[77]

It was also the case that, whereas under Reagan public liaison was dedicated to maintaining fruitful relationships between the White House and conservative activists, the early Bush years were different.[78] Much to the chagrin of right-wing observers, public liaison now worked to build bridges with all sorts of interest groups, even those who were not natural Republican allies:'We opened the doors to meetings with all sorts of people on child care, on welfare reform, on campaign finance reform . . . and we just got lambasted by the right wing.' Later in Bush's term, the spirit of accommodation was less apparent: 'Everybody kind of pulled up the gate a little bit and we could no longer get the President's time for groups that were not supportive.'[79]

Reflecting the President's reservations about public liaison, Sununu placed it under the communications umbrella and made provision for it to be led not by an Assistant to the President, but by two Deputies, Kilberg and Sichan Siv. In the Reagan years there had been a paid staff of close to 60 whereas under Bush that would be reduced to between 11 and 16.[80] While broadly agreeing with the President's scepticism about public liaison, Kilberg conceded that 'we were much too small, we were hampered . . . we had no support staff whatsoever and we had to rely on interns . . . you just cannot operate in an optimum manner with that small a staff.'[81]

A number of presidential aides remarked to this author on the inadequacies of communication in general in the Bush White House and there has been some tendency to lay the blame at the door of staff responsible for this function.[82] However, this may be less than fair. To take one example, the great communications débâcle of the Bush presidency arose from the budget deal of 1990 between the White House and congressional leaders. This definitive event in the history of the Bush Administration will be considered in more detail in Chapter 6 but for the moment it should be noted that it is hardly appropriate to blame communications staff for this catastrophe.

During the negotiations that led to this ill-starred deal, Demarest, the Director of Communications, was completely excluded from the inner circle of policy-makers and he and his staff had no forewarning of the agreement struck with congressional leaders, including the explosively controversial reversal of the President's electoral pledge of 'no new taxes'. Moreover communications staff were not told in advance that the President, in a televised address to the nation, would ask Americans to contact legislators to urge them to support the deal.[83] Public liaison staff, in other words, were given no opportunity to prepare the ground for the appeal by the President, which, not surprisingly, backfired miserably.

The inadequacies of the communications 'shop' in the Bush White House are surely best explained by the personality and leadership style of the President himself. Even if the press and right-wing commentators got some of the details wrong it seems that George Bush's lack of interest in speech-making was the key factor in the undoubted downgrading of speech-writing. As Peggy Noonan said about speech-writers after she had left the Bush entourage: 'They're intrinsically important, but are they important in terms of the political pecking order? They're just above the people who clean up after Millie (the President's dog).'[84]

The very fact that Bush and his closest advisers allowed the Assistant responsible for communications to be totally excluded from the budget negotiations in 1990 surely says much about the low priority accorded his function. The contrast with the standing of someone like Michael Deaver on Reagan's staff is revealing. One of the most experienced and senior figures in the Bush White House, Clayton Yeutter, in reflecting on the Administration's difficulties in getting its message across, commented ruefully: 'I sometimes wonder whether the greatest communications genius in the world could have made that happen.'[85]

CHIEF OF STAFF II – SAMUEL SKINNER

Anyone who doubts whether there were any advantages of consequence to Sununu's style of managing the White House would be well advised to speak with senior staff who also served under his successor. Such witnesses provided me with a picture of an organization descending into chaos after Sununu's replacement by Samuel Skinner. By no means was this entirely attributable to the new Chief of Staff. Indeed, part of the blame rests with Sununu for he left behind a demoralized and faction-ridden staff. His brutal style coupled with his determination to concentrate decision-making in domestic policy in his own hands had contributed much to the demoralization. And the collapse of collegiality in the Bush Administration dated from the 1990 budget deal, for which Sununu bore a large share of the responsibility.

Skinner had been Bush's campaign manager in Illinois in 1988 and had then been appointed to the Cabinet as Secretary for Transportation. Regarded as one of the better Bush appointments, Skinner became Chief of Staff at the end of 1991.[86] The timing of his arrival could hardly have been worse with the White House in considerable disarray. Apart from the difficulties arising from Sununu's tenure, the President's standing in the polls was in steep decline and his former Attorney General, Richard Thornburgh, had recently been well beaten in a crucial US Senate election in Pennsylvania. To add to these difficulties the recession was deepening and Patrick Buchanan was preparing to challenge the President for the Republican nomination.

These circumstances would have tested the most talented of

administrators, but, within a short time, Skinner was seen to be well out of his depth. He introduced some restructuring of the White House and made it more inclusive, but the effect seems to have been to add to the weakness of an already foundering Administration. Senior staff spoke of innumerable, interminable meetings 'where nothing ever got decided and nobody tracked what happened in one meeting as opposed to another meeting and where there were no implementation procedures.'[87] Preparations for the 1992 State of the Union message degenerated into what Kilberg described as a 'circus . . . where there was nobody in charge. Under Sununu we would have had things running like clockwork, and decisions would have been made and actions would have been implemented.'[88] Further evidence of the confusion under Skinner was provided by John Keller. 'There was no leadership, it was management by committee; you couldn't get a decision out. There were different meetings being scheduled at different times of the day. There were different participants but on the same topic; different answers would come out of them and you wouldn't know which one to trust.'[89]

Another staff member recognized that it could be said in Skinner's defence that, unlike Sununu, he was concerned to run the White House by consensual methods:

> Sam tried very hard to seek a way to find consensus and as a result a lot of times decisions were delayed and we found ourselves in meetings upon meetings when Sununu would have said 'do it'. It was a very different style of management. [Both] were trying to serve the President to the best of their ability, but were just very different in style.[90]

One of the most senior members of Bush's entourage was severely critical of Skinner as an administrator.'Sam just doesn't have administrative skills . . . he would either have a decision on his desk forever and just not make it, or he would swing to the other extreme and make a capricious decision in fifteen seconds . . . you can't do that and sustain the credibility of the place and [maintain] the respect of the people that work there.' Consequently, Skinner's standing in the White House was quickly undermined: 'He undercut himself with his own shortcomings.'[91]

How is the Skinner appointment to be explained? It should

be said first that he was a fervent Bush loyalist who had served the President in the 1988 campaign and had been something of a presidential troubleshooter as Secretary of Transporation. Moreover, in the latter role, Skinner was believed to have been a particularly good administrator. In addition, Skinner had strengths that his predecessor lacked. A contest-winning salesman with IBM early in his career, he was a notably outgoing and friendly man with 'an ability to get on with almost anyone, including Democrats'.[92] There was little chance of Skinner abusing senior members of Congress in public, or of launching gratuitous, verbal assaults on interest group leaders.

Unlike Sununu, Skinner was not impervious to pain, with one source describing him as 'very, very sensitive to criticism.'[93] Indeed in several respects the one chief of staff was the obverse of the other. 'Sununu certainly had his shortcomings. He was an autocratic chief of staff and that's not the ideal personality for the job. He had fundamentally sound management and administrative skills [but lacked] human relations skill. Sam Skinner was the opposite, he had great human relations skills, everybody loved Sam, but he had horrible management skills.'[94] It may be that the ideal chief of staff would be a combination of Skinner and Sununu, and James Baker, who replaced Skinner in the summer of 1992, came close to filling the bill, but his appointment came too late to save Bush from electoral defeat.

4 A Guardian's Agenda

By definition guardians have only limited agendas. As conservators they are largely content with things as they are. They are not driven by the reformist zeal that characterizes other presidents and they are deeply sceptical as to what can be achieved by governmental action. As Stephen Hess said of Eisenhower: 'His aspirations as president were limited to two overriding objectives: peace abroad and a balanced budget at home. In keeping with those aspirations, his view of the presidential role was circumscribed.'[1] George Bush's ambitions were similarly modest.

In campaigning for the presidency in 1988 he revealed no grand vision of how the world should be remade. Unlike fellow Republicans such as Goldwater and Reagan he did not see himself as any sort of crusader; he offered himself to the voters not as an architect of fundamental change, but as a leader dedicated to broadly preserving the status quo, as a candidate who would be a guardian president. The previous administration had moved the country in new directions and that movement needed to be consolidated and built upon. Some modifications and adjustments were needed, a case could be made for modest incremental change, but nothing more than that.

From the beginning Bush made no apology for being a reactive leader, believing that he was especially well qualified to deal with problems as they arose. Early in his presidency it was reported that his decision-making was characterized by 'a case-by-case approach that is centered on the details and circumstances immediately at hand and less on ideology or concern about consistency . . . [he] is confident that if he makes enough of what he calls the "right decisions," his actions will cumulatively move the country in the right direction.'[2]

Grandiose schemes of social engineering like the New Deal and the Great Society held little appeal for Bush: 'I have no great love for the imaginings of the social planners.'[3] Politicians needed to guard against arousing undue expectations, and the value of legislation as a vehicle of reform was, in any case,

86

doubtful. Many of the objectives of would-be reformers were best met by private rather than public action; by charities and voluntary work rather than by governments.

Contrary to the liberal Democratic craving for expanding the role of government, Bush was dedicated to shrinking the size of government wherever possible, to ensuring 'that government intrudes as little as possible in the lives of the people.'[4] And, as a conservative Republican, he was particularly averse to government interference in the economy. He saw it as his responsibility to 'set the economy free' by keeping taxes low, diminishing the burden of regulation, reducing public expenditure and promoting free trade.

Governance for a president like Bush was a low-key, low-profile affair with little room for ideology or flamboyant rhetoric. Leadership was best effected through conciliation, compromise and behind-the-scenes negotiation rather than by noisy confrontation. The first rule for those responsible for the making of public policy was 'do no harm' and chief executives had a duty to restrain Congress in this regard. They needed to act as a bar to undesirable legislation, using the veto, or the threat of its use, to modify bills, or to keep them from the statute book altogether. Finally, for a guardian president no part of his job is more important than the conduct of American foreign policy. This is his principal preoccupation and it is here that his skills as a crisis manager are likely to be most severely tested.

Bush not only saw himself as a guardian in the White House, he also faced notably unpromising circumstantial variables, making a nonsense of simple comparisons between his achievements in office and those of other incumbents. FDR, for example, became president during a period of domestic emergency and enjoyed the support of vast majorities in Congress. Similarly, Johnson's much admired performance as chief legislator in the early years of his presidency was made possible by massive congressional support and the mood of the country engendered by the Kennedy assassination. Reagan, in 1981, could reasonably claim a mandate for change and for six years had the advantage of a Republican controlled Senate.

There was no emergency and no clamour for change in January 1989. Both the public opinion polls and the 1988 election results were rightly interpreted by Bush as signifying a desire among the American people for continuity rather than anything more than marginal change. As George C. Edwards commented at the time: 'I don't see any great demands in the country for policy change. The period is just not one for great change.'⁵ Shortly before he entered the White House Bush himself specifically eschewed any desire to embark on a dramatic 'first hundred days' in the time-honoured manner of FDR. Bush said: 'I've been a part of this administration and it isn't like there is a need for radical change.' He acknowledged that action would be required to deal with the deficit, but beyond that he planned to build on the 'tremendous successes' of the Reagan years. 'That's at least the approach that I'm going to bring to the job . . . People understood that when they were voting. They weren't looking for a radical shift.'⁶

Even if Bush had not been a guardian president and had entertained activist ambitions the line-up of party strength in the House and the Senate after the 1988 elections would have made the fulfilment of any such agenda most unlikely. With large Democratic majorities against him in both houses Bush's standing *vis à vis* Congress as he took up office was the weakest of any president elected in the twentieth century, an unenviable distinction which had previously belonged to Richard Nixon. In 1969 there were 58 Democrats and 42 Republicans in the Senate, compared to 55 Democrats and 45 Republicans twenty years later. However, in the House in 1969, Nixon could claim the support of 192 Republicans whereas Bush, in 1989, had to work with 175 Republicans as against 260 Democrats.⁷

These are some of the factors that need to be kept in mind in evaluating the Bush presidency. We need to understand how he saw his role rather than measuring him against yardsticks provided by his political opponents. He had neither the desire for, nor a mandate for, fundamental change and was content to be a reactive rather than a visionary leader. Instead of an activist or an expansionist in the manner of liberal Democratic and even some Republican presidents Bush was a minimalist seeking to limit the reach of government. Nowhere was this more the case than in economic policy where, as he saw it, government meddling could be harmful to the self-correcting mechanisms of a free market economy. It was incumbent on presidents to engage in defensive activity designed to prevent the passage of legislation harmful to the national interest and the management of foreign policy was their paramount. These are the conditions under which Bush assumed the presidency and they provide the terms on which he is entitled to be judged.

A LIMITED AGENDA

In assessing the effectiveness, or capacity for statecraft, of any president the crucial question is what policies did he espouse and how far did he succeed in imposing them on the political system? In the case of a guardian president this may seem to present difficulties in that, by definition, such chief executives take up office unencumbered by ambitious policy programmes. Nevertheless, limited though it was in scope, George Bush could not avoid having an agenda of some sort when he ran for the presidency in 1988. A quandary for a guardian is that he doesn't want to do very much, but can hardly afford to say so. The voters are bound to ask what he intends to do if elected and will be unimpressed by purely negative answers. In campaigning Bush often spoke as if his experience and qualifications were alone sufficient to merit his election, but the realities of electoral politics required that he also offer some specifics.

In accepting the Republican nomination Bush said: 'I'm a man who sees life in terms of missions – missions defined and missions completed.' He went on to outline the elements of a programme before concluding: 'This is my mission. And I will complete it.' Necessarily Bush's 'mission' did not include major change; his principal purpose would be securing and building on the gains of the Reagan era. 'The most important work of my life is to complete the mission we started in 1980. And how, and how do we complete it? We build on it.' The previous administration had restored the strength of the American economy and 'with the right leadership it will remain strong.' Economic success was dependent on growth and this would continue provided the United States maintained its 'commitment to free and fair trade [and] by keeping government spending down and by keeping taxes down.' From this flowed Bush's ill-fated pledge of 'no new taxes'.

He also undertook to create 30 million jobs in eight years, to improve the educational system and to work for a drug-free America. In addition, disabled people were to be brought into the mainstream and environmental concerns were to be accorded a high priority. While distancing himself from Reagan's fiercely anti-government rhetoric Bush emphasized in his acceptance speech the need to keep government in its proper place and stressed the virtues of voluntary organizations, 'a brilliant diversity spread like stars, like a thousand points of light in a broad and peaceful sky'.

As Bush saw it, reviving the innate strength of the American economy had been one of President Reagan's most significant achievements, a development paralleled by a necessary strengthening of the nation's defences which had, in turn, brought great gains in international affairs. Bush undertook to continue with this policy of 'peace through strength', tempered by further cuts in strategic and conventional forces. Another high priority would be efforts to accomplish a total ban on chemical and biological weapons. At the Convention Bush also made the first of a number of appeals for a 'kinder and gentler nation' in which harmony and tolerance prevailed and where the evils of materialism and corruption were eradicated. In the same spirit Bush in his inaugural address invoked the timeless ideals of 'duty, sacrifice, commitment, and a patriotism that finds expression in taking part and pitching in'. Bush was then not entirely without an agenda. In his acceptance speech and elsewhere he did lay out a broad outline of what he hoped to achieve, a limited programme which can be used for evaluative purposes.[8]

Some years ago, James MacGregor Burns noted that since Franklin Roosevelt, 'the classic test for greatness in the White House has been the chief executive's capacity to lead Congress.'[9] Clearly for a guardian president, imposing himself on the legislature is somewhat less crucial than for dedicated activists like Roosevelt and Johnson et al., but for all that the effectiveness of any president is greatly dependent on his ability to get Congress to conform to his wishes.

In this regard the Bush administration began in a most unpromising fashion with the defeat in the Senate of the President's first nomination for Secretary of Defense John Tower. This rejection of a Cabinet nominee was only the ninth in the history of the United States and the first since 1959.[10] Furthermore, no president had ever before been denied a Cabinet choice in his first term. This humiliating setback at the outset of Bush's presidency had ominous implications for his leadership. As one magazine noted, 'A primal commandment for new Presidents, particularly those faced with a Congress controlled by the opposition party: Thou shalt avoid early defeats. The opening days are the time when Congress and the public – and foreign leaders – are sizing up the new man. The perceptions they form early are likely to color their view of the President throughout his term.'[11]

On its face the selection of Tower had seemed to be a sound choice. A good relationship with Congress is essential for any Secretary of Defense and Tower had for 24 years (1961–1985) been a member of the Senate himself; Congress moreover, is notorious for treating its 'own' kindly. It is also valuable for presidents to place in key Cabinet positions appointees whose loyalty can be relied upon and Tower had ben a close political ally of George Bush for a quarter of a century.

In explanation of this disastrous reverse commentators focused on the inexperience and tactical errors of John Sununu, the Chief of Staff, Frederick McClure, the chief lobbyist, and those who worked for them. As an exercise in legislative liaison the effort to get Tower confirmed was unimpressive. The crucial vote in the Armed Services Committee took place when the President and his Chief of Staff were in Japan, vote counting proved unreliable and the administration managed to offend deeply the most important congressional player of all in the nomination process, Senator Sam Nunn of Georgia, the chairman of the Committee.

The President's staff failed to appreciate how damaging allegations of womanizing, conflict of interest problems and excessive drinking were to Tower's case. Ultimately, the latter charge proved to be the most telling with Nunn announcing: 'I cannot in good conscience vote to put an individual at the top of the chain of command when his history of excessive drinking is such that he would not be selected to command a missile wing, a SAC (Strategic Air Command) bomber squadron or a Trident missile submarine.'[12] On 23 Febuary 1989 the Tower nomination was rejected by the Committee in a straight party line vote of 11–9, a decision that was confirmed by the full Senate on 6 March by a vote of 53–47. Senator Dole, the Minority Leader, and other Republicans, excoriated the Democrats who voted solidly against the nomination, for partisanship, whereas the President adopted a more moderate tone, regretting the 'groundless rumors' that lay behind the rejection, while adding: 'Now, however, we owe it to the American people to come together and to move forward.'[13]

This comment was more in line with the conciliatory sentiments that Bush had expressed at his inauguration and a few weeks later the advantages in such an approach were seen in the agreement struck with Congress over aid to the Contras. This agreement, discussed further in Chapter 7, was the result of quiet, painstaking negotiation behind the scenes, and represented a notable triumph for the White House to set against the Tower fiasco.

As we have seen, guardian presidents are not disposed to be activists in the White House. It is not in their nature to proliferate legislative initiatives, a stance which, unfortunately for them, runs counter to the 'dominant perspective' of American politics. That which says that a good president, 'is one who makes government work, one who has a program and uses his resources to get it enacted. The good president is an activist: he sets the agenda.'[14] Presidents are expected, moreover, to get away to a fast start, to 'hit the ground running', to emulate, as best they can, the spectacular success of Franklin Roosevelt in his first 'hundred days'.

At the end of the first hundred days of the Bush presidency, White House staff went out of their way to downplay the significance of such benchmarks. And yet given the 'dominant perspective' they felt obliged to brief newsmen on the President's achievements so far. As one senior aide put it, 'while we do not acknowledge the significance of the first 100 days we acknowledge that everybody is going to write 100 day stories.'[15] In conducting such briefings there was little to point to that had actually been completed other than the Nicaragua accord and a budget agreement negotiated with the legislature in a similar spirit of conciliation and compromise, but widely criticized as being largely meaningless.[16] Initiatives that the Administration were said to have in train included a plan to rescue savings and loan institutions and legislation to deal with third world debt, child care, education and ethics in government.

The slimness of Bush's legislative record in the early months of his Administration was charitably received, even in the liberal press, but media comment became far more severe later in 1989.[17] Newspapers were now inclined to make much of the analysis of congressional rolls calls by the *Congressional Quarterly* showing that Bush won only 63 per cent of the votes on which he took an unambiguous position in 1989, the lowest figure for any elected first-year president since CQ began compiling such figures.[18]

A notably trenchant attack against 'The Can't Do Government' was launched by *Time* magazine highlighting the various pressing problems both at home and abroad that were not receiving attention, and holding the President, in particular, responsible for this state of affairs. In a response wholly fitting for the press spokesman of a guardian president Marlin Fitzwater retorted: 'You liberal writers are just like the Democrats in Congress. You think Government isn't doing anything unless it's taxing and spending and creating new bureaucracies.' For their part the writers of the article concluded with the alternative, and much more fashionable view of what a president's role should be:

> The conservative complaint that only liberal elitists think that Washington must actually *do* something is self-evidently silly. Of course the government must do something. That is why it exists: to act in ways that improve the lives of its citizens and their security in the world. The list of missed opportunities and ignored challenges is already much too long. The sooner Government sets about doing its job again, the better.[19]

Not all the challenges went unanswered however and in 1990 Congress approved a sweeping environmental reform bill as well as legislation to provide relief for disabled Americans. Bush himself and members of his staff have invariably cited these two enactments when asked to identify the principal, domestic policy achievements of his presidency.[20]

THE 1990 CLEAN AIR ACT AMENDMENTS

For some years before Bush became President Congress had been wrestling with the clean air issue. This was a problem desperately difficult to solve given the divisions and conflicts of interest across the country in such matters and the vagaries of a regime of separated powers, weak parties, potent pressure groups and legislators tied closely to their constituents. Environmentalist members of the House and Senate were convinced that existing laws needed to be strengthened, but they were opposed by others worried about the costs of any such changes to business and consumers and the consequences for employment. 'Few argued against the value of clean air, but the potential price in lost jobs and increased costs to industry and consumers left Congress intractably divided for a decade.'[21]

Those in Congress who pressed for change were concerned by the failure of the Environmental Protection Agency to fulfil the promises of the Clean Air Act of 1970, particularly during the eight years of the Reagan Administration. Any attempts to move forward on clean air during the Reagan era faced resistance from the White House and from formidable congressional barons, men such as Representative John Dingell of Michigan, Chairman of the Energy Committee and resolutely opposed to the passage of bills harmful to the automobile industry. Similarly, Senator Robert Byrd of West Virginia, the leader of the Senate Democrats, used his control over scheduling to thwart acid rain proposals that he believed would damage the sulphur coal mining industry in his state. In short, with regard to the clean air issue, there was a log-jam on Capitol Hill, an impasse unlikely to be broken without leadership from the White House, which, rather surprisingly, Bush was to provide.

In accepting his party's nomination Bush endeavoured to distance himself from Reagan on the environment issue saying specifically, 'we must clean the air.' In some respects Bush was an unlikely champion of the environmental cause. As Reagan's chairman of the Task Force on Regulatory Relief he had been the Administration's point man for deregulation, a role which found him enthusiastically endorsing various EPA authored changes in regulations designed to dilute the effects of earlier clean air legislation.[22] Nevertheless, Bush, in June 1989, honoured his campaign commitment by presenting to Congress a clean air proposal, an initiative applauded by one not usually sympathetic source, as follows: 'Mr Bush, simply by joining the debate in a serious way, has moved the middle ground. The question seems no longer to be whether there will be the new law that circumstances require, but how soon and what kind.'[23]

The debate sparked off by the Administration's proposal was taken up in the Senate by the Environment and Public Works Committee which, in late 1989, reported out a bill far stronger than either the President's bill, or a corresponding measure under consideration in the House. The Senate Committee bill, like other versions including that finally signed into law, had four main sections. One of these involved tightening the controls on emissions from motor vehicles; a second was concerned with urban smog; a third dealt with toxic air pollutants and a fourth was aimed at acid rain.

The heavy costs implied by the Senate bill, estimated at $42 billion by the EPA, antagonized both industry and the White House with the President threatening to veto any measure with a cost more than 10 per cent higher than the $19 billion price tag put on his bill. Subsequently, a month of negotiations behind closed doors by representatives from the Senate and the Administration produced a compromise measure behind which Senate leaders and representatives of the White House were able to unite. It was reported by Roger Porter, Assistant to the President for Economic and Domestic Policy and Bush's chief negotiator on the clean air bill, that 'The President is extremely pleased with this agreement.'[24]

Progress on clean air in the Senate was greatly helped by the replacement of Robert Byrd as Democratic leader by the environmentalist Senator George Mitchell of Maine who battled to fend off amendments that would have destroyed the deal worked out with the White House. Byrd, however, while no longer leader, was Chairman of the all-powerful Appropriations Committee. He was also a highly skilled parliamentarian and, drawing on both these resources, he came within a hair's breadth of derailing the compromise worked out between the Senate and Bush's staff. This was brought about by Byrd sponsoring an amendment to provide generous compensation for high-sulphur coal miners expected to be thrown out of work by the acid rain control provisions in the proposed legislation. An original estimate of costs to the taxpayer of $1.4 billion led to pressure on Byrd to modify his plan, but even $700 million was too much for the White House which let it be known that the President would veto any bill including such a provision. Byrd's amendment was eventually beaten back by a 49–50 vote, a result that turned on bad weather preventing one Senator from returning to Washington, the flightiness of a few of the votes promised to Byrd, and the veto threat.[25]

Negotiations in the House were no less fraught and the outcome was similarly threatened by numerous amendments, including a proposal approved by a vote of 274–146 calling for a $250 million programme for unemployment and retraining benefits for workers who lost their jobs. President Bush expressed his displeasure at these provisions and, during the conference stage, there were indications that they might lead to the bill being vetoed. In the event, after further negotiation on this matter with the White House, the Senate and the House approved a clear air package which was then signed into law by the President on 15 November 1990.[26]

There has been some dispute as to the significance of the Clean Air Act of 1990. The President described it as 'the most significant air pollution legislation in our nation's history' and his Counsel went even further in describing it as 'the most sweeping environmental statute in the history of the world'.[27] Elsewhere the gains from the Act were seen as marginal and the burden of costs that it imposed remained a matter of great concern to industrial interests that would resurface to damage Bush later in his presidency.

Reference to these latter sentiments provoked a typically robust response from C. Boyden Gray, the President's Counsel and a major player on the clean air issue in the Bush White House. He said: 'I'd go up against anybody that the costs were negative; that is the Clean Air Act, as it was passed, reduced costs on the American public in comparison to what it replaced. Sure it added some costs, but overall the benefits vastly exceeded the costs.' Gray went on to argue that the Clean Air Act was a truly 'great piece of reform legislation' of great benefit to the American economy. The 'ultimate' test of any reform bill:

... the marketplace test [was] productivity. Manufacturing productivity, service productivity, the ultimate test is productivity. [Some critics argue that such legislation] renders us unproductive, you're wasting dollars, you're not competitive. The fact of the matter is the US has uncontested the best air quality of any industrialized country on earth. Uncontested the best manufacturing productivity growth and service growth ... [Let] the facts speak for themselves. We have the best air quality [and] we have the most competitive industry.'[28]

If the Clean Air Act is to be seen as a mark of Bush's effectiveness, of his ability to translate goals into policy realities, it has to established that it was, in a real sense, *his* bill. This too is open to dispute with some claiming that the bill 'originated in the Congress, among Democrats.'[29] There is obviously something in this argument; like any complex, controversial bill its success depended on a number of key actors both in Congress and the White House. Nevertheless, Bush's role was surely crucial as the Democratic Chairman of the Conference Committee, Senator Max Baucus of Montana, generously conceded on the Senate floor: 'George Bush turned around the previous administration's point of view. The Reagan administration was very much opposed to clean air. The Bush administration is very much in favor of clean air. George Bush deserves major credit.'[30]

There seems to be little doubt that without Bush's initiative in June 1989, his commitment and the efforts that he and his staff put into negotiating with Congress there would not have been a Clean Air Act. This was, by any standard, an impressive exercise of presidential leadership as his chief lobbyist in the House at the time later claimed. 'Congress had struggled for years ... to re-write the Clean Air Act. They were never able to do it until they got the leadership and the cooperation out of the president. Now there were people within our party who didn't like that because they didn't want any [change] but there's no chance in the world all those disparate factions could have been brought together without the leadership of the President.'[31] Some confirmation for this accolade is provided by a more neutral observer Paul Quirk, who says that the Clean Air Act was, 'probably Bush's principal self-initiated domestic policy accomplishment', one achieved in the face of 'regional and sectoral conflicts . . . so intense and complicated that some doubted that any bill could obtain a majority.'[32]

THE AMERICANS WITH DISABILITIES ACT

The Americans with Disabilities Act, so often wheeled out by Bush and his staff as another of his greatest accomplishments, is hardly in the same league in terms of presidential input. It was not a Bush bill to the same degree as the Clean Air Act and its passage was far less problematical. In sending a clean air proposal of his own to Congress in June 1989 Bush had moved the legislative process forward in an infinitely troublesome area, whereas disability legislation was already progressing through the system when he became President.

The need for such a bill had been first advanced by the National Council on Disability in 1985 which then prevailed on the Republican Senator Lowell Weicker of Connecticut to draft the first version of the ADA bill in 1987. On Weicker's electoral defeat in 1988 sponsorship of the bill was taken up by Senator Tom Harkin, Democrat of Iowa, while, in the House, the main sponsor originally was Representative Tony Coelho, Democrat of California. After the latter's resignation responsibility for the bill in the House fell primarily to Representative Steny Hoyer, Democrat of Maryland, later commended for 'skillfully shepherding [the ADA] through substantive and procedural obstacles in 1989 and 1990'.[33]

In campaigning for the presidency Bush came out strongly in support of the ADA. In his acceptance speech at the 1988 Convention he said, 'I am going to do whatever it takes to make sure the disabled are included in the mainstream. For too long they've been left out. But they're not going to be left out anymore.' Immediately before he took up office, the President reiterated his commitment. In a speech at the Department of Health and Human Services he said, 'One step that I've discussed will be action on the Americans with Disabilities Act, in simple fairness, to provide the disabled with the same rights afforded other minorities.'[34]

Nevertheless it is evident that the Bush Administration did not originate this bill and it is not inconceivable that it would have passed even without the President's enthusiastic support. The public, for instance, appeared to be solidly behind the idea of change with a Gallup poll in 1989 establishing that 81 per cent of Americans believed that existing policies with regard to the disabled were inadequate.[35] And it was not easy for anyone to oppose such a bill, as a *Reason* editorial noted: 'The ADA is the nicest bill to come along in a long time. Only the scum of the earth would oppose protecting [the disabled] from discrimination. It wouldn't be nice.'[36]

The chances of disability rights legislation passing were also helped by the personal interest of many of the prime movers. Coelho was himself an epileptic as was Hoyer's wife. Senator Harkin had a brother who had been deaf since childhood. Senator Edward Kennedy, Democrat of Massachusetts, and Chairman of the Labor Committee, had a mentally retarded sister and a son who had lost a leg to cancer. The Minority Leader in the Senate, Senator Robert Dole, Republican of Kansas, had suffered serious injury in the Second World War and was partially disabled. Finally a daughter of George Bush's had died of leukaemia and two of his sons suffered some form of disablement.

A starting point for many of those who campaigned for changes in the law to benefit the disabled was the 1964 Civil Rights Act which made illegal discrimination in employment and public accommodations based on race, sex, religion or national origin. The ADA was modelled on the 1964 Act, but was necessarily much more far reaching. The earlier legislation was primarily directed against discriminatory practices preventing black people from obtaining employment or using restaurants, hotels, cinemas, swimming pools, etc. It was designed to correct the adverse consequences arising from racial prejudice in the white majority. The ADA, however, was concerned not just with majority attitudes, but with providing the facilities whereby disabled people could enjoy fuller lives. As Pat Wright of the Disability Rights and Education Fund put it: 'Sometimes there are barriers that prevent people from getting in to be discriminated against. The problem [for the disabled] has been getting them in the door.'[37]

Under the ADA establishments were required to make new or remodelled facilities accessible to disabled people seeking jobs or endeavouring to make use of public accommodations;

existing facilities were to be similarly modified where that was 'readily achievable'. Whereas the 1964 Act did not incur substantial costs this could not be said of the ADA:

> The bill's scope is vast. New apartment blocks and business buildings – restaurants, grocery stores, dry cleaners – must be made accessible to the disabled, for instance, with ramps and widened doorways: employers must make 'reasonable accommodations' for employees with disabilities: hotels' and car rental companies' new pick-up vans must have wheelchair lifts; public transit must do the same, and must also provide door-to door service for people who can't get to the bus stop.[38]

The massive costs arising from these requirements provided the basis for strong opposition to the ADA by business interests and their many allies in Congress. Many of Bush's critics on the right of the Republican party moreover were deeply troubled by the additional burdens being placed on industry and commerce and pointed to the ADA (and the Clean Air Act) as 'significant drags on the country's economic recovery'.[39] At first sight there was indeed some incongurity between a President supposedly committed to the free market and his willingness to impose large additional regulatory costs on business. C. Boyden Gray, the senior White House aide principally responsible for the ADA, vigorously rebutted such allegations arguing that the legislation was entirely consistent with Bush's conservative principles.[40]

Gray claimed that the ADA was the 'greatest welfare reform ever pulled off', and a few statistics illuminate that point of view. A survey of disabled persons in 1985 showed that 66 per cent of disabled persons aged 16–64 were not working and 65 per cent of those not employed said that they would prefer to work.[41] Elsewhere it was estimated that the unemployed disabled collected 'federal disability and welfare checks, costing nearly $60 billion a year'.[42] With some reason therefore Gray argued that the largest consumer of welfare in the country was not 'the black community, not the unwed mothers drawing Aid for Dependent Children, it is the disabled.'[43]

When Gray and Michael Boskin, the President's Chairman of the Council of Economic Advisers, sat down at the beginning of the Bush Administration to ponder the implications of the ADA they focused on the question: 'How can you justify doing this if it's going to undermine your regulatory principles?' They believed they had the answer to their question after Boskin had calculated the benefits and set them against the costs. This revealed that by making it possible for disabled people to get off welfare, to earn their own living and pay taxes, the benefits 'completely dwarfed the costs of the plan and that was the basis on which we proceeded.'

Gray spoke rather bitterly of the failure of the press to give Bush credit for empowering the disabled and said further, 'It is not as much appreciated now as it will be in about ten years as the baby boom generation hit their wheelchairs and their canes and their whatever, and then people will realize as the population really ages how important it was to prepare for that eventuality.'[44] Bobbie Kilberg, Deputy Assistant to the President for Public Liaison, also stressed Bush's interest in empowerment. In an emotional address at the signing of the ADA:

> He talked about giving people the opportunity to be in the mainstream economically, with a sense of self-worth . . . he believed very strongly in giving everybody a chance to participate fully in society and giving everybody a chance to earn their own way. Yes, he didn't like the idea of regulation and he's very strongly in favor of a free market, but he also had a very strong social conscience.[45]

To set against these laudatory interpretations there are the views of those on the right of the Republican party troubled by the added burden of regulations and unconvinced that such legislation made more than a marginal contribution to the pressing social problems of the United States. It is also necessary to bear in mind that despite Gray's adamant insistence that the ADA 'would not have happened without [Bush], no question about it', it can be argued, as I have suggested above, that the President's role was less important than that; his part in it was undoubtedly important, but it is far from clear that the ADA can be simply simply regarded as his accomplishment.[46]

THE POINTS OF LIGHT MOVEMENT

If there is reason to doubt just how far the ADA can be categorized as a Bush accomplishment there is no question whatsoever as to who deserves the credit for the 'Thousand Points of Light' initiative even if the ideas behind it had been aired on a number of occasions by Reagan.[47] However, this is not an achievement taken at all seriously by Bush's many critics across the political spectrum. From the start cartoonists lampooned the idea, with Herblock, for example, showing a drunk asking for a 'thousand pints of lite'; elsewhere it was assailed as a trivial, opportunist programme born out of *noblesse oblige* and unlikely to make a serious contribution to the amelioration of deep-rooted social problems.[48]

Such criticisms are, however, beside the point for the purposes of this analysis. I am not concerned here with judgements as to the desirability of Bush's policies, but with his effectiveness in the sense of gaining acceptance of those policies. In pursuing that line of inquiry it becomes very clear that while Bush's adversaries in the media and elsewhere did not think highly of the thousand points of light policy it was, for the President, of the greatest importance, as he indicated as he prepared to depart from the White House:

> If I could leave but one legacy to this country, it would not be found in policy papers or even in treaties signed or even wars won; it would be [a] return to the moral compass that must guide America through the next century, the changeless values that can and must guide change. And I'm talking about a respect for the goodness that made this country great, a rekindling of that light lit from within to reveal America as it truly is, a country with strong families, a country of millions of Points of Light.[49]

However much it was derided by Bush's critics, the points of light phrase encapsulated ideas central to his presidency. It first entered the lexicon of American politics in Bush's acceptance speech at the 1988 Republican Convention.[50] As is so often the case with catchy political slogans the meaning behind it was, at first, not at all clear. Bush made use of it in a passage of his speech apparently concerned with reaffirming the advantages of American pluralism:

We are a nation of communities, of thousands of ethnic, religious, social business, labor union, neighborhood, regional and other organizations – all of them varied, voluntary and unique. This is America: the Knights of Columbus, the Grange, Hadassah, the Disabled American Veterans, the Order of AHEPA, the Business and Professional Women of America, the union hall, the Bible study group, LULAC, 'Holy Name' – a brilliant diversity spread like stars, like a thousand points of light in a broad and peaceful sky.[51]

Elsewhere in the same speech Bush called for a 'kinder and gentler nation', deplored materialism, self-centredness and blind ambition and alluded to the merits of voluntary service.

Further elaboration of these ideas appeared in Bush's inaugural address where he noted the limited contribution that government could make to the alleviation of social problems, stressed the inherent goodness of the American people and reflected on the possibility of putting that strength to use:

I am speaking of a new engagement in the lives of others – a new activism, hands-on and involved, that gets the job done. We must bring in the generations, harnessing the unused talent of the elderly and the unfocused energy of the young . . . I've spoken of a thousand points of light – of all the community organizations that are spread like stars throughout the nation doing good . . . The old ideas are . . . timeless: duty, sacrifice, commitment, and a patriotism that finds its expression in taking part and pitching in.[52]

Several months later Bush provided the clearest statement yet of the thinking behind the thousand points of light initiative. His starting point was the high level of commitment to voluntary service already existing in the United States which had helped 'countless Americans find self-respect and dignity'. It was now necessary to extend substantially these efforts; there were limits to what government could do, it 'can't rebuild a family or reclaim a sense of neighborhood.' Throwing public money at problems had been shown to be futile in the past and the 'key to constructive change [lay in] building relationships not bureaucracies.'

The President recalled the various forms of community service that he and his wife had been involved in during their time in Texas; he noted the sense of self-fulfilment that such work brought, and continued: 'Today more than ever, we need community service to help dropouts, pregnant teens, drug abusers, the homeless, AIDS victims, the hungry and illiterate.' To relieve the pain and isolation of such people required the voluntary help of individual Americans as well as schools, churches, businesses and civic groups. 'For this is what I mean when I talked about a Thousand Points of Light: That vast galaxy of people and institutions working together to solve problems in their own backyard.'

Urging citizens and organizations to extend community service to all parts of the nation, Bush stressed the non-governmental nature of the movement being created: 'This is not a program, not another bureaucracy.' Using a form of words which he was constantly to reiterate in speeches during the remaining years of his presidency, Bush said 'from now on in America any definition of a successful life must include serving others.' The objective of the thousand points of light initiative as it now emerged was, the President said, 'to carry this belief to every person in the land.'[53]

The strategies for implementing this policy were developed by C. Gregg Petersmeyer, appointed to head a new division within the White House, the Office of National Service. Petersmeyer could be said to be a classic Bush appointment. While a generation younger, Petersmeyer's background and education was very similar to Bush's with the *New York Times* suggesting that 'he might be described as a man not only of kindred political views but one of kindred build, kindred blue suits and kindred résumés.'[54]

Whereas Bush had been educated at Andover and Yale and, as a young man, worked in the oil industry in Texas, his protégé attended Choate, Harvard and Oxford before being employed in the natural gas business in Colorado. Petersmeyer's father, the head of a television station in Texas, was a Bush acquaintance and Petersmeyer himself first encountered the future President when he worked as a summer intern in the Nixon White House in 1969. Subsequently, when Bush became Chairman of the Republican National Committee Petersmeyer was a staff assistant in the White House, where the two men 'spent a fair amount of time together.' When Bush served in China in the 1970s, Petersmeyer stayed with him for a month where 'we played tennis every day, we had three meals a day together, we travelled some together.' In 1980, Petersmeyer worked briefly in Bush's campaign for the Republican nomination; he kept in touch with the Vice President when he moved to Colorado in 1982 and, at his instigation, became 'very close friends' with his son Neil; in 1988, he became Chairman of Bush's campaign in Colorado.

In terms of background, loyalty and an understanding of his thinking about politics, Petersmeyer could hardly have been better qualified to put into practice the core idea of the Bush presidency. Moreover Petersmeyer took very seriously indeed his responsibility, as a member of the White House staff, to pursue the President's agenda even though the specifics of that agenda were often difficult to discern. 'I always thought to myself, what would the President want to do here? . . . I knew him well enough to know that if he thought about what I was thinking about he'd probably want to do it this way. And so when he saw all the things I was doing he went along with them because it made sense.'[55]

From his experience of working in the Nixon White House Petersmeyer knew how valuable an independent relationship with the President could be, it gave such persons 'an extraordinary advantage in the rough and tumble of debate'. Petersmeyer had such a relationship with Bush; technically he was subordinate to the Chief of Staff, but in practice reported directly to the President. 'I was able to operate under the protection of George Bush . . . I felt I had a responsibility to him, as opposed to a responsibility to the Chief of Staff.' Thus the creation of a points of light infrastructure came about as a result of 'using the President's imprimatur without explicitly seeking or acquiring formal approval within the machinery of the White House.'[56]

Escaping in this way from the close control of policy-making otherwise exercised by John Sununu and his ally Richard Darman was facilitated by two factors, the absence of significant budgetary consequences and the Chief of Staff's lack of interest in Petersmeyer's project. 'That portion of the presidency happened to be a portion that he wasn't particularly interested in, but it was nonetheless important to George Bush.'

The high priority of Petersmeyer's work for Bush was reflected in his initial appointment as a Deputy Assistant to the President and his later promotion to an Assistant; it can also be seen in the substantial amount of time that Bush gave to the points of light enterprise throughout his presidency. Petersmeyer's task, as he saw it, was to lead:

> an effort to use the presidency to call people to a type of engagement in the most serious social problems of our time. To show people how they could do that should they want to respond to that call and to support it in certain ways. We developed a basic strategy the objective of which was, ideally, to cause every American to engage in a direct and consequential way in helping to solve these serious social problems.[57]

The strategy of the points of light movement had five components: changing people's attitudes to community service; identifying notably successful and valuable examples of individual and collective community service; discovering and encouraging leaders; establishing supporting institutions; and reducing the vulnerability of volunteers to legal liability.[58]

Bush has often been criticized for failing to make sufficient use of his office as a 'bully pulpit' and has himself conceded that this was one of his shortcomings. Under Petersmeyer's prodding, however, it seems that the President did resort to the bully pulpit on behalf of the points of life movement. In a number of ways the weight of his office was thrown behind a comprehensive effort to move the country in a particular direction. In other words, a chief executive normally sceptical of crusades did, in this area at least, embark on a wide-ranging exercise in moral leadership, striving to convince his compatriots of the value and rewards of voluntary community service.

The President's public utterances provided the linchpin of the points of light strategy with Petersmeyer assiduously injecting the 'theology' of voluntary service into as many of Bush's speeches as possible. It is estimated that during his presidency he spoke on the subject in more than 500 speeches and public pronouncements and, by constant repetition, sought to make a mantra of 'from now on in America any definition of a successful life must include serving others.'[59]

The second part of the strategy involved identifying notable contributions to voluntary service by individuals or groups, giving them presidential recognition and publicizing them through the media as examples for other Americans to emulate. In November 1989 the White House began a process whereby the President, on a daily basis, formally recognized the voluntary service efforts of an individual or group. On 22 November 1989 the first of these presidential Points of Light to be named was a newspaper *The Memphis Commercial Appeal* of Tennessee, which, in July 1989, had embarked on a series 'highlighting citizens who have made community service a central part of their lives.'[60] The 100th Point of Light to be recognized was Barbara Tomblinson, of Kansas City, Missouri who once homeless herself, had founded 'a non-profit corporation which provides transitional housing assistance for homeless families'. The final and 1020th Point of Light, identified on the day that Bush left office, was the Mariucci Inner City Hockey Starter Association of St Paul, Minnesota, an organization of 28 volunteers that 'teaches inner-city children aged six to eight to skate and play hockey.' The President met with representatives of 675 Points of Light and Vice President Quayle met with representatives of a further 103.[61]

The amount of time and effort invested by the Bush White House in the Point of Light awards was quite unprecedented. In Petersmeyer's words it was a programme of 'constant parable telling' by the President: 'it was never the most important thing happening that day, it was typically not among the top four things happening [but] it was always there. And over time it had an impact on the way people, including the hard-nosed press corps, saw this President.'[62]

To publicize the awards Marlin Fitzwater, the President's Press Secretary, issued daily press releases to 45 media outlets. The White House press corps gave them little attention, but at the local level each Point of Light generated an average of four or five newspaper stories and two items on radio or television; overall, it is estimated that approximately 8000 news stories appeared.[63]

In addition to making speeches and honouring exemplary individuals and groups President Bush worked to encourage the participation of leaders in government, business, education, entertainment, sports and youth organizations. He established an independent non-profit organization, the Points of Light Foundation, to be funded 50 per cent by the private sector and 50 per cent by Congress. This institution, initial funding for which was included in the National and Community Service Act of 1990, was intended to 'promote the ethic of community service, disseminate information about successful local activities to other communities across the Nation, and stimulate the development of new leaders and their community service initiatives.'[64] The foundation advertised extensively, set up educational programmes and local volunteer centres and provided technical assistance to corporations. The President also called for the creation of an independent institution to provide legal advice and assistance to volunteer programmes, an initiative that led to the setting up of a National Center for Community Risk Management and Insurance.

What did these and the many other activities that constituted the points of light movement actually achieve? How far, in other words, did the President succeed in completing what is described in a document put out over his signature as the 'defining mission' of his administration?[65]

Significant policy change normally requires the mustering of supporting coalitions and epic struggles with the legislative branch, but this initiative was of a different sort. Apart from the $25 million in funding included in the National and Community Service Act, no additional authorization legislation was required. In essence, this was a presidential campaign trying to effect a consequential change in popular attitudes. Rather than enlisting the aid of government on behalf of reform this was an attempt to bring home to the American people that there were limits to what government could do; that voluntary community service was not only essential to the eradication of serious social problems, but was necessary to the self-fulfilment of those who became volunteers.

In this instance presidential effectiveness had little to do with the passing of bills; it turned instead on how successful a White House sponsored campaign of public education was. When pressed on this point Petersmeyer alluded to Advertising Council surveys that found that the points of light slogan 'was recognized by an exceptionally high number of the American people a year or two into the Bush presidency. And [found] that there was no [significant] difference between Republicans and Democrats in those who thought well of it.'[66]

There is also evidence of an increase in volunteerism during the Bush years. According to Gallup poll figures in 1990 54 per cent of 2727 American adults surveyed said they had done some volunteer work compared to 45 per cent who had answered similarly in 1988. In New York City, furthermore, it was estimated that inquiries about volunteer opportunities increased between 1990 and 1991 by 28 per cent; similar increases were also reported in other cities, 16 per cent in Kansas City and 20 per cent in Houston.[67]

There are several possible explanations for the new interest in volunteerism at the end of the 1980s. As the economy moved into recession social problems intensified – unemployment went up and homelessness became more common, as did as other forms of distress, creating a greater need for voluntary workers. Economic decline by putting people out of work also made them available for volunteer work in a way that they had not been hitherto. In addition, the cuts in funding for social programmes at all levels of government in the 1980s had made social service agencies more dependent on the efforts of volunteers. Having said all that experts in the field conceded that the points of light campaign had played a part of some significance in stimulating voluntary activity.[68]

CONCLUSIONS

If Bush's record in fulfilling his agenda in domestic policy is to be used for evaluative purposes it has to be said that it was, at best, mixed. In economic policy he singularly failed to build on Ronald Reagan's record as he had undertaken to do at the 1988 Republican Convention. This can be demonstrated by a few statistics. The average annual rate of growth of GNP had been 2.3 per cent during Reagan's first term and 3.2 per cent in the second, whereas for Bush's incumbency it was 0.9 per cent. Reagan had managed to cut substantially the rate of growth of domestic spending; it grew by an annual average of 0.87 per cent in his first term and 0.19 per cent in the second. During Bush's presidency, by contrast, the average annual growth rate of domestic spending was 7.54 per cent. The Reagan administration could claim to have created 18 million new jobs over two terms and Bush spoke jauntily in

1988 of '30 million in 8', but, in fact, less than a million new jobs came into being in the four years that he held office.[69] In late 1991 it was established that despite the President's supposed commitment to deregulation his administration had 'witnessed the broadest expansions of government's regulatory reach since the early 1970s.'[70] And most damaging of all, Bush proved unable to keep his most sacred campaign pledge of 'no new taxes' – a disastrous failure for his presidency discussed at length in Chapter 6.

Bush was also unable to deliver much of significance on his undertakings before taking office to improve the education system and to work for a drug-free America. Nevertheless, as we have seen, Bush did have some success in meeting his limited agenda. He spoke in 1988 of the need to 'clean the air' and submitted to Congress a bill of some importance that eventually resulted in important legislation. He had promised to do what he could to ensure that the disabled were brought into the mainstream of American life and he played a significant part in the passage of notably advanced legislation. The founding of the points of light movement meant little to Bush's critics whether on the left or the right, but for a guardian president progress in such matters was especially gratifying. Guardian presidents are also anxious to hold the line against undesirable change, another area where Bush could claim some success, as the next chapter will demonstrate.

5 'Preventing Bad Laws'

Modern presidents, whether Democrat or Republican, are expected to be activists in the White House. It is routinely argued that it is incumbent upon them to advance proposals for change and to mastermind their enactment into law. As a new president takes up office the problems of governance are reduced to activist clichés. He is advised to 'hit the ground running' and is expected to exploit fully the opportunities offered by the 'honeymoon' relationship with Congress that is is assumed will prevail during the early months of his presidency. At the end of his 'first hundred days' in office media pundits and others will calculate how successful he has been in gaining the cooperation of Congress, estimates that will be reactivated at the end of each year in office and again at the conclusion of his term. According to calculations of this type George Bush was consistently found wanting. As we saw in the previous chapter, he was accused of 'hitting the ground crawling' and of failing to take advantage of the 'honeymoon': analysts found his achievements in his first year to be slim and were similarly unimpressed by his legislative record throughout his presidency.

CONGRESSIONAL QUARTERLY SCORES

Plausible evidence of Bush's failure to impose himself on the legislature seemed to be provided by the annual presidential success scores calculated by the *Congressional Quarterly*. By examining speeches and other statements by the president, or his authorized spokesmen, CQ decides, where possible, what his position is on a given congressional roll call vote. Presidential success is then calculated by totalling the percentage of roll call votes where the chief executive had a clearly stated position and his view prevailed.

The application of these criteria to Bush's presidency present a most unflattering picture. Leaving aside the very special case of Gerald Ford, Bush's presidential success rate of 62.6 per cent in his first year in the White House was by far the

111

worst of any president since records began in 1953. Comparable first year success rates were Eisenhower 89 per cent, Kennedy 81 per cent, Johnson 93 per cent (in 1965), Nixon 74 per cent, Carter 75.4 per cent and Reagan 82.4 per cent. On the face of it, these figures provide convincing evidence of Bush's failure to make good use of the honeymoon period.[1]

Similarly, Bush's success rate in the final year of his term at 43 per cent was 'the worst performance of any president at any point in his term since CQ began keeping score 39 years ago.'[2] Bush's success rate over the whole of his presidency averaged 51.8 per cent, the lowest of any first-term president since 1953 – by comparison Eisenhower averaged 79.7 per cent, Kennedy 84.6 per cent, Johnson 82.2 per cent, Nixon 74.4 per cent, Carter 76.6 per cent and Reagan 72.3 per cent. Again the gap between George Bush and other modern presidents was large, with even a fellow guardian like Eisenhower exceeding his average success score by a margin of 28 per cent.[3]

Congressional Quarterly scores are eagerly seized upon by commentators as concrete evidence of how a president is faring, whereas they need to be handled with care. Such figures undoubtedly do provide useful yardsticks of presidential effectiveness and those cited above contribute something to an analyis of the Bush presidency. On the other hand, such calculations, while not without relevance in the case of activist presidents, have much less to say about conservative guardians.

As a number of scholars have shown there are difficulties with CQ presidential success scores.[4] In the first place, no account is taken of the wide variations in party support in Congress; that is to say, there is no difference in treatment between presidents who encounter the perils of divided government and those who do not. This makes a mockery of simple comparisons between, say, Johnson and Nixon, or even Carter and Bush. It is also the case that success scores are based on roll-call votes alone, whereas many important questions turn on voice votes, may be decided by party leaders or in committee, or may not come to a vote at all. Thus a proposal from Bush early in his term 'to open the Arctic National Wildlife Refuge never came to the House or Senate floor, and all the 1989 tests of his clean-air proposal took place in committee.'[5]

There is also, under the CQ scoring system, no attempt to differentiate between votes, or to weight them in terms of their significance. In 1989 the highly significant vote to reject John Tower's nomination as Secretary of Defense was given the same weight as innumerable, routine, unanimous confirmations. In such calculations votes of great importance are rolled together with the trivial and, as Anthony King pointed out, that is to ignore the fact that 'some congressional outcomes matter far more to presidents than others. In 1919, Woodrow Wilson would probably have been content with a *Congressional Quarterly* support score of near zero if he could have got the Senate to ratify the Treaty of Versailles.'[6]

CQ scores moreover are liable to distortion by the inclusion of roll-call votes on matters which are non-controversial and which are decided by near unanimous votes and may therefore inflate levels of presidential support. It is also the case that there may be a multitude of votes on similar or related questions and this too may give an artificial impression of presidential support; the Senate, for instance, 'took 116 roll call votes on the 1964 Civil Rights Act.'[7]

It is, however, with regard to the veto power that limitations in CQ scores become especially pertinent in the case of guardian presidents – chief executives particularly mindful of their responsibility to amend or to prevent the passage of undesirable legislation. As Nick Calio, head of Bush's legislative liaison operation, put it: 'I think in terms of [CQ's] ratings vs. our internal ratings, there's a real difference. CQ rates every vote and there are some we don't care about. And there are some votes CQ rates as a loss, but that we considered a win because we showed veto strength. So they don't really reflect the complicated reality.' In other words, account must be taken not just of Bush's notable success in sustaining vetoes, but also of his use of veto threats to shape, or to cause the withdrawal of bills that met with his disapproval.[8]

THE VETO POWER

Conservative Republicans have attacked George Bush for being excessively conciliatory towards Congress, but such analyses take insufficient account of his veto strategy. As Richard Rose has pointed out: 'A guardian president can accept Congress being in opposition hands, whereas an expansive President depends more for success on congressional approval of White House proposals. Confronted with an activist Congress, a guardian President can fulfil his role by vetoing bills.'[9] Out of Bush's 44 vetoes only one was overridden, a level of success that no other modern president has equalled.[10] Among other enthusiastic vetoers Nixon was overridden five times in respect of 24 vetoes of 'nationally significant legislation' whereas Ford was similarly overridden on 12 vetoes out of 42 of national significance. Modern presidents (1933–81) have, on the average, had a quarter of their vetoes of nationally significant legislation overridden.[11]

The rationale underlying Bush's veto strategy was provided by Nicholas Calio, originally head of legislative liaison in the House and subsequently in overall charge of congressional relations. 'There were many things that, in our view, Congress got involved in [which] it really shouldn't – in micro managing markets, in micro managing foreign policy . . . There were a lot of things we felt needed to be stopped . . . on all sorts of issues we felt the legislation wasn't in the best interest of the country and so, to use the only tool the President had to stop it and to [thereby] "make policy" we had to use the veto.'[12] As this statement confirms, the veto power assumes particular importance for those who labour on behalf of a guardian president. And, it should be noted, there was ample support for the negativism of the guardian position, for the determination of such presidents to prevent the passing of bad laws, in the debates held at the Constitutional Convention in 1787.

The Founding Fathers were anxious to place in the president's hands some sort of veto on the actions of the national legislature for, in the words of Alexander Hamilton, such an arrangement would give the executive 'the power of preventing bad laws'. Moreover, the very fact that the veto existed and might be brought into play would act as a restraint on lawmakers:

A power of this nature will often have a silent if unperceived, though forcible, operation. When men engaged in unjustifiable pursuits, are aware that obstructions may come from a quarter which they cannot control, they will often be restrained by the bare apprehension of opposition from doing what they would with eagerness rush into if no such external impediments were to be feared.[13]

Another heavyweight in the Convention, Gouverneur Morris declared that 'the public liberty [was] in greater danger from legislative usurpations than from any other source' and the possibility that 'bad laws will be pushed' meant that 'a strong check will be necessary.'[14] The justification for a veto, according to George Mason, arose from the fact that the legislature 'must be expected to pass unjust and pernicious laws. This restraining power was therefore essentially necessary.'[15] While the veto power and the guardianship posture arouses the ire of those who favour activism in the White House, both were fully supported by those who drew up the Constitution.

The principal author of Bush's veto strategy appears to have been Roger Porter, Assistant to the President for Economic and Domestic Policy. As a political scientist who had studied the history of presidential vetoes Porter was well qualified to apprise President Bush of the possibilities inherent in the device.[16] He recognized that it could be not just a means of outright rejection, but also a tool available to presidents for shaping legislation as it moved through Congress. 'One of Porter's major beliefs was that the veto should not always be considered the end of a bill's evolution but only part of an ongoing process of compromise.'[17]

Relevant experience was another of Porter's strengths. He had served in the Ford White House where the veto had been freely used; indeed, according to Spitzer, writing in 1988, 'Ford was the only twentieth century president to design and pursue a calculated veto strategy.'[18] There were, of course, parallels between Ford and Bush; they were conservatives and guardians and in both cases their position *vis-à-vis* Congress was weak. Lacking any sort of electoral mandate and weakened further after the 1974 mid-term elections Ford was obliged to resort to a veto strategy.[19] Similarly, as we saw in the previous chapter, Bush, in 1989, had less party support in the House and Senate than any other newly elected modern president and his extensive use of veto threats could be construed as 'a sign of a weak position in Congress.'[20]

The threat of a veto makes it possible for chief executives to exercise considerable influence on the legislative process. According to one source, the Bush Administration used the veto power like a ratchet, with spokesmen privately mentioning the possibility of a veto at the committee stage of a bill; if that failed to have the desired effect White House communications staff would let it be known that a veto might occur before, where necessary, a public wielding of the veto threat by the President himself.[21] Bush moreover established a reputation for following through on his veto threats; in this respect at least, he was stronger and more effective than Reagan. According to Terry Eastland: 'In general, Reagan did not have as much veto credibility as Bush.'[22]

David Stockman, Director of the Office of Management and Budget in the Reagan Administration, complains of the reluctance of that president to use veto threats. For example, in testifying before the House Budget Committee in March 1981 Stockman said that Reagan would veto a one-year tax cut if it was passed by Congress instead of the succession of cuts over three years that the Administration was seeking. Such aggression troubled pragmatists in the White House like James Baker and Richard Darman bent on deal-making with congressional leaders. They convinced Reagan that his 'general principle of not announcing vetoes in advance' had been violated and Larry Speakes, the Press Secretary, was commissioned to disassociate the President from Stockman's comment.[23]

The exceptional effectiveness of Bush's veto strategy was highlighted in 1991 when it was reported that not only had he vetoed 21 bills without once being overridden, but, in addition, his veto threats were proving to be major factors in determining the fate of many bills.[24] On a wide range of issues, the Democratic leadership in both houses now felt obliged to accept that a veto-proof two-thirds vote, rather than a simple majority, was essential for the passage of legislation. As one Democratic leader, Representative Vic Fazio of California, ruefully commented: 'We have fallen into the trap of thinking that if we don't have a two-thirds vote we should do nothing.'[25] These were, no doubt, comforting words for a President so committed to limiting the reach of government.

Some have questioned the use of the veto as an instrument of policy rather than for constitutional purposes.[26] However, Hamilton argued that it had two purposes: the first was concerned with the Constitution and the second with the substance of policy. The primary purpose of the veto was to make it possible for the president to defend himself against the propensity of the 'legislative body to invade the rights of the executive'. The secondary purpose of the veto related to matters of policy – it would aid the president in preventing the 'passing of bad laws through haste, inadvertence or design.'[27] The use of the veto for policy purposes was also anticipated by James Madison when he said:

> It would be useful to the legislature by the valuable assistance it would give in preserving a consistency, conciseness, perspicuity and technical propriety in the laws, qualities peculiarly necessary, and yet shamefully wanting in our republican codes. It would moreover be useful to the community at large as an additional check against a pursuit of those unwise and unjust measures which constituted so great a portion of our calamities.[28]

For President Bush and his principal adviser on constitutional matters, his Counsel, C. Boyden Gray, the dangers of congressional encroachment on the rights of the executive were particularly grave in the foreign policy realm. Accordingly, four of the nine vetoes exercised in 1989 were concerned with protecting presidential prerogatives in foreign affairs. The first of these was directed at a resolution approving arrangements for the co-development with Japan of the FS-X, a fighter plane. Congress included in the resolution certain conditions which would become relevant if the plane went into production. Bush saw these conditions as infringing on his freedom to engage in negotiations with another country. 'In the conduct of negotiations with foreign governments,' the President insisted, 'it is imperative that the United States speak with one voice. The Constitution provides that that one voice is the president's.'[29]

A second foreign policy veto was cast in 1989 against a foreign aid appropriations bill, partly for reasons of policy substance, but also on constitutional grounds. Congress, in light of the Iran Contra affair, included in the legislation certain prohibitions on how aid to other countries might be used. The President and his advisers saw these restrictions as a constitutionally unwarranted encroachment on the right of the executive to conduct foreign policy. On 21 November 1989 Bush vetoed another bill with Iran Contra ramifications, that authorizing funds for the Department of State and other foreign policy agencies. Part of the bill 'prohibited executive officials from giving funds to other countries to carry out activities banned by law.' The President's legal advisers regarded such restrictions as unconstitutionally circumscribing his 'responsibility to protect national security by representing US interests abroad.'[30] Similar concerns about presidential prerogatives led Bush to veto a bill designed to waive the visa restrictions on Chinese students after the Tiananmen Square repression of June 1989. In 1990, a further three bills were vetoed in defence of the presidential prerogative in foreign affairs. Two of these were concerned with international trade, whereas the third was yet another arising from the congressional backlash against the Iran Contra débâcle.[31]

In substantive policy matters Bush used the veto power most frequently to reject abortion-related legislation. There were no less than ten such vetoes in 1989–92. In 1989 HR 2990 included provision for federal funding of abortions in cases of rape and incest where they were 'promptly reported' to the relevant authorities, language unacceptable to the President and which led to a veto. In the same year, appropriations legislation for the District of Columbia was twice vetoed because it would have made possible abortions funded out of locally raised tax revenues. The foreign aid appropriations bill referred to above was also vetoed partly because of abortion concerns.[32]

Debates on the abortion issue in the 102nd Congress (1991–92) showed evidence of movement in favour of abortion rights, but Bush repeatedly used his veto power to hold the line against further liberalization. 'In 1991, both chambers voted to jettison five separate abortion-related restrictions. But Bush vetoes and repeated veto threats prevented any policy changes.' The following year the President vetoed four bills 'because of abortion language, while abortion-related language was dropped from the final versions of three other measures to avert threatened vetoes.'[33] The Bush Administration's resourceful use of the veto to shape national policy on abortion points to the dangers of making too much of CQ scores as a measure of presidential effectiveness.

On the face of it, 43 out of 44 vetoes upheld, plus an untold number of successful veto threats would seem to represent useful evidence to set against popular perceptions of Bush as a weak and ineffectual President, incapable of imposing his priorities on Congress.[34] Some on the right of the Republican Party however, were not impressed. One of these was Charles Kolb who, as Deputy Assistant for Domestic Policy, had an inside view of the workings of the Bush White House from mid-1990 onwards.

Kolb argues that Bush's veto strategy was, in truth, ultra cautious with the Administration generally unwilling to resort to the veto except when victory was assured. The President 'would rarely veto legislation unless he knew in advance that he had the votes necessary to sustain the veto. The issue was counting heads, not standing on principle. If Fred McClure or Nick Calio, his two assistants who headed his legislative shop, told him he was shy on votes, Bush rarely applied the veto. Simple as that.'[35]

This charge was vehemently rejected by some of Kolb's senior colleagues. Calio, for instance, who was very much in the front line when it came to sustaining vetoes, questioned Kolb's claim to knowledge of decision-making at the highest level and continued: 'Putting together the votes for most of those vetoes was extremely difficult. If you look at the numbers we had available on the Republican side . . . [it is evident that] we had to rely on getting some Democratic votes as well. George Bush did not veto things when they were in the bag, George Bush vetoed things as a matter of principle, with all due respect to Charlie.'[36] David Demarest was no less scathing describing Kolb's analysis as 'staggeringly inaccurate' and insisting that Bush was a man of principle. 'We got 39 [*sic*] vetoes and sustained all but one. On many occasions, I'm not going to say a majority, but on a number of occasions, we were in a situation where most of us thought we could not sustain the veto and it was the President saying, "Yes we are [*sic*]".'[37]

James Cicconi went further in defending Bush as a man of integrity who used the veto courageously and honourably:

He wielded the veto with great success throughout his presidency on a lot of issues of principle, where in many [cases] . . . it was predicted he would easily be overridden and humiliated. I can recall when he vetoed sanctions against China. He felt extremely strongly on that issue and our legislative liaison chief said at the time that [the President] announced his decision, that we didn't have single vote, not a single vote to sustain that veto. We had to work to sustain it, but he firmly believed that the proper course of action was not to isolate China. That it would destroy so much of what we were working to achieve in the world.[38]

Nevertheless Kolb is not alone in claiming that Bush picked his veto fights rather cautiously. James Sundquist remarked that 'Bush has been careful in selecting his targets. When he knows that he is going to lose, he goes ahead and signs the bill.'[39] Yet this argument cannot be carried too far. An examination of Bush's vetoes does show that on many occasions the margin of success in sustaining them was very close, most notably in the Senate.[40]

The veto of the FS-X fighter plane was upheld by the bare minimum of 34 votes required in the Senate. The veto of the bill waiving the visa requirements of Chinese students attracted 37 votes after an intensive lobbying campaign by the White House. In May 1990, the veto of an Amtrak authorization bill was upheld with 36 votes; the following month a Hatch Act amendments veto obtained 35 votes. One of Bush's most controversial vetoes was of the 1990 Civil Rights Act, another which was upheld by the bare minimum of 34 Senators. In 1991, the veto of an unemployment benefits bill survived 'a major effort to override the veto' by a vote of 65–35.[41] Another epic struggle in 1992, that referred to by Ciconni above, saw 38 votes sustain a veto on legislation concerning MFN ('most favoured nation') status for China, and the same number of Senators prevented a veto of a 'Motor Voter' registration bill from being overturned. Several of the abortion-related vetoes in the House also only narrowly escaped being overridden.[42]

In defence of Bush's veto strategy it can also be said that he and his advisers understood that a degree of caution in wielding the veto could be a source of strength in that it gave greater credibility to his threats to veto. As the Republican Representative Steve Gunderson of Wisconsin remarked: 'When he talks veto, people take it seriously.'[43] Reagan's veto threats, by contrast, were less effective, with members of Congress able to take comfort from the fact that the President often backed down from veto threats and was overridden on a number of occasions. According to *US News and World Report*:

'Ronald Reagan vetoed only 78 bills in eight years and was overridden nine times. As his administration wore on, he made the mistake of threatening more and more vetoes, then backing off without extracting important concessions from Democrats. That damaged his credibility.'[44] In that sense Bush, it could be argued, was the stronger of the two chief executives, but such views carried little weight with conservatives like Kolb who wanted the President to be more adventurous; to be less protective of his record in sustaining vetoes and to be prepared to go down with all guns blazing where necessary.

At first sight the arguments within Republican ranks over Bush's use of the veto highlight the differences between his pragmatic, reactive, guardian style of leadership and the more ideological crusading approach of Reagan. Kolb, who is clearly a Reaganite, was appalled to find among his colleagues on the White House staff a 'real resistance to doing anything when they knew they might lose'. He wanted the Administration to take principled stands, to say simply: 'We are going to veto these appropriations bills and we don't care if we are over-ridden because they are wrong, or they are too expensive . . . why not take a position of principle and if you win it you win it, if you lose it move on to the next thing.'[45] However, we must set against such complaints the frustration that David Stockman endured in the previous administration in the face of Reagan's repeated unwillingness to use the veto against appropriations bills.[46]

Any calculation of George Bush's effectiveness in meeting his agenda needs to take account of his use of the veto power. Advised by shrewd strategists like Gray and Porter, Bush used the veto as the Founding Fathers intended, first to defend the presidency in the never-ending struggle with the legislature over prerogatives, and second as a means of shaping policy outcomes. Not just abortion, but also US policy towards China, civil rights, minimum wage, family leave and many other impor-tant issues provoked the veto. As a guardian Bush made relatively little effort to advance legislative proposals of his own, but was successful in modifying or 'preventing bad laws' emanating from his Democratic opponents. As the President said in defence of his record when he faced re-election: 'I wasn't elected to do it the way the liberal Democrats that control Congress want, and so I've had to stand up to them.'[47]

As might be expected Bush's repeated flaunting of the veto led to irate comment on Capitol Hill. 'The president is ruling the country by the rule of 33 plus one,' said Senator Dale Bumpers, Democrat of Arkansas. 'It doesn't matter what 535 people think. What matters is 34 people in the Senate.'[48] Similarly Richard Gephardt, the House Majority Leader, said: 'If you are looking for George Bush's domestic program, and many people are, this is it: the veto pen. The president's veto pen is more powerful than the votes of 66 senators and 289 representatives. He has used it to thwart the will of the American people, to defend the status quo of a declining economy, to preserve the privileges of the powerful, and to deny the positive role of government as an agent of renewal and change.'[49]

Leaving aside for a moment the partisan rhetoric, Bumpers and Gephardt were, of course, analytically correct; the veto, like the filibuster and judicial review, is a flagrantly counter-majoritarian device. In theory, 501 national legislators could be in favour of a policy, but could then be defeated by 34, a mere fragment of the whole. Less than 7 per cent of the total membership of Congress could theoretically thwart the wishes of 93 per cent Nevertheless, the use of the veto both as a self-defence mechanism and for policy-shaping purposes is fully in accord with the intentions of those who devised the Constitution. In addition, however, Bush used signing statements to protect his prerogatives and to influence policy outcomes, and this device, defined by George Edwards as a 'type of unofficial item veto', was constitutionally far more dubious.[50]

SIGNING STATEMENTS

Signing statements enable presidents to place on record their reservations about some part of a bill which they are nevertheless willing to sign. Statements allow a president to 'express the intent not to enforce a provision of the bill on the grounds that it is unconstitutional. He may state that it is against the policy of the administration. Or the president may give his interpretation of some provision of the statute.'[51] The use of signing statements is a long-established practice and was deployed, among others, by Andrew Jackson, Woodrow Wilson, Richard Nixon, Jimmy Carter and Ronald Reagan.[52]

It is charged against George Bush that he made excessive use of signing statements, turning them into 'sovereign powers for shaping or escaping laws and for governing without Congress by voiding or revising key provisions in congressional enactments.'[53] The uses of signing statements can be illustrated by the one issued by Bush when he put his signature to the National Community Service Act of 1990. The President began by expressing his pleasure at that part of the bill which provided for initial funding for one of his most favoured projects, the Points of Light Foundation, but then went on to express doubts about other parts of the Act. He was troubled by the degree to which paid rather than unpaid volunteers were to be employed in community service and he rejected as unconstitutional certain limitations on presidential appointees to a commission to be set up under the statute. In addition, Bush noted that prohibitions in the act on the transfer of funds from one account to another without congressional approval represented a legislative veto and were therefore unconstitutional.[54]

The substantive policy position expressed in this signing statement squared with the stance of a guardian president, sceptical of what government could do and reluctant to extend its reach. The statement was also consistent with Bush's determination, guided by his Counsel, the ubiquitous C. Boyden Gray, to resist what they perceived as congressional encroachments on the powers of the executive. This latter concern was particularly relevant in the realm of foreign policy. Thus in signing the Foreign Relations Authorization Act in 1990, the President referred to provisions that 'raise consitutional difficulties' and intimated that he would regard some of these as advisory rather than binding. In signing the Foreign Relations Authorization Act for Fiscal Years 1992 and 1993, the President went out of his way to make a sweeping assertion of executive power:

'Article II of the Constitution confers the executive power of the United States on the President alone. Executive power includes the authority to receive and appoint ambassadors and to conduct diplomacy. Thus, under our system

of government, all decisions concerning the conduct of negotiations with foreign governments are within the exclusive
control of the President.'[55]

Quite apart from the constitutional dubiety of such a large
claim, it is not difficult to understand why presidential signing
statements are the source of great indignation on Capitol Hill.
The signing of a bill is supposedly the concluding stage of the
legislative process – at that point a bill becomes a law. And yet,
by a signing statement a president may effectively undermine
the force of a law on either substantive or constitutional
grounds. Unlike the veto, moreover, there is no means whereby
the legislature can recoup the situation. Saving intervention
by the courts, which past precedent would suggest is unlikely,
the chief executive is given the last word in the policy-making
process and the separation of powers principle is violated.[56]

It has been argued by Charles Tiefer that, contrary to the
popular impressions of a pathetically weak President buffeted
by an unruly and partisan Congress, Bush in truth, used signing
statements, vetoes and other strategies in a flagrant effort to
govern without the legislature. That he attempted, in other
words, to bring about a 'semi-sovereign' presidency.[57] Tiefer
mounts a formidable, if distinctly one-sided case with his professional allegiance to the United States Congress as acting general
counsel to the House of Representatives, evident on every page.
For this observer Tiefer's analysis takes insufficient account of
the undeniable fact that constitutional development in America
has culminated in a situation where the responsibility for
policy-making, for national leadership, falls primarily on the
President in both domestic and foreign policy.

As Theodore Sorensen said in a book based on his experience in the Kennedy Administration: 'No one else has [the
President's] power to lead, to inspire, or to restrain the Congress
and country. If he fails to lead, no one leads . . . The nation
selects its President, at least in part, for his philosophy and his
conscientious conviction of what is right – and he need not
hesitate to apply them.'[58] All manner of obstacles are placed
in the way of presidents as they attempt to meet their responsibility to lead and the circumstances of divided government
may make their task immeasurably more difficult. In attempting
to impose himself on the policy-making process, whether to

initiate change, or to prevent change from occurring, presidents are likely to resort to whatever weapons they can lay their hands on, even those that are constitutionally suspect. While Tiefer is undoubtedly correct in arguing that the Founding Fathers were most anxious to guard against the emergence of an all-powerful executive, it is also the case that they were no less determined to resist the inevitable encroachment by the legislature on presidential prerogatives.[59]

And it is not as if members of Congress were paragons of constitutional propriety. In 1994, for instance, President Clinton's attempts to govern were constantly frustrated by the incessant use of filibuster threats: 'Under Rule 22 of the Senate the only way to close debate is to get 60 senators to concur. By using the filibuster liberally, conservative forces in the Senate have thwarted the Clinton administration's legislative agenda time and again.'[60] Just like signing statements, filibusters were used in the past selectively and infrequently, unlike their regular use today. Furthermore, the constitutionality of the filibuster is as much open to challenge as the signing statement.

President Bush has been criticized for being weak, for not providing sufficient leadership, yet Tiefer would have preferred him to have been even weaker. He should, it seems, have sat idly by while Congress seized control of the policy process and wilfully eroded presidential prerogatives. This is to ignore the fact that the legislature and the executive in the United States are engaged in a constant battle to maintain their respective positions in the 'separated system' provided for by the Constitution.[61] This was of course, anticipated by the Founding Fathers: Madison famously made reference to the 'tendency in the legislature to absorb all power into its vortex' while Gouverneur Morris worried that the executive would be so weak 'that there is the justest ground to fear his want of firmness in resisting encroachments.'[62] Similarly, Hamilton, in making the case for the veto, said that without it the president 'would be absolutely unable to defend himself against the depredations of the [legislative branch]. He might gradually be stripped of his authorities by successive resolutions or annihilated by a single vote. And . . . the legislative and executive powers might speedily come to be blended in the same hands.[63]

The never ending struggle between the branches is, of course, liable to be even fiercer than usual in circumstances of divided government and it is surely the case that presidents are obliged to do what they can to defend their office against assaults from ambitious, parochially minded, sometimes unscrupulous and often ruthlessly partisan members of the legislature. Certainly, this has been the view of past presidents, some of whom enjoy heroic status among Democratic legislators who supposedly squirmed under the lash of the 'semi-sovereign' Bush. Thus Dean Acheson reported that Truman was moved by the passionate conviction that 'his great office was to him a sacred and temporary trust, which he was determined to pass on unimpaired by the slightest loss of power or prestige.'[64] Similarly, Kennedy's faithful aide Sorensen said that a president 'must strive always to preserve the power and the prestige of his office, the availability of his options, and the long range interests of the nation.'[64]

CONCLUSIONS

The discussion in this chapter does something to offset perceptions of Bush as a do-nothing, passive figure in the White House, incapable of imposing his leadership on the legislature. It has been argued here that CQ scores have to be treated with care and that they are especially limited in what they contribute to our understanding of the legislative leadership records of conservative, guardian presidents. Presidents, as I have repeatedly said, are entitled to be judged on their own terms and, viewed charitably, Bush's veto strategy, devised and implemented by some of the shrewdest minds on his staff, appears to have been moderately successful; allowing a 'resource poor' president to play a not insignificant part in shaping the substance of policy and to defend his prerogatives against encroachment, most notably in the realm of foreign policy.[66] In this regard at least Bush appears to have been a rather stronger chief executive than his predecessor.[67] Similarly, signing statements, while questionable constitutionally, helped to make it possible for Bush to be rather more effective in office than is sometimes suggested.

6 The 1990 Budget Crisis

The tortured efforts by President Bush and congressional leaders to agree a budget in 1990 raised fundamental questions about the American political system. The difficulties encountered exposed the extraordinary fragility of party discipline in the national legislature, emphasized the problems of divided government and once again cast doubt on the very governability of the United States. For the purposes of this study, however, the budget crisis of 1990 is especially interesting as a defining event for the presidency of George Bush, one which revealed major flaws in his style of presidential leadership.

NO NEW TAXES

At the Republican Convention in 1988 the future President, in reflecting on how economic policy would develop when he was in the White House, said: 'The Congress will push me to raise taxes, and I'll say no, and they'll push me again, and I'll say to them, "Read my lips; no new taxes".' Bush had been under pressure to make such a commitment for some time. During the primaries he had resisted the entreaties of campaign advisers like Lee Atwater and James Pinkerton that he should sign an anti-tax pledge to help him fend off the challenges of Jack Kemp and Robert Dole.[1] Such reluctance was understandable, for while Bush was a conservative, instinctively resistant to tax increases and had been a meticulously loyal Vice President, he had never been a devotee of Reaganomics. Unlike his predecessor, he bracketed an enthusiasm for low taxes with a belief in government. As one unnamed close adviser later explained: 'Some days he gets up and says "Jesus Christ, you know we ought to hold taxes down." Next day he gets up and finds out that we got to cut funding to some special education program and he gets all worked up.'[2]

This lack of certainty had caused Bush to haver on the tax issue prior to the 1988 Convention; on some occasions he had taken a hard anti-tax line, while on others he appeared to be unwilling to rule out tax increases in some circumstances. Such shilly-shallying troubled members of his staff either because of their own supply-side inclinations or for strategic reasons, with some convinced that signing up to an anti-tax pledge would help dispose of allegations that Bush was an ideological wimp lacking in firm convictions and would sharply define his candidacy. Others like Craig Fuller, the Vice President's Chief of Staff, worried that a fixed position on taxes would detract from Bush's ability to govern if elected. Similarly, Richard Darman, recognizing that whoever was elected would have to deal with the burgeoning budget deficit, decried the irresponsibilty of making such a pledge.[3] Charles Kolb suggests that initially Darman concealed his opposition to the pledge for opportunistic reasons, but leaving that aside, there is little doubt that he was against it from the beginning.[4] These concerns were overridden by those whose focus was campaigning rather than governing with Peggy Noonan, at the urging of Jack Kemp, incorporating the pledge in Bush's acceptance speech and vigorously fending off attempts to remove it.[5]

Immediately the election was over the President came under pressure to go back on his 'no new taxes' promise. Initially, the National Economic Commission was the main source of that pressure. Established in 1987, the NEC was a high-powered, bipartisan body set up to consider how the ever-growing federal deficit should be dealt with. The commission had devised a deficit reduction scheme including both spending cuts and tax increases, and on 7 December 1988 an outline of the proposal was placed before the President-elect. At this stage Bush flatly refused to countenance tax increases reportedly saying: 'There's no possibility I can even consider this. I'll have no credibility with the American public, if before I even get sworn into office, I support a program that increases taxes.'[6]

By early 1990, however, the situation had changed. The economy was looking less healthy with the budget deficit set to become even larger than anticipated and the possibility looming of swingeing cuts in government expenditures becoming necessary under the provisions of the Gramm-Rudman-Hollings legislation. This law, otherwise known as the Balanced Budget and Emergency Deficit Control Act of

1985, established maximum deficit levels and required across-the-board spending cuts if those targets were not reached. No one was more conscious of these problems than Richard Darman, now Director of the Office of Management and Budget and in the process of becoming one of the three most influential members of the White House staff, the others being John Sununu, the Chief of Staff, and Brent Scowcroft, the National Security Adviser.

RICHARD DARMAN

From the outset opposed to the 'no new taxes' pledge, Darman had, for some months, been working behind the scenes to convince the President of the adverse consequences of an ever-increasing budget deficit. He argued that the situation could only be brought under control by striking a deal with Congress requiring cuts in government expenditures coupled with increased taxes. As James Cicconi put it: 'Our Budget Director became entranced with the notion of being able to do a deal to help cure the problem on the deficit . . . and set about over the course of the better part of a year . . . to convince the President, gradually step by step, that a budget deal involving taxes was really the only way to deal with the problem and essential to the well-being of the nation.'[7] Charles Kolb also claims that Darman talked Bush into the budget deal.[8]

Other senior members of Bush's staff have testified to the extraordinary influence that Darman came to exert over the President in the making of economic policy. Two factors that help to explain Darman's hold over Bush and his dominant position within the White House were his exceptional intelligence and his extensive experience of working in the upper echelons of previous Republican administrations. One presidential aide estimated that the Budget Director was about '30 IQ points forward of Bush'.[9] Another spoke of him as a 'brilliant, brilliant man' while C. Boyden Gray noted that Darman's cleverness, in conjunction with his superior understanding of the system, allowed him to manipulate situations to his advantage: 'If you are as smart and as clever and experienced as Darman you can manipulate the process to control it to your political end, or your programmatic end.'[10]

Deputy Chief of Staff, Andrew Card, provided an illuminating description of Darman's dazzling ability to monopolize information and thereby dominate the domestic policy decision-making process in the Bush White House:

> Dick Darman is very bright and he does his homework; he is probably the most diligent person I've met in government. He does his own work, he is not staff-dependent; he reads, he understands; he is also very opinionated. He also knows that information is power . . . and he disseminates that information when he wants to. It used to be frustrating because sometimes he would blindside everybody else in the room with his information. He would pull out this little document in a policy reading with the President, and nobody else in the room would have seen the information he put on the table, but they didn't want to say 'Dick, I haven't seen that before, where did you get that?' And you didn't have the information to attack the document so therefore the document stood. I think the President maybe sometimes was swayed towards Dick Darman's bias because of the way [he] managed the information.[11]

A similar, if slightly different, slant on Darman's influence over Bush was provided by Clayton Yeutter, another of the genuine heavyweights in the Administration, who had known and worked with the Budget Director since the Nixon years.

> Darman is so skilful at making himself appear indispensable. He's been around in government so many years that he's just good. He's smart, clever, sometimes ruthless, and he knows that knowledge is power. There is no better knowledge base than the Office of Management and Budget, and he used it skilfully to persuade President Bush of his indispensability. No one is indispensable, of course, but the perception thereof made Dick Darman one of the most powerful people in the executive branch for many years.[12]

Even the Chief of Staff, John Sununu, who possessed an intelligence and a self-confidence no less formidable than Darman's, seems to have succumbed to the idea that the Budget Director was indispensable. In conversation with Bobbie Kilberg Sununu explained: 'The President needs Dick, he's the only one with a coherent [budgetary] policy.' With rare modesty Sununu denied that he could perform such a role himself saying 'No, I don't have the knowledge, Darman has.' Kilberg concluded that 'even as brilliant as Sununu was he was cowed a little bit by Darman's knowledge of the budgetary process.'[13]

By mid-1990 the Director of OMB and the Chief of Staff, whose egos had been widely expected to clash, were working closely with one another and had together become the principal arbiters of domestic policy. As Sununu's deputy saw it, 'while people thought they would do battle with each other [they] ended up becoming real allies.'[14] This gave Darman access to the power he craved while allowing the relatively inexperienced Sununu to benefit from the Budget Director's understanding of the labyrinthine workings of the federal government and, in particular, his mastery of the budgetary process.[15]

THE 1990 BUDGET DEAL

In May 1990, the President, in calling on congressional leaders to participate in a summit with Administration officials designed to address the budget deficit, let it be known, through his press secretary, that discussions would start with 'no preconditions' and would proceed 'unfettered with conclusions about positions taken in the past'. This was, not surprisingly, interpreted as a signal that Bush would now countenance tax increases, a conclusion which Sununu tried surreptitiously to dispel by saying that 'no preconditions' meant that the Democrats were at liberty to propose tax increases, but 'it's our prerogative to say no. And I emphasize the no.'[16]

The Chief of Staff's statement alarmed Democratic leaders suspicious of being manoeuvred into a situation where they would have to take the blame for any increases in taxation. In subsequent meetings with Bush the Democratic leadership insisted that he clarify his position on taxes.[17] This led to a statement drafted by Darman and issued in the name of the President which said, in part:

> It is clear to me that both the size of the deficit problem and the need for a package that can be enacted require all of

the following: entitlement and mandatory program reform, *tax revenue increases*, growth incentives, discretionary spending reductions, orderly reductions in defense expenditures and budget process reform, to assure that any bipartisan agreement is enforceable and that the deficit problem is brought under responsible control.[18] [My italics]

By those three italicized words Bush jettisoned the defining issue between the parties, horrified many members of his own party in Congress, appalled conservative Republicans in general, shattered morale among White House staff and sowed the seeds of his defeat in 1992. For the moment, however, Bush's concession made it possible for budget negotiations between congressional leaders and Administration officials to proceed behind closed doors. These continued fitfully for three months with agreement on a package of cuts and tax increases, largely orchestrated by Richard Darman, finally being reached on 30 September.

This deal, it was claimed, would reduce government borrowing by approximately $500 billion over five years. Defence and domestic discretionary spending were to be cut by $182 billion; entitlements such as Medicare and farm subsidies were to be reduced by $106 billion; interest payments on the national debt would be reduced by $65 billion and new taxes and user fees for government services were expected to raise $148 billion.[19] While the agreement included a whole range of tax increases covering commodities such as gasoline, tobacco, alcohol and heating oil it did not include an increase in income tax, the one thing the Adminstration was most anxious to avoid.[20]

The President and his staff now lobbied members of Congress hard and Bush, on 2 October, made a nationally televised address to the people to urge support for the package. He described the budget deficit as 'a cancer gnawing away at our nation's economic health' and, while he accepted that the bipartisan budget agreement was less than perfect, it was 'the best . . . that can be legislated now.' Bush admitted that the agreement included tax increases which he was not 'a fan' of, but income taxes would not go up and those tax increases that were included 'should allow the economy to grow' by reducing the deficit and allowing interest rates to be lowered. The

President warned, 'if we fail to enact this agreement our
economy will falter, markets may tumble and recession will
follow' and concluded by making a direct appeal to the
American people:

'I ask you to understand how important and, for some, how
difficult this vote is, for your congressmen and senators.
Many worry about your reaction to one part or another.
But I want you to know the importance of the whole. And
so I ask you to take this initiative: Tell your congressmen
and senators you support this agreement . . . Your senators
and congressmen need to know that you want this deficit
brought down.'[21]

Despite these dire warnings and exhortations the House of
Representatives refused by a large margin to ratify the budget
compromise that had been worked out between the White
House and congressional leaders. The House as a whole
voted it down on 5 October by 254–179; the Democrats opposed
it 149–108 while the Republicans voted against 105–71. Many
Democrats opposed the agreement because they saw it as
being balanced unfairly against their natural constituents. They
were troubled by cuts in Medicare and welfare progammes
and believed that the suggested tax increases would hit the
middle class and and the poor hardest while leaving the wealthy
relatively unscathed. Conservative Republicans on the other
hand were mortified by the President's willingness to renege
on his repeated pledge to not increase taxes.[22]

In the days immediately following this humiliating set-back
President Bush, in an abortive effort to frighten Congress into
submission, vetoed a continuing resolution designed to prevent
the shutting down of essential government services now that
authority for spending money had elapsed. After a further
three weeks of negotiation and adjustments a budget resolution was cleared by the House and the Senate on 27 October.

This new package passed largely because it had now been
made more 'progressive' and thereby more palatable to
congressional Democrats. More of the burden of reducing the
deficit, in other words, was to be placed on those of means
and the pressure relaxed somewhat on the less well off. Thus
the top marginal income tax rate was increased from 28 per
cent to 31 per cent; Medicare cuts were to be less swingeing;

proposed increases in gasoline taxes were almost halved and a new tax on home heating oil was eliminated altogether.[23]

Overall, however, the final version of the Omnibus Budget Reconciliation Act of 1990 differed little from the earlier deal.[24] It was designed to reduce the deficit by $492 billion over five years – $137 billion of that was to be realized by revenue increases, $99 billion would be obtained by cuts in entitlements and other mandatory spending programmes, while $184 billion would come from cuts in other appropriations. The remainder was to be realized by savings on interest payments on the national debt.[25] Most significantly perhaps the 1990 legislation also included important procedural changes designed to make a reality of attempts to reduce the deficit. The much derided Gramm-Rudman-Hollings legislation was, in effect, repealed and in an effort to contain increases in spending it was now agreed that appropriations bills would have to stay within specific caps for discretionary spending. There would be one such cap for defence, one for foreign aid and a third for domestic expenditures. New spending under either of these headings would have to be offset by decreases elsewhere under the same heading. 'Bills exceeding the caps would be out of order for floor consideration.'[26] Despite the inauspicious circumstances of its birth the budget finally agreed in 1990 was seen as a modest but not unimportant step towards bringing the deficit under control.[27]

A CRISIS OF GOVERNABILITY

The budget débâcle of 1990 can be seen as a crisis of governability, demonstrating not just the fallibility of Bush and other leaders, but also revealing structural defects in the American political system. As Janet Hook said in writing at the time of the defeat of the first budget deal: 'It is a seismic political event that exposes the architecture of power in Washington, unsettling the relationship between political leaders and their followers, between the two parties, and between Congress and the public.'[28]

The fact of divided government obviously contributed to this crisis and yet that is only part of the explanation. In the 1950s, despite divided government, President Eisenhower enjoyed a reasonably constructive relationship with Congress, whereas close to 40 years later the conditions were markedly different. Congress had now become an intensely individual-istic institution where the old adage 'to get along go along' associated with the legendary former Speaker Sam Rayburn had become outmoded, where an ethos of 'every man for himself' prevailed.[29]

By the 1990s the proliferation of direct primaries and the ever-expanding role of television in electoral politics had turned congressional campaigns into personal rather than party affairs, and legislators elected almost entirely by their own efforts were bound to be less susceptible to party discipline. A former member of the House, Perkins Bass of New Hampshire, in referring to the budget crisis said: 'When I was in Congress we had a lot of party discipline. There's no discipline I can see today. Congress can't take on the entitlements, or the other tough budget choices, because there's no discipline.'[30]

This situation had arisen in part as a consequence of congres-sional reforms introduced in the 1970s, which had sharply tilted the balance of power in favour of the rank and file while making party leaders and committee chairmen weaker than they had ever been before.[31] As another former congressman, Joel Pritchard, a Republican from the state of Washington, said: 'In Congress today everyone runs for office as a political entity of his own. Without a strong party connection, there's no coherent philosophy for them to connect to; it's everyone for himself.'[32] During the budget crisis the Minority Leader in the House, Robert Michel, spoke of his role in terms that would have appalled congressional titans of previous eras, 'You just have to keep begging and begging and begging.'[33]

Given the line-up of party forces in the House of Representatives, passage of the first bipartisan budget agree-ment required that the leaders of each party obtain the support of half their followers – 130 Democratic votes and 89 on the Republican side. The fact that neither came close to these modest objectives with only 108 Democrats and 71 Republicans voting with the leadership provides dramatic testi-mony of the weakness of party in Congress. This was, after all, a critical issue, and one where Bush and congressional leaders lobbied hard and yet they failed to convince even 50 per cent of their followers to support a bipartisan package.

Among the Democrats only 14 out of 27 standing committee chairmen voted Yea while a mere six out of 13 appropriations sub-committee chairmen voted in favour of the deal.[34]

The most serious divisions, however, were among the House Republicans where the conservative wing led by the Minority Whip, Newt Gingrich, was in open revolt against the President's reversal of his 'no new taxes' undertaking. For a long time the Republican Party had been divided between devotees of supply side economics and those with more traditional views as Gingrich himself explained: 'There is a clear difference between those of us who believe passionately in growth incentives and those with the traditional view that reducing the deficit is more important. It's a debate that has been going on for 15 years.'[35] Initially, it seemed unlikely that conservative Republicans in the House would go so far as to humiliate their own President on such a critical issue, but party loyalty was, in the end, strained beyond reasonable limits by the insensitive tactics of the principal White House negotiators. The President's televised appeal to the voters to pressure their representatives into compliance backfired and the defection by Gingrich was crucial. He was the second-ranking Republican leader in the House and, as Minority Whip, was normally responsible for marshalling votes behind the party leadership, whereas on this occasion, he actively undermined Michel's capacity to deliver the votes of half of his party colleagues.

In defence of the Bush Administration, it can be said that the budgetary crisis of 1990 was, in part, brought about by systemic problems. It was a victim of the chronic individualism that now characterizes the national legislature in the United States. It failed also because of the astonishing fragility of American parties, with the Republican Party in the House on this occasion revealing profound divisions over the direction of economic policy. On the other hand, it is difficult to avoid the conclusion that this crisis might have been avoided by more skilful leadership from the White House.

A CRISIS OF LEADERSHIP

The President himself, his Chief of Staff and his Director of the Office of Management and Budget must bear the heaviest responsibility for the budget débâcle of 1990. The dominant role of Sununu and Darman in the making of domestic policy in the Bush Administration has been attested to by a number of insiders. As Edie Holiday put it, the two men 'were very powerful; they were able to basically command the domestic agenda.'[36] The Assistant to the President for Communications argued similarly that after about three months 'Sununu and Darman were wielding tremendous influence, not only in the shaping and the direction of the President's policies, but also in how he advanced those policies . . . in terms of having a complete picture of what was going on they were the only two that had that.'[37]

Earlier, I touched on some of the reasons why these two aides were so influential in the Bush White House. Sununu's intellect, his tough cop demeanour and his links with conservative Republicans complemented the President's patrician, ideologically agnostic and more decorous approach. Darman, for his part, had made himself seemingly indispensable by dint of his lengthy experience in government, the sharpness of his intellect and his mastery of the arcane mysteries of the budgetary process. However, none of these factors would have counted for so much if the President had not been so disinterested when it came to matters of domestic policy.

With characteristic transparency Bush blurted out his preference for foreign policy at a press conference during the budget crisis: 'When you get a problem with the complexities that the Middle East has now, and the Gulf has now, I enjoy trying to put the coalition together and keep it together . . . I can't say I just rejoice every time I go up and talk to Rostenkowski about what he's going to do on taxes.'[38] John Keller, Director of Presidential Advance and a dedicated Bush loyalist, spoke of the difficulty of engaging the President's interest when it came to domestic issues. 'Getting him excited about agriculture and things like that was like pulling teeth; you could see it when you did those sort of events . . . he was doing it [only] because he had to do it.'[39] The same point was made by Clayton Yeutter who contrasted the President's responses in press conferences to questions on foreign policy with those on domestic matters: '[With] an international question, his eyes would sparkle, his voice would get stronger, he would answer it in a persuasive way . . . When it got to a domestic policy question it was sort of "Jeez, do I have to answer this God awful thing".[40]

This all too evident lack of interest in domestic affairs by the chief executive created a vacuum that Sununu and Darman eagerly sought to fill. In budgetary matters Darman was allowed to become the prime mover. Aided and abetted by Sununu, he manoeuvred to marginalize other senior figures in the White House who otherwise might have acted as counterweights in this area – notables such as Nicholas Brady, Secretary to the Treasury and a close friend of the President; Michael Boskin, Chairman of the Council of Economic Advisers, and Roger Porter, Assistant to the President for Economic and Domestic Policy.

Both Bush loyalists and Reaganite conservatives in the White House have pointed the finger at Darman as an overbearing, unprincipled manipulator who led the hapless George Bush into the budget quagmire. Thus the infinitely loyal Bobbie Kilberg found Darman to be 'extraordinarily bright but arrogant'; David Demarest believed the Budget Director was 'too brilliant for his own good' and according to Andrew Card the President 'was politically, poorly served by Dick Darman'.[41] Among the conservatives Connie Horner deplored Darman's penchant for wheeling and dealing and his lack of attachment to principles. She accused him of favouring 'deals rather than standing fast to ideas . . . he did not believe in the no new taxes pledge. He thought it was a stupid idea and was quite happy to draw the President into a repudiation of it.'[42] Another conservative, Charles Kolb, devotes much of his book to the excoriation of Darman and charges that Bush's 'apostasy on taxes was the result of a palace coup orchestrated by Darman. By convincing Bush that the chief threat to the economy was the budget deficit, Darman managed to con Bush away from the one message that had sustained and galvanized Republicans since 1978: economic growth through lower taxes.'[43]

The many critics of the Budget Director within the Bush Administration may have overstated their case and there is much to be said for William Kristol's more measured view. He perceived Darman as 'a very shrewd operator who had his own views on what should be done, but at the end of the day he was doing what the President wanted him to do and what other forces in the White House wanted him to do.'[44] James Pinkerton argued similarly that Darman's budget deal strategy 'appealed to Bush's anti-Reagan instincts' and believed that the President was taken in by the Budget Director, effectively saying: 'If you leave all this to me, I will take care of it and all you've got to worry about is foreign policy.'[45]

It seems that not all the blame for this crisis of leadership can be heaped on Darman, and his close ally Sununu. As a guardian President Bush was only too pleased to have the opportunity to concentrate on what he saw as his primary responsibility, the conduct of foreign and national security policy. This became even more the case after 2 August 1990 and the invasion of Kuwait by Iraqi forces. Unquestionably Darman was on the pragmatic rather than the ideological wing of the Republican Party, but so was Bush. The President moreover shared his Budget Director's scepticism about Reaganomics and almost certainly made the no new taxes pledge more for electoral reasons rather than out of economic policy convictions. Darman had a proclivity for elite deal-making away from the public view, a style of decision-making that Bush himself preferred. Rather than the President being brainwashed and manoeuvred into the budget deal by Darman and Sununu there is good reason to believe that they doing what he wanted them to do.

For all that, the Chief of Staff and the Director of the budget office were deeply implicated in several strategic errors of great consequence. As Bush's most influential advisers on domestic policy they appear to have done him a major disservice by allowing the fateful reversal of his no new taxes pledge to dribble out via a five-line statement pinned to the White House press office bulletin board. According to one source there was no attempt to 'staff' properly this enormously significant announcement. 'Did it go through Boyden [Gray]? No. Did it go through Jim Cicconi? No. Did it go through "speech"? No. Did it go through Marlin Fitzwater? No. Did it go through anybody but Sununu and Darman? No.'[46]

Other senior White House staff were deeply shocked by the manner of Bush's U-turn on taxes, by what Cicconi described as 'cavalierly reneging on a pretty sacred commitment.' In expounding on the nature of that commitment Cicconi said,:

There are very few pledges that have been made in American politics that have been made so clearly and with such obvious intent that it be taken as much more than a typical political promise. When you not only say 'I am not going to raise taxes' but you [also] say 'read my lips' it was as if he'd said, 'I really mean this' and 'I can be believed'. To renege on that after only a year and a half, no matter what the rationale, was fated to divide the party and alienate the American people, and that is exactly the effect that it had.[47]

John Keller took a more relaxed view of the President going back on his pledge, but despaired of the failure of the Administration to 'spin' the issue effectively:

[The President] made a decision which actually was probably the right thing to do for the American people, for the economy, for the country. He realized, although this never came out, that one cannot always be held to campaign promises. You cannot predict the future, or how current events are going to affect your decision-making . . . [Unfortunately there] were no road trips, no events, no spin, no anything around that whole thing. We just got eaten alive; it was like making an announcement and then sitting in the Oval Office and waiting for them to chew you up, which they did.[48]

In an earlier chapter I noted how Nick Calio, the Administration's head of legislative liaison in the House of Representatives, received no forewarning of the abandonment of the tax pledge, even though this development was bound to make his job immeasurably more difficult. After the announcement had been made however, Calio participated in the debate in the White House on how the President should now proceed. Like Keller, Calio argued that the President needed to actively and publicly sell the change of policy:

He should have gone on TV immediately and said 'Look this is something I don't want to do. I said no new taxes, but here is where our economy is and here is what we think needs to be done – the deficit is the problem . . . I know this will hurt me politically, but I am supposed to be your leader and, as your leader, I am going to say I made a mistake to say never. But now we have to go forward; here is why we are doing this. If you are going to take it out on me politically you are welcome to, but I have to do what I think is best for the country and I hope you will come with me'.[49]

Instead of following Calio's excellent advice the President, in the middle of a press conference, 'made some kind of short statement that nobody picked up at all, and was meaningless in terms of the public relations that needed to be done.'[50] One cabinet member subsequently placed the blame for this presentational disaster primarily on Darman, who would not:

> . . . admit that it was a mistake, because Darman didn't make mistakes . . . But what Darman missed was how damaging it would be to break that . . . pledge . . . [He] totally missed the political significance of that. So did the other executive branch participants . . . And they were totally nonchalant about it. They really thought nobody would pay any attention; that this was just another campaign promise and nobody pays any attention to campaign promises.[51]

These critics from within the Administration, all of them Bush loyalists, surely made, admittedly with the benefit of hindsight, a number of telling points. Darman and Sununu should have recognized that the no new taxes pledge was far more than an ordinary campaign promise; they should have seen that the cavalier abandonment of such a 'sacred commitment' was bound to outrage conservative Republicans and to damage significantly the President's standing in the country. It could be argued that the deterioration in economic circumstances since the election made necessary a change of course, but the rationale for such an important change needed to be spelled out in detail to the public by the President. By openly and courageously facing up to the fact that he had made a mistake and explaining why the good of the country required a budget including increased taxes, Bush would have stood a far better chance of minimizing the damage to his party and retaining the trust of the American people.

The President and his closest advisers were also badly mistaken in adopting a strategy of putting together a budget by deal-making with congressional leaders behind closed doors. This attempt to take the politics out of intensely political matters was ill-advised. The fiercely democratic spirit that infuses the

American system makes elitist decision-making arrangements particularly inappropriate and neither the public, nor rank and file members of Congress, were pleased to be presented with a *fait accompli* on such a politically sensitive matter. At a press conference, after the first budget deal had been rejected, the President was asked whether the behind closed doors strategy had not been a mistake: 'Don't you think though, the secrecy was an impediment? [The budget deal] fell like a lead balloon . . . So had you not negotiated more in public, more public dialogue, more debate, don't you think you would have been better off?'[52]

The President blandly brushed this criticism aside doubting that anyone opposed to raising gasoline taxes would have been more likely to accept them if the matter had been the subject of public debate. This was an especially revealing response, indicating a lack of faith in what can be accomplished through the democratic process.

Dealing with highly contentious matters in secret was also unwelcome to members of Congress of both parties. Thus a California Republican in the House, Bill Thomas, in commenting on the rejection of the first budget deal said 'What this vote proved was that closed door sessions don't work; the whole process should begin and end with full public debate.'[53]

Another House Republican, Arthur Ravenel of South Carolina asked his colleagues: 'Are we in charge as we were sent here to be, or have we become a house of political eunuchs?' On the Democratic side Benjamin Cardin of Maryland observed: 'Even if we weren't happy with what was going on, we'd be a lot more comfortable if we knew what was going on.'[54] Meanwhile his party colleague, Dan Glickman of Kansas, said: 'Eight men met in secret for several weeks to prepare this budget, that is not the democratic way to do business.'[55]

To add to the resentment provoked by the Administration's strategy of secrecy the handling of the legislature by Sununu and Darman was, in other ways, insensitive if not inept. Neither man was well liked on Capitol Hill. The Budget Director was well known for brash intolerance of those he deemed to be his intellectual inferiors, an attitude that made him less than popular among conservative Republican representatives who, in any case, doubted his ideological credentials. Rightly enough, they regarded Darman as a traditional Republican, with little time for the tax pledge or the supply-side faith. The Chief of Staff was less vulnerable on ideological grounds, but his brutish behaviour towards legislators had been a liability before and now proved, once again, to be counterproductive.

Republican members of the House, already smarting from having been excluded from the budget discussions that had gone on through the summer of 1990, might have expected some quiet diplomacy from a White House badly in need of their support when the first budget deal came to the floor of the House. The President's lobbying was suitably low key, but Sununu after a moderate beginning, adopted a different approach. In addressing the House Republican Conference, the Chief of Staff outraged his listeners by saying: 'By the way, none of you guys want to have the President come to your district, to be on a platform with him with a big audience of constituents and have him turn and say, "Why aren't you with me on this deal?" ' [56] One indignant Congressman responded, 'I know George Bush, and he would never do anything like that', leading Sununu to reply, 'George Bush is a much nicer guy than I am.' [57]

These acrimonious exchanges badly damaged the President's cause. In the first place Sununu's threat was seen as an empty one that merely served to alienate potential supporters. As we saw earlier, Bush, arising from his own service in the House and the friends he still had there, had adopted a conciliatory approach to Congress and there was no reason to suppose that this was now to be abandoned. Moreover, the Chief of Staff's abrasive comments helped to drive moderate Republicans into the arms of conservatives already appalled by the President's reversal on taxes. A senior Republican member of the House reportedly said of Sununu's intervention: 'I bet you that of the 176 members of the conference, at least 100 of them were undecided at that point. You could feel the tide turn. All of those people who wanted to help shifted to "no" and it was downhill from there.' [58] Another Republican said 'Sununu insulted the conference. Some of us who felt bad about voting against the President before the conference now feel good about it.' [59] In these new circumstances, Newt Gingrich, the leader of the conservatives, felt sufficiently emboldened to go public with his opposition to the budget deal, a defection of the greatest consequence.

The President's most influential advisers on the budget also erred in insisting on keeping information on the budget negotiations even from senior White House colleagues. From the outset of the Bush Administration there had been a downplaying of the role of those who worked in Communications, Legislative Affairs and Public Liaison and now their exclusion from discussions on the budget deal proved to be a costly mistake.

Several senior staff expressed their indignation at being totally shut out of the negotiations . Bobbie Kilberg reported that 'the only people with any idea of what was in the budget deal in the White House were Sununu and Darman.'[60] James Cicconi observed that 'virtually the entire senior staff were kept in the dark on this; the only people that really knew what was going on were Sununu and Darman.'[61] The dangers in such an approach were pinpointed by Edie Holiday; she noted that 'Dick Darman wanted total control over those issues and didn't want anybody to know what they were doing,' and went on to say 'as a result there was not an apparatus working to prepare the necessary public relations or communications strategy, that would have helped to sell the reasons' why the budget deal was necessary.[62]

The same point was elaborated in some detail by Kilberg who, as one of the two people in charge of the Office of Public Liaison, was responsible for maintaining healthy relationships with business and other interest groups sympathetic to the Administration. These organizations could be expected to play a pivotal role in ensuring public and congressional acceptance of any budget agreement. However, as Kilberg explained, during the budget negotiations Public Liaison was placed 'in an absolutely impossible position because we were totally cut out of the loop . . . Darman let nobody know what was going on, absolutely nobody. [Consequently], we could not defuse anger, help build coalitions, help get support for what was going on, because we didn't have the foggiest notion of what was going on, and neither did any of the interest groups.'

Kilberg went on to recount how she was summoned to the White House on the Sunday morning when the budget deal was to be announced. After the announcement was made in the Rose Garden:

'Sununu turned to me and said 'Sell it.' I said 'Sell what? How am I going to sell this when for the last three months I have been stonewalling all of these people? Telling them that we couldn't have their input; telling them they weren't part of the game. And now you want me to turn around and tell them to start selling this. What do I do?' And he said, 'Just do it.'

Having outlined the impossible situation in which Public Liaison had been placed Kilberg nevertheless tried to meet her responsibilities by turning to Darman and saying 'OK here is a piece of paper [listing] all the groups we need to touch base with between now and Tuesday. And between now and Tuesday I need you here for this briefing and there for that briefing.' Darman, however, declined to be so instructed saying, before turning away,'I will brief when I care to brief on what I care to brief about and you will not direct me.'[63] This arrogant, wilful refusal to draw on the expertise, the contacts and the relationships nurtured by Kilberg and her colleagues was another reaction most unhelpful to the acceptance of the budget agreement.

President Bush suffered a humiliating setback when he urged the American people, during his 2 October television address, to call upon their representatives to support the first budget deal. In the event, far greater numbers of constituents appear to have demanded rejection rather than support for the agreement. According to Kilberg the calls from constituents to their members of Congress ran something like six to one against the budget deal.[64] Part of the explanation for this humiliating rebuff surely lies in the failure to prepare the ground adequately for the President's appeal. Again according to Kilberg, neither she, her boss David Demarest, Assistant to the President for Communications, or Nick Calio, the President's chief of legislative affairs in the House, had any advance warning that the President's address would include such an appeal and it appears that the relevant wording was only added to the text of the President's speech shortly before Bush spoke. With some feeling Ms Kilberg said: 'No other White House would ever have done that without having decided it at least a day before, without having told public liaison, without having public liaison all organized and ready to go.' Immediately after the President had spoken the Office of Public Liaison began working the phones, but 'our association folks were so mad they couldn't see straight. They said, "You're on your own on this one. Forget it. You tell us after the speech that this is what you're expecting us to do just days ahead of the vote." I said, "I didn't know." They said, "How could you not know?" I said, "Nobody knew." They said, "How is that possible?" '[65]

It is evident that George Bush, in 1990, was poorly served by his Budget Director and his Chief of Staff. Their obsessive determination to monopolize information, to keep details of the budget negotiations secret from rank and file members of Congress, from the public, and even from their senior White House colleagues, was a fundamental and damaging mistake. Sununu and Darman failed abysmally to anticipate the political fallout that was bound to arise from the President going back on a constantly reiterated, specific promise that formed the centrepiece of his 1988 campaign.

Both men, moreover, had difficulty in concealing their contempt for Congress, and the Chief of Staff's abrasive tactics in dealing with legislators were especially ill-judged. Sununu acted as if he was still the governor of a small state with a part-time legislature rather than the agent of a chief executive facing a Congress with formidable powers in divided government circumstances. As one Republican House member said of Sununu: 'He's an extraordinarily bright and intellectual man. But his basic problem is that was effective as a governor dealing with people who were part-time legislators. Frankly, you can bully them around. You don't get anywhere in this town by bullying people around. That lesson has not quite soaked through.'[66]

It should also be noted that the White House includes specialists in communications, in legislative liaison and in public liaison; these groupings of staff possess expertise, resources and contacts invaluable to a president as he struggles to gain acceptance of his policies. It was foolhardy in the extreme for Sununu and Darman to go out of their way to cut such people out of the 'loop', to exclude these specialists from the decision-making process, to deny them the opportunity to make use of their expertise and to prepare the ground for the announcement of the budget deal.

'THE BUCK STOPS HERE'

Harry Truman famously placed on his desk a sign which said 'The buck stops here', a slogan that should be kept in mind by all those Bush loyalists inclined to heap blame on senior advisers for his failures.[67] To be sure, Sununu and Darman had their shortcomings, but Bush selected them in the first place and persisted in keeping them on despite the mounting evidence of their inadeqacies. Sununu only left after the 'Air Sununu' scandal had made his position untenable and Darman remained until the very end. According to one source, when Samuel Skinner replaced Sununu as Chief of Staff, he 'tried to get Bush to get rid of Darman . . . but Bush wouldn't do it and he should have, that was a big mistake.'[68]

The selection of competent staff is one of the tests of effective leadership and if the White House functioned imperfectly during the budget crisis of 1990 the responsibility for that rests ultimately with George Bush. As is the case with any president, Bush's staff and the organization of the White House were reflections of his character and his style of leadership. Richard Darman was a pragmatist and an elitist; he disdained ideology and delighted in making deals behind the scenes with other members of the elite. This type of leadership was all of a piece with the President's patrician, managerial approach. He too had a penchant for 'cutting deals with other leaders. His is the insider game. His weakness is in sensing outside perspectives and in extending the ambit of discussion. This is not because, like Reagan, Bush has strong passions about the substance, but because his style of operation is fundamentally boardroom politics and brokerage among "proper gentlemen".'[69]

As I argued earlier, it was the President's extravagant lack of interest in domestic policy that created the vacuum that his two egotistical, belligerent aides leapt to fill. It was his lack of engagement that allowed them to act without inhibition, monopolizing information, offending legislators and cutting out of the decision-making process other senior White House staff. If Bush had been more 'hands-on' in this area, in the way that he was in matters of foreign policy, it is probable that neither Sununu nor Darman would have been appointed. Or if they had managed to secure appointment we may presume that their displacement would have been less; conceivably, they would have been less able to exclude other staff from the decision-making process, and their removal would have become highly likely when their behaviour became damaging to the President's purposes.

The widespread belief that Bush was not interested in domestic policy tended to feed the suspicion that he was a man without deeply held views on economic policy. These concerns were especially prevalent among those on the right of his party who had not forgotten his denunciation of supply side theory during the 1980 primaries as 'voodoo economics'. This notably significant comment revealed the fault line in Bush's party that has for years divided the Reaganites from more traditional, more pragmatic Republicans. The former had been reassured by Bush taking the tax pledge in 1988, whereas their worst fears were confirmed by his apparently casual abandonment of that undertaking. It does not make sense to exonerate Bush from responsibility for taking a step that disastrously divided his party, and ultimately destroyed his presidency, on the grounds that he was talked into it by Richard Darman for, in the end, it was the President's decision and his alone.

Several Bush loyalists whom I spoke to robustly defended him against the charge that his willingness to renege on taxes was evidence of his lack of convictions. One of those who worked closely with the President and knew him well, James Cicconi, insisted that the no new taxes promise was made sincerely; when he 'made that pledge he meant it and he fully intended to keep it.' Eventually, however, he succumbed to Darman's persuasion, accepting that:

> A budget deal involving taxes was really the only way to deal with the [deficit] problem and was essential to the well-being of the nation. George Bush does have an inner core of conviction [one] that is rooted in doing what is right for the country regardless. The Budget Director understood this and was able to appeal to that gradually over time to swing him around to the notion that this was the only way to help the country . . . In George Bush's mind it probably amounted to "Look, you can either adhere to your commitment for the sake of foolish consistency, or you can do what

is right for the country and seize the moment for an historic agreement with Congress that will finally get the deficit under control and ensure future generations of prosperity." . . . The George Bush I know probably said to himself, "I am willing to take the heat for reneging if it is in the best interest of the nation." . . . There are many occasions on which he stood up to political heat because of that integral conviction. I don't think the budget deal showed him to be cynical. Certainly a lot of the American public concluded that, but I don't think it was a correct conclusion.[70]

This explanation presents Bush as a man of principle forced to change course out of a concern for the national interest. It is also the case that Bush's change of tack was entirely consistent with a guardianship approach to presidential leadership. As Chapter 1 made clear, guardian presidents have no preordained plan for change; they take the view that presidents should be skilled managers who deal with problems on an *ad hoc* basis. Such an approach presupposes pragmatic flexibility rather than the sort of ideological certainty associated with Bush's predecessor. However, it is surely the case that making an iron-clad commitment in the first place was inconsistent with a guardian style of leadership, and the fact that George Bush nevertheless did so serves to reinforce the allegation that the pledge was made principally for electoral reasons.

Further reason to question the President's motives and to doubt the quality of his leadership in domestic policy was provided by his weaving back and forth on the capital gains issue during the budget crisis. Since the beginning of his presidency, Bush had been pressing on Congress the case for a reduction in capital gains tax. In addressing a joint session on 9 Febuary 1989 he had said: 'I propose that we cut the maximum tax rate on capital gains to increase long-term investment. History is clear. This would increase revenues, help saving and create new jobs'.[71]

During the budget negotiations capital gains had been a central issue, but the Democrats had been been resistant to a reduction in the rate which they saw as a windfall for the wealthy. They would only countenance such a cut if it was offset by higher rates of income tax on those with large incomes. The negotiators failed to reach agreement on this matter in the summer ultimately because the Republicans' aversion to an income tax increase outweighed their enthusiasm for a capital gains tax reduction. After the defeat of the first budget deal on 5 October the possibility of some such trade-off was reopened.

At a press conference on the morning of 9 October the President was asked whether he was willing to contemplate a higher income tax rate for the wealthy in an exchange for a capital gains cut. He replied: 'That's on the table. That's been talked about. And if it's proper, if it can be worked in the proper balance between the capital gains rate and the income tax changes, fine'.[72] Later that day, however, 17 Republican senators descended on the White House to put it to the President that any such deal was not possible in the short term; their virtually unanimous advice was, according to Senator Pete Domenici of New Mexico, 'Get it off the table.' Senator Bob Packwood of Oregon emerged from the meeting to announce: 'The President agreed, our unified position was we will not go up on the rate, not 1 per cent, not 2 per cent, not one penny . . . we will leave the rates where they are, drop capital gains and do nothing about the rates.' The following morning Robert Dole, the Senate Minority Leader, put a different gloss on Bush's position: '[He] did not make any decision yesterday, even though that was reported. He listened to us. He did not announce his position at all. He did not acquiesce in what we said.'[73]

When asked, on a trip to Florida, to clarify the confusion that had arisen, Bush most unhelpfully said: 'Let Congress clear it up.' Rather more damagingly, when out jogging, the President, on being asked whether he was ready to give up on a capital gains cut, pointed to his backside and said: 'Read my hips.'[74] On his return to Washington Bush met with a delegation of House Republicans on 11 October after which Congressman Bill Archer of Texas reported to the press that the President was ready to accept a tax increase in return for a capital gains cut: 'He is willing – and I think he will speak to you today about this – he is willing to equalize or level the rate at 31 per cent . . . in exchange for a 15 per cent capital gains rate . . . I'm telling you that he told us today that he has been consistently for this all the way through.' Within hours, however, the President's position changed again, when he said through his press spokesman that 'he did not believe that such a compromise was now possible'.[75]

To summarize the foregoing fiasco, in the course of two days the President appeared to make several U-turns on a central issue of economic policy. He began on 9 October by saying that a trade-off between capital gains and income tax rates was 'on the table'. After meeting later that day with Republican senators he left those like Packwood with the clear impression that no deal was possible. The following morning, Dole inferred that, in fact, the President was undecided on the matter and Bush, when pressed to resolve the confusion, made only flippant response. Subsequently, he gave congressmen reason to believe that a deal was back on the table only to deny that this was so later the same day.

Not surprisingly, this display of 'rampant indecision' brought about many unflattering newspaper headlines across the country, precipitated a sharp fall in the President's public opinion poll ratings and further damaged his standing in Congress with one Democrat in the House, Thomas Downey of New York gleefully observing: 'Our president has now taken more positions on taxes than Nadia Comaneci.'[76] Meanwhile, conservative Republicans like Gingrich were appalled by the President making a wisecrack about what they looked upon as a sacred campaign commitment and regarded his behaviour during this episode as further proof of his lack of any settled beliefs in economic matters.

President Bush's leadership during the 1990 budget crisis was shown to be badly flawed; not only was he chronically indecisive, throughout he failed to make effective use of his office as a bully pulpit. In an earlier chapter I commented on Bush's disinclination to use rhetorical appeals in support of policy objectives and this weakness now became glaringly apparent. As a good loyalist, Edie Holiday faulted other senior staff for not impressing on Bush the need to go to the country to explain why it was necessary to go back on no new taxes, but this is surely disingenuous.[77] An experienced leader like Bush should have seen for himself that if he was to abandon such a central and often repeated undertaking, a programme of public education beforehand would be required.

As Stuart Eizenstat, chief domestic policy adviser in the Carter White House, noted in a rather prescient article written in

June 1990 before the budget had become a crisis issue, presidents had broken campaign promises before and survived
relatively unscathed. FDR, for instance in the 1932 campaign
promised to reduce spending and to balance the budget and
then did precisely the opposite in office. However Bush needed
to understand that 'the people will forgive a breach in a major
campaign commitment if the president can convincingly
demonstrate that external circumstances have changed.'
Roosevelt had done this impressively in 1936 and gone to win
re-election in a landslide. 'In Bush's case, circumstances have
indeed changed, but not in ways that are immediately evident
to the average citizen. That's why it is essential that if the president does agree to raise taxes, he explain to the people why
new circumstances have required it. Otherwise he risks
provoking a degree of public cynicism that could be dangerous
to his presidency.[78]

As I indicated earlier, there were some in the upper reaches
of the Bush White House who urged the President to go to
the country to explain why it was necessary to renege on his
promise, but he chose to ignore such voices. He did so presumably because such advice was unpalatable to him, because he
had little talent for public speaking, had no faith in what it
could accomplish and, in any case, did not see such activity as
an essential role for presidents. Even though it should ideally
have come months earlier it is not inconceivable that inspired
use of the bully pulpit after the first budget deal might have
saved Bush and his colleagues from disaster. Instead the
President made a brief, insipid television address that was unac-
companied by any careful preparing of the ground and had
all the effect, according to one source, of a 'whisper in a hurricane'. Indeed, the *Congressional Quarterly* reported that:
'Unexpectedly, those selling the budget found momentum
slowed in the 24 hours after Bush's speech. Far from producing
a groundswell of support, it seemed to have increased
constituents' awareness of its painful provisions.'[79]

Even ardent Bush loyalists in the White House agreed that,
irrespective of the merits of the budget deal, its presentation
to the public was a disaster. Ron Kaufman said: 'It wasn't the
deal itself, it was the way it was sold . . . It wasn't what we did,
it's how we did it; it's not what you say, it's how you say
it.' Similarly, Andrew Card said: 'We did a lousy job of

communicating to the public as to why we were where we were and what the consequences of failure were.' According to the Cabinet Secretary, Edie Holiday: 'I saw it as a failure of communications as opposed to a policy failure . . . [we could] have managed the policy change had it been conducted properly.'[80]

The inability of Bush and his Administration to communicate effectively with the American people and to mobilize support behind his budgetary policy in 1990 stands in stark contrast with the high professionalism in such mattters of Ronald Reagan and his colleagues. Not only was Reagan himself a master communicator, his staff, when crucial votes were at stake, worked tirelessly to organize support for his policies in the country – contacting interest groups and campaign contributors to get them to bring pressure to bear on members of Congress.[81] This was precisely the sort of input that Bush's communications staff could have provided if he had not allowed them to be sidelined by Sununu and Darman.

Unlike Bush, Reagan was devastatingly effective in making set-piece speeches on television and testimony to his ability to use that medium to bring members of Congress into line was provided by former Senator Laxalt: 'While Reagan very often could not convince [legislators] on given major policy issues,' Laxalt said, 'they'd better not cross him because he'd get on television and appeal to their constituencies and build up enormous constituent pressure . . . On issue after issue, I saw Reagan change the complexion of Congress on key votes because he had that capability.'[82] By his own admission, Bush lacked that capability and his ability to gain support for his policies in Congress was further eroded by his insider, kid-glove style in dealing with senators and representatives. 'George Bush might be too nice for his own good' Norman Ornstein suggested during the budget crisis.'Every one of those House Republicans knows that if they defied him on this vote the president would be real unhappy, but within a couple of weeks they'd each get a handwritten thoughtful note saying let "bygones be bygones." Nobody out there really feared any serious consequences from this.'[83]

If a president's ability to achieve his policy objectives is the criterion by which he may be legitimately assessed, Bush, in 1990, failed by some margin to meet this test. He was first forced to abandon a hallowed campaign commitment with grave consequences for the unity of his party. He then suffered humiliation when, despite his televised appeal for its accep- tance, the first budget deal was rejected. A second budget deal then only became possible after the President had given further ground to his opponents. To put it another way, the budget crisis was a defining event for the Bush presidency demon- strating several deficiencies in his approach to leadership. His choice of Sununu and Darman for key roles was mistaken, as was his willingness to allow them wide-ranging freedom of action. No modern president can afford to be as disinterested in domestic policy as George Bush was and his preference for insider decision-making, out of the public view, was ill-advised in domestic affairs. His indecisiveness and his evident lack of convictions when it came to economics, and in domestic policy generally, badly undermined his credibility. Finally, Bush's presidency was crippled by his reluctance to mount the bully pulpit and his uninspired performances when he grudgingly did so.

In reflecting on their experience in the Bush White House various senior people have identified the budget imbroglio of 1990 as a pivotal occurrence. Vice President Quayle observed: 'If you want to look for the place where things first went wrong, I'd pick the "budget summit" of 1990.'[84] Much the same point was made by James Cicconi: 'In our White House there is a dividing line between what happened before the budget agreement and what happened after . . . the budget agreement, in many ways was one of the seminal events of the Bush presidency. In my view, his defeat in the 1992 elections flowed directly from the budget agreement.' In reviewing the reasons for Bush's loss in 1992 the conservative Pinkerton mentioned the ending of the Cold War, 'the dry rot of twelve years in power . . . and the budget deal.'

Several of those who were there have confirmed how the atmosphere inside the White House itself was dramatically, if not disastrously, transformed by the budget deal. It shattered 'staff morale in the White House to an extraordinary degree' according to Cicconi, while also destroying the 'collegiality' that existed for the first year and a half of the Bush Administration. This was confirmed by Ms Kilberg: 'After the budget deal the whole domestic White House operation changed dramatically, everybody was suspicious of everybody and everybody started doing their own thing.' In this new atmosphere where 'staff were shocked and more than a little rebellious' the Chief of Staff and his ally the Budget Director, those who had fostered the budget deal, were driven into 'a death embrace with each other. It became them against the world, them against the rest of the staff.'[85] The prevalence of this distinctly unhealthy state of affairs has been remarked upon by Charles Kolb: 'After the deal was concluded, Darman and Sununu became locked together in a fraternal death embrace. Anyone who criticized their deal or who proposed policies even slightly at odds with the legislation was treated as a leper. Policy-making ground to a halt.'[86]

The President's conduct during the budget crisis severely damaged his credibility as a leader and eroded respect for his competence in economic policy. The budget deal 'undermined [Bush's] credibility' in the words of Nick Calio, a view Vice President Quayle and many other Americans shared.[87] According to a *Time*/CNN poll taken on 10 October 1990, Bush's approval rating slumped to 59 per cent from 74 per cent on 23 August, while only 34 per cent now thought he was doing a good job in handling the economy compared to 56 per cent who thought he was doing a poor job.[88].

To add to all this, the rebuffs that Bush suffered over the budget in 1990 did immense harm to his 'professional reputation' defined by Richard Neustadt as the standing of a president in the 'Washington community'. That community comprised not only members of Congress and those within the administration, but also 'governors of states, military commanders in the field, leading politicians in both parties, representatives of private organizations, newsmen of assorted types and sizes, foreign diplomats (and principals abroad)'.[89] In Washington itself the defeat of the first budget deal sparked off ruminations by leading politicos on the possibly dire consequences for the President. Robert Strauss, a former Chairman of the Democratic National Committee, remarked to the press: 'You know and I know that when they smell blood in the water, they go in this town.' Meanwhile Jody Powell, who, as President Carter's press secretary, had first-hand experience of the weakening of a presidency, said: 'Any time you get beat, it makes people inclined to think they can beat you again.'[90]

Another seriously adverse result of the budget débâcle was the heavy damage inflicted on Republican Party unity. The White House 'ideas man', Pinkerton spoke of the agreement on the budget breaking 'the spine of the Republican Party's morale'; Calio referred to it as 'undermining party unity' and Cicconi reported that the 'party was clearly divided on this issue.'[91]   The candidacy of Patrick Buchanan in the 1992 primaries was a direct result of the divisions in the party brought about by the budget deal.

Bush's reactions under the pressure of a significant threat to his renomination added weight to the suspicions of those inclined to doubt whether he was a man of convictions. In a radio broadcast in the spring of 1992 the President described his abandonment of the no new taxes pledge as the worst mistake of his presidency. What was remarkable, however, was the stress Bush laid on political considerations in explaining why the change of course was a mistake: 'Listen, if I had to do that over, I wouldn't do it. Look at all the flak its taking.' The President admitted that Republican voters were 'just overwhelmed by the fact that I went for a tax increase' and were giving him 'political grief' as a consequence.[92] Elsewhere he said: 'If I had it to do over, I wouldn't do what I did then, for a lot of reasons, including political reasons.'[93]

These admissions provide an example of Bush's tendency, on occasion, towards transparent honesty, but they also reveal the misplaced distinction he was inclined to make between campaigning and governing. In addition, they gave renewed currency to the allegation that he was a political wimp. As one of his most senior and loyal advisers frankly observed: 'He explained [the mistake] on the basis of all the flak he was getting, not on the substance of the issue. The importance of the issue was his credibility and that of his administration. He should have taken it like a man. He should have said "This was wrong. [If] the President of the United States makes major campaign promises [he's] got to live up to them. I didn't, I was wrong, and if I am re-relected in 1992 I'm going to live up to campaign promises".'[94]

Over the long term, one of the most damaging repercussions arising from the budget deal was the dimunition of the American people's trust in George Bush, a critical factor in his 1992 defeat. To lose ground on trust in a contest with a candidate notoriously vulnerable on this score was especially galling for presidential staff, denied what would have been a potent campaign weapon. With understandable bitterness David Demarest claimed that the budget deal 'deprived us of two key arguments that Republicans make – you can trust us [and] we won't raise taxes. It killed us on trust and it killed us on taxes.' It was particularly frustrating to be hurt on the issue of trust 'given Bush's inherent strengths; because if you looked at the poll data, one of his strengths was that this is a decent and honorable man.' That same frustration was apparent in James Cicconi's remark, 'We were not able to take advantage of the far larger questions of trust that revolved around Clinton because we ourselves were vulnerable on that issue.'[95] After the 1992 election, exit polls showed Bush ahead of Clinton on the trust issue, but without the budget deal we may assume the margin would have been far greater, sufficient, perhaps, to have brought electoral success.[96]

7 Guardianship and Foreign Policy

In domestic policy guardian presidents are unambitious if not passive. They are reluctant to take initiatives and are keenly conscious of the limits of the power of government. In dealing with foreign and national security issues, by contrast, they adopt a more activist stance, as Richard Rose has noted: 'A guardian President wants to be more influential abroad than at home.' This was certainly true in the case of George Bush, yet for all that there were parallels between his style of leadership on the domestic front and in international affairs.

In managing foreign policy Bush made much use of private diplomacy, a style not unlike his penchant for behind-the-scenes negotiations with other leaders that he used at home. In domestic policy he was at pains to 'do no harm' and his foreign policy stewardship was similarly marked by prudence, caution and pragmatism. An emphasis on limited government at home was reflected by a limited role for the United States abroad. In both arenas, there was the same inclination to discourage people from expecting Washington to provide solutions to their problems. People should 'look to private organizations for domestic problems, and [should] settle their own problems abroad before expecting the United States to take a hand in imposing a settlement.'[2]

In domestic policy Bush's inadequacies as a communicator were a notable source of weakness and for his critics, this deficiency was also a liability in international affairs. He was to be faulted for failing to articulate a memorable response to the destruction of the Berlin Wall and for not spelling out a convincing rationale to the American people for massive intervention in the Persian Gulf.

Bush was accused of lacking vision in international affairs no less than in domestic policy, but he was unrepentant, seeing no need for a conceptual framework for dealing with foreign policy problems. As he saw it, it was more important that he possessed the experience, the contacts and the understanding necessary for dealing with developments on a case-by-case basis. Consequently, his Administration spawned no grand strategy comparable to containment or detente; there was to be no Bush doctrine to place alongside the Truman doctrine, or the Reagan doctrine. An early attempt to enunciate a strategy of 'beyond containment' was derided in the media, a fate which also befell attempts to define a 'new world order' in the wake of the Gulf War.[3]

The key words distinguishing Bush's approach to foreign policy were prudence, moderation and pragmatism. In the same way that he had no plan for restructuring America at home, he entertained no grand schemes for reordering the world outside. He responded cautiously to the tumultuous changes that occurred on his watch, constantly warning of the dangers of instability and upredictability. Instinctively, he favoured the status quo and often, to the chagrin of conservatives in his party, displayed a preference for dealing with established elites rather than encouraging dissenters.

In January 1993 Lawrence Eagleburger, by then Secretary of State, denied that Bush's foreign policy had been unduly reactive and lacking in vision; he insisted that:

> There was a strategy behind the President's conduct of foreign policy . . . [it] was characterized by pragmatism and flexibility . . . [Admittedly] our approach was often ad hoc [but] a certain degree of ad hockery is a virtue, not a vice, when you are dealing with a world in crisis and in chaos, one in which it is impossible to be certain of anything six months ahead . . . for a long time to come, we will be in a post-revolutionary transitional period which will require of us an ability to react quickly to events. In these circumstances, good instincts are as invaluable as a good plan.[4]

The strategy apparently was, in essence, to not have a strategy at all, but to be ready to respond quickly, and on an *ad hoc* basis, to events as they unfolded. This is not to say that Bush had no foreign policy objectives even though they undoubtedly differed from those of his predecessor. Unlike Reagan, who was an ideologue and an often strident advocate of change, Bush and the circle of policy advisers close to him were moderates and pragmatists, troubled by the rapidity of change while they were in office and convinced that the interests of the United States would be best served by cautiously conservative policies that encouraged stability and minimized departures from the status quo. As one senior member of the National Security Council staff explained it: 'This administration is not ideological. It is conservative with a small "c". It is trying to preserve what is working, not embracing departure for departure's sake. We prefer what is, as opposed to the alternative. We don't want to reinvent the world. This is not an administration that is hellbent on change.'[5]

While the Bush Administration has been criticized for being unadventurous in the international arena, there is a sense in which the President's management of foreign policy was far from timid. He had no doubt that the conduct of foreign policy was an executive responsibility and he and his colleagues vigorously resisted attempts by Congress to encroach on his prerogatives in this area. As I explained in Chapter 5, he did this by resolute use of the veto, by extensive use of National Security Directives and, as will become apparent, most significantly of all, by wide-sweeping and controversial interpretations of his constitutional role in warmaking.

FOREIGN POLICY ADVISERS

In sharp contrast to his marked lack of interest in domestic policy, Bush regarded foreign and national security policy as his forte and there was no possibility of his ceding control over decision-making to senior staff in this area. His closest advisers on such matters were James Baker, his Secretary of State, and his Assistant for National Security, Brent Scowcroft. As might be expected, both men had longstanding and close relationships with the President. No one outside his family was closer to Bush than Baker who had been a friend and confidant for more than thirty years. Baker had managed Bush's unsuccessful Senate campaign in 1970 and on the latter's recommendation was appointed Under Secretary for Commerce in the Ford administration. Subsequently, Baker ran Ford's 1976 campaign and then did the same for Bush in 1980. He served as a notably successful Chief of Staff during Reagan's first term, before becoming Secretary of the Treasury in 1985; he was Bush's campaign manager again in 1988.[6]

The President's relationship with Scowcroft extended back to the days of the Nixon Administration. A former Air Force lieutenant general and holding a PhD in international relations, Scowcroft worked in the Nixon White House as a military aide and became Henry Kissinger's deputy at the National Security Council. Scowcroft became National Security Adviser himself in the Ford Administration and it was at this point that Bush became Director of the Central Intelligence Agency and Scowcroft provided the channel through whom he reported to the President.[7]

For a President bent on keeping the control of foreign policy in his own hands, Baker and Scowcroft were excellent choices. Their loyalty was unquestioned and their world views reflected that of George Bush. To take the Bush-Baker relationship first, the President had far greater knowledge of international affairs than his friend whereas Baker's reputation rested on his astute political sense. Essentially, however, these two men were strikingly similar in their approaches to politics. Neither was remotely interested in ideas and they prided themselves on their unremitting pragmatism. Thus Bush pronounced: 'I am a practical man. I like what's real. I'm not much for the airy and the abstract. I like what works. I am not a mystic, and I do not yearn to lead crusades.' His friend Baker meanwhile, said: 'I'm more interested in the game than in philosophy.'[8]

As Chief of Staff and then Secretary of the Treasury in the Reagan Administration, Baker had been seen as the 'ultimate pragmatist', respected for his problem solving skills and his acute political sense, but also criticized by conservatives for his readiness to strike deals rather than to hold out for the whole loaf of Reagan's ideological agenda and 'for lacking an overall conceptual design'.[9] The same sort of complaints surfaced when Baker became Bush's Secretary of State. Thus a 1989 magazine article with the title 'Vision Problems at State . . .' quoted Frank Gaffney, director of the conservative Center for Security Policy, as saying that Baker 'believes in success for its own sake and often finds specific goals inconvenient. That's not leadership or vision.'[10]

Three years later, the same publication in a piece headed 'Boldness Without Vision' praised Baker for the problem-solving capability he had shown in working out an agreement with Congress on Nicaragua, and for putting together the massive coalition necessary for the war against Iraq, but nevertheless found his performance wanting. 'In a fragmented and challenging new world American foreign policy needs a conceptual overhaul, the kind of coherent vision that it got in a simpler past from such men as Dean Acheson and George Kennan. A seat-of-the-pants approach to international relations, even with its share of short-term successes, will not preserve American leadership.'[11]

While Baker was always one of those closest to the President his duties required him to travel abroad extensively and it was the knowledgeable, experienced, self-effacing Scowcroft who was constantly at Bush's side, aiding and advising him on foreign and national security matters. The President's reasons for selecting Scowcroft as his National Security Adviser are apparent from his autobiography, published in 1987. In that book, Bush noted the tendency, apparent since the presidencies of Kennedy and Johnson, for National Security advisers to stray from their original purpose to 'advise the President with respect to the integration of domestic, foreign and military policies relating to the national security'.

Beginning in the early 1960s, NSC chiefs had assumed a role in the policy-making process that had never been intended; they had become rivals for influence over the conduct of foreign policy with the Secretary of State. However, Scowcroft's conduct during his brief tenure as Ford's National Security Adviser had been exemplary, providing 'a model that every future American president ought to follow in choosing and properly using a national security adviser. Scowcroft scrupulously adhered to the NS charter, seeing to it that the views of all the council members were accurately and objectively reported to the President. He didn't try to make the NSC into a policy-making agency.'[12]

As a member of the Tower Commission set up to investigate the Iran Contra scandal, Scowcroft had been shocked by the evidence uncovered of the misuse of the National Security Council during the Reagan presidency.[13] According to Richard Haass, one of Scowcroft's principal aides, the idea of the National Security Adviser as an honest broker had been lost sight of in the previous administration. Under Reagan the NSC 'was both too weak and too strong. It was too weak at what it was supposed to do and too strong at what it wasn't supposed to do.' In other words, advisers had neglected to be honest brokers, turning themselves into policy advocates and allowing NSC staff to adopt operational roles. 'Scowcroft wanted to bring back a fairly orderly system, much like he had under Ford. Not to go back to Kissinger's heavily controlled thing, but much more of a Ford-like system, where multiple advocacy would be the closest model; where he would play the broker role.'[14]

Scowcroft began by reducing the number of NSC staff from 200 to 150 and by defining his own role in limited terms: 'The President runs the government. He has expert advice from State and Defense, and it is my job to ensure the integration of that advice, to fill in where there are holes, and hopefully to help provide a strategic concept which covers the whole field of national security.'[15] Leaving day-to-day management of NSC staff to his deputy Robert Gates, Scowcroft became, in effect, the President's personal counsellor on foreign and national security policy.[16]

As a political scientist by training who observed Scowcroft in action at close range, Richard Haass had some insightful comments to make about how the National Security Adviser perceived his responsibilities. Those who had studied presidential decision-making had argued that White House policy advisers should be honest brokers. They needed to be close to the President, but should be low-profile individuals without policy management responsibilities, capable of detachment and finding 'satisfaction in pulling the strands of a problem together or in laying out a complex issue for someone else's judgment.'[17] Haass, drawing on his experience of working with Scowcroft, noted that National Security Advisers were somewhat more than honest brokers even though that was their most important role. It might be more appropriate to characterize the adviser as an 'honest balancer'. The brokerage role required them 'to ensure that the options get to the President; that they are well staffed; that the analysis is rigorous; that everyone who wants and deserves to be a player gets to play; that decisions are made and that they're carefully communicated and implemented.' In addition, however, the Assistant for National Security Affairs was obliged to offer the president 'advice and counsel' to be both a 'referee and a protagonist'. This had been how Scowcroft operated, as had Haass himself, and it was up to to others to judge 'whether we did that fairly or rigorously and whether our counselling ever got in the way of our facilitating.'[18]

Even if Baker knew relatively little about foreign policy issues when he became Secretary of State, his Washington experience caused him to be well versed in the political manoeuvring and deadly infighting that had, in the past, detracted from presidential control of the foreign policy process. From the beginning Baker made clear his determination not to become a captive of the career professionals in the State Department; it was his intention to be 'the President's man at State and not State's man at the White House.'[19]

To further that overriding aim, Baker brought with him to the State Department a praetorian guard of senior aides who had worked elsewhere for him before. These were Margaret Tutwiler, who became Assistant for Public Affairs, Robert Kimmit, Under Secretary for Political Affairs, Dennis Ross, director of policy planning and Robert Zoellick counsellor and Under Secretary for Economic and Agricultural Affairs. These four officials formed an inner circle around the Secretary of State: 'They alone had direct access to Baker and were familiar with most of what went on.'[20] Inevitably this attempt by Baker to insulate himself from the wiles of career professionals led to resentment. 'He's running a mini NSC, not State,' a senior diplomat complained. 'We learn what our policy is when we read it in the newspapers.'[21] Ultimately other observers saw Baker's shutting out of State Department specialists while heavily relying on an inner sanctum of advisers as a mixed blessing. 'This management style enhanced his control over policy, but also left him vulnerable to missed opportunities.'[22]

NICARAGUA

The new administration's quite different approach to the management of foreign policy was demonstrated at an early stage by Baker's orchestration of a deal with Congress over aid for the Nicaraguan Contras. In the previous administration, US policy in Central America had been the subject of bitter contention between the White House and Capitol Hill. In President Reagan's mind there was no doubt that Nicaragua was potentially a second Cuba and as such a serious threat to the national security of the United States. The Reagan doctrine entailed supporting anti-Soviet counter-revolutions and, in line with this strategy, Reagan sought to provide military aid to Contra rebels against the Sandinista regime. This had provoked the ire of many Democrats in Congress who succeeded in passing a number of amendments designed to curtail the provision of such aid. It was Reagan's attempts to evade these restrictions that led to the Iran Contra affair, the greatest crisis of his presidency and the most acrimonious episode in executive-legislative relations since Watergate.

In the 1988 campaign Bush called for the renewal of military aid to the Contras, but after the election congressional leaders made it clear that any request to provide such aid would meet with rejection out of hand.[25] Shortly afterwards the five Central America presidents who had for some time been trying to bring about peace and reconciliation in the area, drew up the Tesoro Beach agreement. This allowed for the 'demobilization, repatriation or relocation' of the Contras matched by an undertaking by the Nicaraguan government to provide the conditions for free and fair elections in the near future. In the United States this agreement had a mixed reception with President Bush welcoming the 'positive elements', namely the promise of democratic elections, but questioning whether the Sandinistas could be relied on to honour that pledge once the Contras had disbanded.

Nevertheless, in response to the Tesoro Beach accord and the solid congressional resistance to military aid for the Contras, a new American policy with regard to Nicaragua now began to take shape. Masterminded by James Baker, the Secretary of State, this emphasized the promotion of democracy by diplomatic rather than military means, involved a renewal of humanitarian aid for the Contras and called for the use of sticks and carrots as a means of keeping the pressure on the Sandinistas to deliver on their promise of free elections. 'Carrots could include lifting the trade embargo, improving diplomatic relations, and even restoring US aid to Nicaragua. Sticks could include a tightening of the embargo, further curtailment of diplomatic relations, or if the Sandinistas refused to hold free elections, a possible renewal of military support for the Contras.'[23]

A bipartisan agreement with Congress in line with the above policy was eventually hammered out by Baker after several months of private discussions and 22 days of intense negotiation on Capitol Hill.[24] It was agreed that non-military aid of nearly $50 million would go to the Contras subject to three conditions insisted on by Democrats in the House of Representatives – no Contra funds were to be used for offensive military operations, no funds would go to any Contra human rights violators and aid would not continue beyond 30 November 1989 unless approval was given by four relevant congressional committees.

By adopting a pragmatic approach and engaging in some accomplished deal-making Baker thereby defused an issue that, for some years, had poisoned relations between President Reagan and Congress and adversely affected the conduct of American foreign policy. Some questioned the validity of such case-by-case problem-solving, but the most important criticism in the short term came from within the White House itself.[25]

As I have said, while Bush tried where possible to be conciliatory and accommodating towards the legislature he simultaneously resisted with resolution any encroachment on his constitutional powers. C. Boyden Gray, the White House Counsel, assumed particular responsibility for protecting presidential prerogatives and he took exception to that part of the Contra aid agreement that allowed congressional committees to prevent the President from spending appropriated funds.[26] As Gray saw it, this would be tantamount to an 'unconstitutional legislative veto and set a dangerous precedent for congressional checks on presidential power in foreign affairs.' [27]

On this occasion, Gray was rebuked by the President for speaking out publicly yet his clash with Baker threw light on tensions within the White House.[28] Gray was a conservative and a constitutionalist and, for the moment, he was outgunned by a master pragmatist and deal-maker. The nature of the deal that led to the congressional veto was frankly explained by one of the Secretary of State's lieutenants: 'It was the last little blood out of the turnip. It's the price we had to pay to get the job done, to get a deal. It was a tradeoff. We decided it was time we got our act together so we could do what we need to do on the ground in Central America without being distracted by bureaucratic and political fights up here in Washington.'[29] While the formidable Gray was forced to give ground on this occasion he persisted to the end in vigorous defence of the President's position *vis-à-vis* Congress in the making of foreign policy

PANAMA

Panama and its military dictator General Noriega represented another piece of unfinished business in Central America left behind by the Reagan Administration. Rather embarrassingly for the United States, Noriega had been recruited by the CIA as long ago as 1967 and had been a purveyor of intelligence material to Washington on Cuba and Nicaragua for some years. Indeed, he had been on the books of the agency when Bush himself was the Director of the CIA. The disenchantment of the American government with Noriega began in 1987 and, in early 1988, he was indicted on drugs charges in two US federal courts.

Two months later, President Reagan imposed economic sanctions on Panama and the removal of Noriega from office became a priority of American foreign policy. In 1989, Bush continued in the same vein, renewing sanctions and providing covert support for the opposition when elections took place in May. These were massively fraudulent, with the pro-Noriega coalition claiming to have won by 2:1 while the Panamanian Catholic Church made its own count and estimated that, in fact, the opposition had won by a margin of 3:1.[30] Noriega's continuance in power and his brutal putting down of opposition demonstrations outraged both the Bush Administration and Congress. On 3 October 1989, however, a coup attempt by disaffected members of the armed forces in Panama was crushed by Noriega loyalists with the US military in the country remaining largely on the sidelines, providing only minimal support to the rebels.

The failure of the Bush Administration to support the attempted coup was the subject of fierce criticism in Congress and the media. Many observers saw it as a damning indictment of the President's management of foreign policy. It was charged that he and his advisers had carried caution to excess, thereby wasting an excellent opportunity to unseat a dangerous adversary. Critics focused also on Bush's obsessive concern with secrecy and his tendency to deal with such matters informally, conferring only with a small and exclusive group of advisers while failing to draw on the expertise of the bureaucracy.[31]

It was not long however, before Bush was gifted the chance to redeem his earlier failure. The killing, in mid-December 1989, of a US military officer by members of the Panamanian Defence Forces, in conjunction with the roughing up of a US Navy officer and the sexual harassment of his wife, provided Bush with a pretext for launching a massive military operation against Panama involving 24 000 US troops.[32] Ostensibly, the purposes of Operation Just Cause were to protect the lives of 35 000 Americans, to defend democracy, to combat drug trafficking by taking Noriega into custody and to secure the Panama Canal.

Abroad, the incursion into Panama was widely seen as an exercise in American imperialism. The Organization of American States voted 20–1, with five abstentions, in favour of a resolution condemning the intervention and calling for the immediate withdrawal of US troops. A similar resolution brought before the General Assembly of the United Nations passed 75–20, with 40 abstentions.[33] These condemnations had little consequence within the US where the President's standing in public opinion polls rose sharply and Congress, with a few exceptions, eagerly applauded his decisive action.[34] The Senate Majority Leader, George Mitchell, said that the invasion 'was made necessary by the reckless action of General Noriega', while his counterpart in the House, Speaker Tom Foley, despite some concerns, felt that the President's actions were 'justified'.[35] Such reactions by opposition leaders and others in Congress helped Bush escape condemnation for an action that, some have argued, was both contrary to international law and a flagrant violation of the Constitution.[36]

The invasion of Panama brought to light the hardline influences at work in the Bush White House; those unwilling to concede an inch to Congress in the never-ending struggle between the executive and the legislature over the conduct of American foreign policy. On this occasion, as on others, President Bush effectively treated the War Powers Resolution of 1973 with contempt. That legislation, designed to reassert the war power of Congress, sought 'to insure that the collective judgment' of both branches was drawn on when US forces were to be committed to armed conflict. In furtherance of that end presidents were required to consult with Congress 'in every possible instance' before taking such actions and were then obliged to report to the legislature within 48 hours.

Bush complied with the latter provision, but the decision to commit troops in the first place was, in no sense, an outcome of 'collective judgment'. In fact, the President typically made his decision in circumstances of the utmost secrecy with only a small group of the most senior officials including Baker, Vice President Quayle, Secretary of Defense Cheney, William Webster, the Director of the CIA and General Colin Powell, the Chairman of the Joint Chiefs of Staff, privy to the plan.[37]

There was, of course, no meaningful consultation with Congress whatsoever. The President did inform congressional leaders, but only after the decision to invade had already been taken. A document published in the name of the US House of Representatives Committee on Foreign Affairs mentioned that a few members of Congress were troubled by the constitutional ramifications, yet also limply observed: 'The US intervention in Panama did not raise the issue of the War Powers Resolution in Congress. This was largely because Congress was not in session during the intervention and because the action was supported by most Members of Congress and by US public opinion.'[38]

Such blithe capitulation to the executive branch, principally on the grounds that the end justifies the means, has taken place repeatedly throughout the history of the United States. It allowed Lincoln's reputation to remain unscathed by his violations of the Constitution in defence of the Union, and similar arguments were applied to FDR's several consitutionally dubious actions in the run up to the entry of the US into the Second World War. This is all very understandable, but it does seriously undermine the validity of furiously indignant complaints about unconstitutional behaviour that follow when some members of Congress and some segments of the public decide that the President's ends are not justifiable.[39]

ENDING THE COLD WAR

Caution is the hallmark of guardian presidents. They are at pains not to arouse expectations that cannot be fulfilled and are much concerned to 'do no harm'. They disdain ideology and are disinclined to engage in florid rhetoric; by definition, they harbour no grand schemes for reordering the world and see themselves as reactive leaders, as pragmatists responding to situations as they arise.

For many, however, the Bush Administration was from the beginning marked by an excess of caution.'Ever since he took office, critics at home and abroad have lambasted Bush for what they describe as a halting and reactive approach to the historic changes afoot in the Soviet Union.'[40] Initially wary of of Gorbachev, Bush's staff embarked on a painstaking, five month long, policy review. The Soviet leader meanwhile was pushing ahead with perestroika and glasnost; separatism was on the march in Georgia, the Ukraine and the Baltics; free elections had been agreed in Poland, and the lowering of the Iron Curtain had been set in train by Hungary beginning to dismantle its barbed wire border with Western Europe.

The unprecedented opportunities now on offer and in danger of being neglected by undue caution were stressed by various luminaries. Ronald Reagan was reliably reported to be becoming uneasy about the foreign policy indecisiven* ness of his successor.[41] Henry Kissinger, a former Secretary of State, said: 'We face an opportunity – the greatest in 40 years – to bring an end to the Cold War. International factors have rarely been so fluid. The one thing that cannot occur is a continuance of the status quo.'[42] Very similarly, James Schlesinger, formerly Director of the CIA, observed: 'For the [US] to appear both passive and impassive to Gorbachev is a problem. One needs to strike a balance between caution . . . and responsiveness to the changes going on in the Soviet Union.'[43]

In reply to the allegation that the Bush Administration did not, in those early months, strike the right balance in reacting to developments in the Eastern part of Europe, Brent Scowcroft explained to this author:

> That may be true, but one of the things you have to remember is that President Bush and I, and Cheney and, to some extent,

Baker, had gone through the detente period and the euphoria that was created in the US and Europe during that period, [and] for which we paid a fairly heavy price in the late 70s and early 80s. We were very reluctant to have that sort of thing happen again. So maybe we were over-cautious – perhaps, perhaps. I think it was because we were watching Gorbachev's actions rather than [listening to] his rhetoric. In 1989 he was running around Europe trying to outpromise things in arms control and so forth. It looked like typical Soviet tactics [designed to] split the West.[44]

Gorbachev's reforms within the Soviet Union, however, had had repercussions in the Warsaw Pact countries – setting off opposition movements and leading, during Bush's first year in office, to the overthrow of communist regimes in Poland, Hungary, East Germany, Czechoslovakia, Bulgaria and Romania. The fact that these extraordinary changes occurred relatively peacefully owed much to the restraint displayed, on the one hand, by Gorbachev and, on the other, by Bush. The Soviet leader effectively renounced the Brezhnev doctrine of intervening in satellite countries to put down revolutions while Bush avoided the temptation to make political capital out of the disintegration of the Soviet empire.

Before leaving for a trip to Eastern Europe in July, Bush told his speechwriters: 'Whatever this trip is, it's *not* a victory tour, with me running around over there pounding my chest. [In my speeches] I don't want it to sound inflammatory or provocative. I don't want what I do to complicate the lives of Gorbachev and the others . . . I don't want to put a stick in Gorbachev's eye.'[45] On that same trip, both in Poland and Hungary, the President exercised caution again by appearing to be intent on emphasizing stability at the expense of the forces of change; he seemed to prefer dealing with existing elites rather than encouraging dissident elements. Thus Bush gave succour to the Communist President of Poland, General Jaruzelski, by encouraging him to run for re-election. The President then bestowed his support on Hungarian Communist leaders while telling representatives of the noncommunist opposition: 'Your leaders are moving in the right direction. Your country is taking things one step at a time. That's surely the prudent thing to do.'[46]

A few months later, the caution that pervaded the Bush Administration was reflected in the President's subdued, inarticulate reaction to the pulling down of the Berlin Wall. This was the source of much critical comment in the media and in Congress.[47] The Majority Leader in the House, Congressman Richard Gephardt, said: 'Even as the walls of the modern Jericho come tumbling down, we have a president who is inadequate to the moment.'[48] There was, however, according to Bush's staff, a purpose to the President's reticence; he knew that excessive celebration of the Wall's collapse might well create a backlash by the military and other conservative elements in both East Germany and the Soviet Union. As Andrew Card, the Deputy Chief of Staff explained the President was being urged to:

> Go stand in front of the Wall, [but] he had to say 'Wait a minute. That's smart short-term politics, but it is dumb diplomacy. Let's see how Helmut Kohl reacts. Let's see how Gorbachev reacts. This is a tricky time for Gorbachev; he's probably being pressured by the generals to go in and take East Germany back. Let's step back. Let the world celebrate the Wall coming down. I am celebrating too, but I don't have to be there waving the flag.'[49]

It was while he was in Europe that Bush appears to have decided that Gorbachev was a man he could do business with and that it was time for an informal meeting with the Soviet leader. This led to the Malta summit in December 1989, a crucial event in the process of ending the Cold War. This meeting gave Bush the opportunity to deploy his personal diplomacy skills and to forge a highly productive relationship with Gorbachev. As we saw earlier, Scowcroft had reservations about Gorbachev and was, reportedly, wary of the summit before it took place.[50] Nevertheless when I spoke to him he confirmed how important the meeting had been: 'They did establish then a personal relationship which continued and helped to cut through the enormous encrustation of bureaucracy to bureaucracy, the way the dialogue had taken place up until then.' Scowcroft also went out of his way to stress the importance of Eduard Shevardnadze as a highly desirable influence on Gorbachev at this point.[51]

In one-on-one meetings in Malta, Gorbachev assured Bush that he was determined to avoid the use of force against the breakaway Baltic countries of Estonia, Latvia and Lithuania. In return, Bush made it clear that while the US had never recognized the annexation of these countries by the USSR, provided Gorbachev kept his promise, the American side would act with restraint in making public statements.[52] As testimony to the central importance of the good personal relationship established between the two presidents at Malta, Shevardnadze's deputy, Alexander Bessmertnykh, said two years later: 'If it were not for Malta, the Soviet Union would never have so smoothly surrendered its control of Eastern Europe and the Baltics.'[53] George Bush's taste for personal diplomacy had, on this occasion, proved to be a formidable asset.

In early 1990 US policy towards the Baltics was a highly sensitive matter for all those cold warriors on the right of the Republican party, but Bush, advised by the ultra cautious Scowcroft, was determined to move carefully, taking account of the fragility of Gorbachev's position and fearful of a backlash by hardliners within the Soviet Union.[54] Some of the flavour of the advice Scowcroft was providing at this stage was revealed later when he explained to me:

What we sought to do in Eastern Europe was to move the process as fast as possible without creating an explosion like that of Hungary in 1956 or even like that in Czechoslovakia in 1968. [We feared] creating a reaction from the Soviet Union which would stop it all ... What we wanted to do was to establish a pace that could be sustained [although] we certainly didn't see it moving as rapidly as it did.[55]

In line with Scowcroft's counsel, Bush, at a White House meeting, was reported as saying: 'I don't want to do something that would inadvertently set back the progress that has been made in Eastern Europe ... And so it is delicate ... I'm old enough to remember Hungary in 1956 where we exhorted people to go to the barricades, and a lot of people were left out there alone.'[56]

The caution that was so much a feature of the Bush Administration's reaction to events in Eastern Europe was evident in their handling of Gorbachev. Initially, Bush and his foreign policy team doubted the Soviet leader's motives and sought to keep him at arm's length, whereas later the President came under attack, particularly from the right, for clinging to the Soviet leader too long, and to the disadvantage of Boris Yeltsin. 'Fearing instability in the Soviet Union almost as much as Gorbachev does, Bush has hitched his star to the Soviet president, believing that only Gorbachev can keep the USSR from spinning out of control.'[57]

As General Scowcroft explained it to me, the Administration's rationale for remaining with Gorbachev so long was that even though the Soviet leader's commitment to democracy was questionable, he was moving the USSR in the right direction; he was, moreover, able to carry the military with him. This was essential to one of the most significant developments of all in this period, the reunification of Germany, while also keeping it within NATO. Gorbachev achieved that, whereas it was doubtful whether Yeltsin could have done likewise:

> [He] wasn't a very polished politician at that time. Could he have brought the military along? I don't know, but I guess we were very pragmatic . . . We are frequently criticized for sticking with Gorbachev too long, but nobody I have read has said what would have happened had we turned on him, or what that would have meant, and what the consequences would have been.[58]

A similar defence of Bush's reluctance to abandon Gorbachev in favour of Yeltsin, as so many on the right of his party urged, was provided by James Cicconi:

> If he had [done so] the odds are that the 1991 coup in the Soviet Union would probably have succeeded, and the hardliners would have come back into control. If we had not stuck with Gorbachev, I think it's very arguable that none of these changes would have transpired, or at least been brought to fruition. Certainly not the unification of Germany and probably not the collapse of the Warsaw pact which were strategically the two most salient events.'[59]

With the advantage of hindsight and the evidence available to us now, moreover, the case for questioning Yeltsin's reliability has been reinforced.

It is difficult to apply the central test of statecraft, a leader's fulfilment of his or her agenda, to this part of the analysis. As Eagleburger suggested in the quotation at the beginning of this chapter, Bush had no agenda as such for dealing with the extraordinary occurrences taking place in Europe during his presidency, he was reacting to events. Measured by results, however, it is difficult to deny Bush's achievement in helping to bring the Cold War to a conclusion in a manner that served well the interests of the United States. Massive change of a nature that his predecessors could only dream of took place while he was in office. The arch enemy communism was vanquished with no American lives lost and democratic, capitalist values began to take root in a large area of the world. How far all this can be attributed to Bush and his advisers will remain a matter of endless dispute. It clearly is the case that he was not a prime mover in the sense that Reagan and Gorbachev could be said to be, but that does not detract from his role in managing the change that their actions, in conjunction with other factors, had set in motion. It was not unreasonable for Brent Scowcroft to claim in reviewing Bush's part:

> The fact that these earthshaking developments all took place within about a three year period – Eastern Europe was freed, Germany was unified and stayed within NATO, and the Soviet Union collapsed [all] without a shot being fired – it was pretty remarkable. Fifteen years ago, if you had forecast that people would have said 'You are crazy, you are crazy!' The only way this could happen is in the context of another war. So, I am content to let history speak for itself. These things were going to happen sooner or later, that's clear, but the way they happened, President Bush had an enormous amount to do with it.[60]

The 1988 election placed George Bush in overall charge of the management of the West's response to the massive upheavals already underway within both the Soviet Union and the countries of the Warsaw Pact, and historians are likely to accord him a large part of the credit for a peaceful, mainly successful conclusion to a notably fraught and dangerous period in world history. It can hardly be argued, moreover, that such an outcome was a foregone conclusion. As another senior member of the White House explained, there were many hazards involved: 'There were a lot of predictions that if the Soviet empire ever came to the brink of collapse, if communism ever came to the brink of collapse . . . that could trigger a nuclear war . . . believe me, while I don't think things ever got to that point, there were very hairy moments in the whole process.'[61] As to Bush's methods, many commentators worried about his caution, his obsessive concern with doing nothing imprudent, his penchant for secrecy, his fondness for stability and his preference for dealing with elites rather than going public. Many have argued, however, that these tactics were appropriate for the moment, that this was not the time for ideological clamour or strident appeals, but for the quiet, cautious diplomacy that Bush was so well qualified to provide.[62]

8 The War in the Gulf

George Bush's second year in office provided the two defining events of his presidency, the budget crisis and the war in the Gulf. The former was a leadership débâcle whereas the latter showed President Bush in a far more favourable light, particularly if the analysis is concentrated primarily, as it will be here, on the seven months between Iraq's invasion of Kuwait at the beginning of August 1990 and the cease fire agreed at the end of Febuary 1991. During this critical period Bush's foreign policy leadership is not easy to fault if it is measured simply by the fulfilment of goals. At an early stage the President decided that Iraq's aggression had to be reversed and seven months later he presided over the triumphant achievement of that objective. On this occasion, far from being excessively cautious, Bush came across as a bold and resolute leader who kept his nerve in the face of many dangers and uncertainties.

THE CHRONOLOGY

To review in bare outline the chronology of this crisis. On the evening of 1 August 1990 (early morning on 2 August in the Middle East), word reached Washington that Iraqi forces had moved into Kuwait. The President issued a statement condemning the invasion as 'naked aggression' and calling for 'the immediate and unconditional withdrawal of all Iraqi forces'. Later that night, Bush signed executive orders banning all trade with Iraq and freezing both Iraqi and Kuwaiti assets. Meanwhile Thomas Pickering, the US Ambassador to the United Nations, was instructed to call an emergency session of the Security Council. At that meeting, which went on through the night, a resolution condemning the invasion and calling for immediate and unconditional withdrawal was agreed to by a vote of 14–0 with Yemen abstaining.[1]

This was the first of a remarkable series of resolutions relevant to the crisis in Kuwait passed by the Security Council in the period between 2 August 1990 and 29 November 1990. Of twelve resolutions, five were agreed to unanimously by the

15 members of the Council; three passed by 13–0 with Cuba and Yemen abstaining; one was agreed by 14–1 with Cuba voting against; one received a vote in its favour of 13–2 with Cuba and Yemen voting against, and one passed by a vote of 12–2 with Cuba and Yemen voting against, while China abstained.[2]

At 8 a.m. on 2 August the National Security Council came together and before the meeting began the President told reporters in front of television cameras: 'We're not discussing intervention . . . we're not considering any military option . . . I am not contemplating such action.' Later that day in Colorado Bush appeared to shift his position, saying to the press: 'We're not ruling any options in, but we're not ruling any options out.'[3]

On his return to Washington from Camp David on 5 August, the President, in speaking to the press, spoke of 'Our determination to reverse out this aggression – this will not stand, this will not stand this aggression against Kuwait.'[4] On 6 August the UN Security Council agreed by a vote of 13–0 to impose sanctions against Iraq. On the same day King Fahd indicated his willingness to accept foreign forces to assist in the defence of Saudi Arabia. Two days later President Bush appeared on television to announce to the nation the deployment of American troops to the Middle East saying that 'the sovereign independence of Saudi Arabia is of vital interest to the United States.' The President also stressed however, that 'The mission of our troops is wholly defensive.'[5] This force in support of 'Operation Desert Shield' was to grow to 230 000 men and women by late October 1990. On 25 August the UN Security Council voted 13–0 in favour of a resolution effectively authorizing military action to enforce the sanctions against Iraq agreed earlier. This was the first occasion in the history of the UN that individual countries were authorized 'to enforce an international blockade, an extraordinary diplomatic victory for the administration.'[6]

At the beginning of October the US Congress gave overwhelming support to the Bush Administration's efforts so far to deter Iraqi aggression – the House by a vote of 380–29, and the Senate by a vote of 96–3. On 8 November the President at a news briefing announced that the size of US forces committed to 'Operation Desert Shield' was to be increased –

reportedly by 200 000 – 'to ensure that the coalition has an adequate offensive military option should that be necessary to achieve our common goals.' Three weeks later the Security Council adopted Resolution 678 authorizing the use of 'all necessary means' to enforce Iraq's removal from Kuwait, unless Iraq complied with UN resolutions and withdrew by 15 January 1991.[7]

On 5 December, 54 Democratic members of the US House of Representatives sought a federal court injunction that would have prevented the President from embarking on offensive, military action without first obtaining explicit congressional authorization. This suit was dismissed by US Federal District Court Judge Harold Greene on 13 December on the grounds that there was 'lack of evidence of an imminent clash between the executive and legislative branches, lack of evidence that either the administration is on the verge of launching a war, or that a majority of Congress deems a declaration of war imprudent.'[8]

While never admitting that Congress had a formal role in the ultimate decision to go to war President Bush on 8 January 1991 requested a congressional resolution authorizing the use of force. The Senate on 12 January approved by a vote of 57–42, a resolution that gave the President authority to use military force against Iraq in order to achieve the implementation of the various relevant Security Council resolutions. Later the same day, the House voted 250–183 in favour of an identical resolution.[9] The war against Iraq – Operation Desert Storm – began on 17 January with a bombing campaign. The coalition ground attack was launched on 24 Febuary and ceased on 28 Febuary, following President Bush's televised announcement: 'Kuwait is liberated. Iraq's army is defeated. Our military objectives are met.'[10]

THE WOODWARD BOOK

Early judgements in the media regarding Bush's leadership in the Gulf War tended to be highly favourable.[11] Subsequent analyses have been much more critical and, in most cases, have drawn heavily on material presented in Bob Woodward's *The Commanders*.[12] The latter is an important source, but it needs to be treated with care. There are no footnotes for the many interviews conducted by Woodward and his assistants, and the fact that the book began as a study of the Pentagon needs to be borne in mind.

It has been said of Woodward's account that notwithstanding any doubts about its credibility, it 'has not been publicly disputed by any major figure he quotes.' However, this may come later when all the memoirs have been written.[13] When asked what he thought of Woodward's book, General Scowcroft, the President's closest adviser during this crisis, replied:

> I don't think too much of it. Woodward's typical practice is to start with something that is pretty well accepted fact and then spin from that conclusions and run it out to a degree that it ends up being pure supposition. He does that over and over again, so that you are captured by the fact that he starts with something [accurate] but then he [reaches] unwarranted conclusions'.[14]

Another of those closely involved in the decision-making process was somewhat more charitable, but drew attention to the incompleteness of Woodward's analysis:

> What is there . . . based on my recollection, is fairly accurate [although] not a hundred percent accurate. My problem with the book is what is not there. It [has] a fairly narrow take on things and it's heavily influenced by what I infer, if I use the word carefully, to be his sources, which were heavily from the Pentagon . . . it is just an incomplete story; it doesn't have the way it often looked from the White House, or the State Department.'[15]

Eliot Cohen has also suggested that Woodward's perspective is largely that of the Pentagon with 'James Baker, Brent Scowcroft and even George Bush . . . chiefly heard as offstage voices in a drama that centers on Colin Powell and Dick Cheney.'[16]

NO TIME TO GO WOBBLY

It has been suggested that far from displaying resolute and decisive leadership throughout this crisis, Bush dithered at the outset before weakly allowing himself to be hustled into a belligerent response by Mrs Thatcher and Brent Scowcroft.[17] This does not accord with Scowcroft's version of events. He reports that when the invasion of Kuwait first took place some of the President's advisers threw up their hands and said: 'Well, it's a tragedy, but what [can] you do? Let's make sure [the Iraqis] don't get any further into Kuwait.' Bush, however, was not content to leave matters there; from the beginning he said: 'No. This is an unacceptable move.'[18]

There is, moreover, ample evidence to refute the widely prevalent supposition that President Bush only concluded that Saddam Hussein must be ejected from Kuwait after Mrs Thatcher had stiffened his resolve when they met in Aspen, Colorado, on the day after the invasion. Jean Edward Smith, for instance, heads his chapter on this period with the quotation 'Remember, George, this is no time to go wobbly' and dates it 3 August. It was at this juncture, moreover, that the Prime Minister supposedly performed a 'backbone transplant' on the President.[19] However, some witnesses with powerful claims to know what actually occurred in Aspen have categorically denied the thrust of such stories. Accompanied by his National Security Adviser, the President met with the British Prime Minister who had with her Charles Powell, her Private Secretary. Subsequently, Powell observed: 'It has been said that Mrs Thatcher had to put backbone into the President. That is just wrong. They both arrived there absolutely determined that this was something that could not be tolerated. The genuine sense of outrage on the part of both of them is the thing that I remember.'[20]

With some vigour, Richard Haass, Scowcroft's principal aide for the Middle East, insisted that 'Bush was not wobbly when he went out [to Colorado] . . . I was with him both before and afterwards . . . the idea that somehow she gave him an infusion of backbone . . . I see nothing that supports that thesis.'[21]. Similarly, Scowcroft talked of 'a meeting of minds between Mrs Thatcher and the President . . . they were both heading in the same direction . . . they tended to reinforce each other.'[22]

The Prime Minister did use the 'no time to go wobbly' expression nearly three weeks later, but in a totally different context. Towards the end of August the National Security Council had

to decide how to respond to Saddam's flouting of the sanctions against Iraq agreed on 6 August. Some took the view
that the US should unilaterally enforce the blockade if necessary, whereas others were more cautious. In the words of
James Baker: 'The question was whether we should proceed
under Article 51 [of the UN Charter], which we were all
agreed we had the full legal right to do. Or whether, in order
to keep the coalition together, we should take a little bit longer
and try to get another resolution from the Security Council
in order to authorize the use of force to enforce the embargo.'[23]

This clearly became a fiercely contested issue in NSC meetings. As Brent Scowcroft remembered it, it was necessary to
decide: 'Would we intervene unilaterally, or would we go to
the UN not knowing whether we would get authority? We
were divided on the issue; I wanted to move [unilaterally] and
Secretary Baker did not.' The State Department was particularly conscious of the fact that the Iraqis were actively
attempting to separate the USSR from the US and Baker
recalled 'counselling [the President] to see at least if we could
not bring the Soviets along.'[24]

The Secretary of State rather than the National Security
Adviser won this particular battle for the President's ear and,
once convinced, Bush moved to bring Mrs Thatcher around
to the same view. The Prime Minister's conversion was not
achieved without difficulty, for conscious of her own problems
with the UN over the Falklands she 'felt that the Security
Council Resolution which had already been passed, combined
with our ability to invoke Article 51 of the UN Charter on self-
defence, was sufficient.' And despite the changes wrought by
the ending of the Cold War 'the fact remained that if one
could achieve an objective without UN authority there was no
point in running the risks attached to seeking it.'[25]
Notwithstanding her reservations, Mrs Thatcher finally fell
into line and it was this point according to Scowcroft that she
famously said: 'all right George, all right, but this is no time
to go wobbly.'[26]

As we have seen, a resolution was successfully obtained
from the Security Council on 25 August and, in retrospect, it
was surely just as well that this additional authorization was
sought. The success of the allied cause was ultimately much
dependent on keeping an inherently fragile coalition together

and if the Soviet Union had broken away the consequences might well have been disastrous.

PERSONALIZATION AND POLICY-MAKING ON THE HOOF

The President's National Security Adviser rejected the allegation given currency in several studies of the war that Bush personalized this conflict excessively and made far too much of supposed parallels between Saddam Hussein and Adolf Hitler.[27] As Scowcroft explained it, when these events were taking place Bush was immersed in a book on the Second World War. He was reading about:

> . . . the invasion of Poland at the outset of the war and the horrors that the Nazis perpetrated [there]. That was where he started calling Saddam Hussein a fascist and [suggesting that he] was like Hitler . . . It came right out of that book and him seeing the similarities of the two. But it was not personalized in any deep sense. [His reaction] was based on what he felt was an important movement not only against the US national interest, but as a destabilizing factor in a world which was getting into a turmoil.[28]

Scowcroft agreed that the parallels between Hussein and Hitler were overdrawn, and admitted that 'some of us worried a little bit about that', but excused these lapses on the grounds that they were rhetorical clichés of the sort that Bush, like any politician, was likely to use out on the campaign trail. Finally, in answering the charge of personalization, Scowcroft insisted that 'if in fact it had been a personalized issue the President never would have stopped when he did.' The implication being that Bush would have permitted US forces to go on to Baghdad, not stopping them, as he did, short of Hussein's removal.[29]

Critics of Bush's leadership during the Gulf War have argued that the processes of decision-making were unstructured with the President prone to make policy on the hoof without sober consideration and appropriate consultation with the military and other specialists. Woodward, for example, makes much of the Chairman of the Joint Chiefs of Staff, Colin Powell, feeling obliged to inform himself of changes in US policy by keeping abreast of the President's public utterances: 'It was his habit to excavate Bush's public statements. The Chairman had to know the President's policy, and this President tended to lay out at least some of his thinking in speeches and comments to the press. Sometimes the policy came out carefully and incrementally. Other times Powell discovered surprises.'[30.]

In the early days of the crisis, if Woodward is correct, Powell was deeply troubled by the President in his public remarks appearing to move policy goalposts without consulting with senior advisers like himself. Initially, on 2 August, the President had told the press that military intervention was not under consideration. There had then been discussions within the Administration, which Powell had been privy to, regarding the possibility of committing US forces to the Middle East as a defensive measure to prevent any attempt by the Iraqis to move into Saudi Arabia. But then on 5 August, Powell, we are told, was stunned to see the President on television arriving at the White House from Camp David and angrily saying 'This will not stand' in reference to the the aggression against Kuwait. 'There had been no NSC meeting, no debate. The Chairman could not understand why the President had laid down this new marker, changing radically the definition of success. It was one thing to stop Saddam from going into other countries like Saudi Arabia; it was very much another thing to reverse an invasion that was accomplished.'[31] The impression created by comments such as these that Powell was 'out of the loop' when crucial decisions were made was crisply and flatly denied by Scowcroft: 'I don't think that [Powell] was ever out of the loop at all.'[32]

More detail was provided by Richard Haass. He did not accept that the military could reasonably claim to be unpleasantly surprised by Bush's public remarks on 5 August: 'People had their day in court and the military was often asked their views. Even if they were not specifically asked for, they were sitting at the table and could have offered them.' Prior to Sunday, 5 August, there had already been three meetings of the NSC on Thursday, Friday and Saturday to discuss the crisis: 'We were all there; you had a chance to talk about these things. People were given the chance to talk about what we should do . . . Everyone was basically saying we have got to resist . . . So when the President said "This will not stand" on

Sunday . . . [while] he was very emotional . . . the policy ought
not to have come as a surprise to anyone.'[33]

THE DECISION-MAKING PROCESS

Not surprisingly, General Scowcroft was unimpressed by
suggestions that the crisis had not been properly handled within
the White House. One source for instance claims that 'rational'
procedures were notably absent and argues that the President
and his National Security Adviser 'alone determined' the crucial
steps towards war with Iraq. Another critic meanwhile claimed
that:

> Throughout the crisis, Bush acted with a small coterie of
> subordinates. Expert opinion was screened out, and the NSC
> rarely met in structured fashion. Means and ends were never
> reconciled, policy alternatives were not canvassed, structured
> analysis was not rendered. The executive branch of the
> government moved at the President's command and no insti-
> tutional checks were provided.[34]

These charges were countered by Scowcroft: 'The analysis
was very dispassionate and the conclusions were [arrived at]
calmly and analytically. The objectives and the means to achieve
them [were worked out] in what, to me, is a model way. [We]
had to understand what the problem was. What we thought
we wanted to do about it, and after we had done it would we
be able to get out.' The Administration's first concern was to
'get some force over there and to send a strong signal to Saddam
Hussein that we would defend Saudi Arabia. We tried very
hard to send that message.' The second decision taken was
'that the conquest of Kuwait would not be allowed to stand.
[This] did not immediately translate into a plan for a military
operation; it was originally translated into a general force
build up that would allow us to keep our options open.'

In the early weeks it was necessary to decide how big a force
would be required to defend Saudi Arabia; the advice from
General Schwarzkopf, the field commander, was that 100 000
troops would be needed and this provided the basis for the
first military build-up. Then the President said: 'We need to
keep our options open beyond that. That is the minimum that

we have to do for now, [but] what does it take to keep our options open.' It was this that led to a continuation of the build-up far beyond the early prognostications, given that Hussein continued to put forces into the area.

None of this precluded the possibility of a diplomatic solution to the crisis, although Scowcroft, by his own admission, always doubted that Saddam would leave Kuwait peaceably. In defence of the Administration's decision to not let sanctions run indefinitely Scowcroft said this grew out of a careful consideration of which side 'would be favored by a long drawn out deadlock.' The military consensus had been:

> . . . that we needed to act before Ramadan . . . that a military operation late in the spring and into the summer would be a very, very difficult operation. So unless sanctions operated in the very short term, in a matter of a few months, we would have almost a year to wait. In a year the outrage and the cohesiveness of the Arab world was likely to erode . . . therefore we had a time window basically between August, when the attack was launched, and some time in March.[35]

The criticism given the widest currency in the literature on the Gulf War is the claim that policy-making was restricted to an inner circle that quickly developed a consensus on a military solution and gave scant consideration to alternative courses of action.[36] While accepting that decision-making was limited to a small group Scowcroft made no apology for that: 'It included basically everyone who would have attended a National Security Council meeting . . . all of the principal national security decision-makers participated. The meetings were not large . . . since staff were informed only to the minimal amount.' The latter restriction was deemed necessary for reasons of security. 'We felt it was important when we began planning for a military solution that it should stay closely held so that we would not signal to Saddam Hussein what it was we actually had in mind.'[37]

Given his background as a political scientist, Richard Haass's perspective on matters of process is of particular interest. He agreed that decision-making had been restricted to 'a fairly small group', but went on to explain that 'there was a multi-layered cake.' There were 'lots of people at the lower level';

then there was a small group of deputies at the intermediate level. This included Haass himself, Robert Gates, the Deputy National Security Adviser; CIA Deputy Director, Richard Kerr; Robert Kimmit, Undersecretary for Political Affairs at the State Department; Admiral David Jeremiah, Deputy Chairman of the Joint Chiefs of Staff; and Paul Wolfowitz, Under Secretary for Policy at the Department of Defense. At the top, the number of National Security Council principals varied. There 'could be a few, could be as many as nine or ten, it was often eight. But the principals had a chance to influence the deputies and the deputies had a chance to influence the principals.' When the crisis was at its height the deputies 'met every day; often several times a day, either personally or electronically [via a video link].'[38]

As he was one of those involved and had been particularly 'responsible for dispensing good process a lot of the time' Haass recognized that he might be thought to be biased. Nevertheless he was dismissive of the allegations that a proper airing of alternative courses of action had not taken place, that adhocracy rather than multiple advocacy had occurred. Academic students of decision-making have stressed the value of ensuring that a suitably wide range of viewpoints are properly represented in the process, that major participants are given a full hearing and that all options are thoroughly considered – multiple advocacy, it has been argued, is essential. If a president draws advice from only a small group of intimates there arises a danger of 'groupthink'; the consideration of options is likely to be incomplete and an artificial consensus behind one course of action may develop.[39]

Haass was aware of this literature, but denied that it was relevant in this case. 'This was very clear multiple advocacy. This was not adhocracy . . . I have trouble thinking of a more carefully managed process . . . When I add up all the meetings the deputies had and then all the meetings the principals had, there was an extraordinary amount of interaction and of structured consideration.' This was the case in the process leading up to the war and for 'most of the pursuit of the war' even if things got 'messier' toward the end. During these later stages the process was 'not quite as deliberative as it might have been because things happened rather suddenly' and as 'everybody was on the road in different places it was difficult to pull things together.' After the war's end, in coping with events occurring in northern and southern Iraq, decision-making 'got a little less tidy . . . but it was still considered, it was still deliberative [even if] it wasn't quite as formally done as in some of the earlier sessions.'[40]

In answer to those critics who claim that all the options were not fully aired, Scowcroft said:

> There was a strong debate about all these issues . . . [even if] we all came down generally in the same place . . . [there were differences with] me out in front on the military side and Colin Powell maybe on the other end . . . [However,] President Bush put together a national security team that was generally like-minded. They were not poles apart. That was one of the reasons we were effective; because we did have a general consensus. We were all facing in the same direction on national security issues. While we had hours of vigorous debate, it was not visceral or ideologically moti-vated. It was analytical. 'Can we do this?' 'Is this the right way to go?' It was practically oriented, rather than emotion-ally or ideologically.

The value of a vociferous naysayer, or devil's advocate compa-rable to George Ball in the Johnson White House, was lost on Scowcroft.[41] The fact that 'we all came to a common conclu-sion doesn't seem to me to be a bad [thing]. I don't think you have to have somebody that says you are a fool and that you cannot go that way to have a thoughtful conclusion.' Of Colin Powell's role Scowcroft said: 'He was I think the most reluc-tant of the [decision-making] group and the least willing to entertain the military option. I think that was clear.' When asked whether it was true that Powell had not stated his reser-vations particularly strongly, Scowcroft replied: 'No, he did not. And as a matter of fact I think he never spoke of them directly to me.'[42]

The National Security Adviser discounted suggestions that the President's inner circle made insufficient use of outside experts in its decision-making during the Gulf War.[43] 'Did we have every Middle East expert in the world [in]? Not at all. But we did draw on [such] people. We had one or two groups of outside Middle East experts in with the President. We had them talk about Saddam Hussein [and] about Iraq. To talk

[also] about what was going on in the Iraqis' mind, and what was the impact throughout the Arab and the Muslim world.' According to Scowcroft's account there were also fairly regular discussions with Congress: 'We consulted quite frequently with the Congress, both individually and in groups. While the general tenor of the Congress was negative, we got key support from some members [such as Les Aspin, the Chairman of the Armed Services Committee in the House] that gave us a lot of confidence that we were going the right way.'[44]

Both Scowcroft and Haass, however, agreed that the Administration had erred in not keeping Congress informed about the decision, at the end of October 1990, to double the number of US troops in Saudi Arabia. Bush waited until the mid-term elections were safely past before announcing that he had 'directed the Secretary of Defense to increase the size of US forces committed to Desert Shield to ensure that the coalition has an adequate offensive military option should that be necessary to achieve our common goal.'[45] This was a crucial decision, for given this level of commitment, war became a virtual certainty, short of a most unlikely total withdrawal by Iraq. Congress however, had no foreknowledge of this decision, even though congressional leaders had been regularly briefed on the Gulf crisis by the White House. As Tom Foley, the Speaker of the House, explained: 'There was a call from Secretary Cheney in the morning – not very elaborate, just an announcement – the Administration was doubling the forces – this, of course, had never been discussed with the congressional leadership group that had been visiting the White House in recent weeks.'[46]

In accepting that the Administration had made a mistake in not keeping Congress better informed on the doubling of forces Scowcroft said that he thought that the President had made it sufficiently clear that 'we were going to put enough force in there to keep our options open.' Nevertheless, in retrospect he could see 'we were inadequate in our briefings to Congress to prepare them for that.' Richard Haass went further, describing the doubling decision as 'probably the worst handled piece of decision-making of the crisis . . . it was clumsily done particularly in the consultative area with the Congress.' Partly this was because Baker was away drumming up support for what eventually became UN Security Council Resolution 678, that which authorized the use of force, but the doubling decision 'was a bit rushed through and it created more problems with Congress than necessary.'[47]

It is argued in one of the most fiercely critical studies of the Gulf War that George Bush adroitly brought public opinion along with him; first in support of the defence of Saudi Arabia and then behind the decision to launch an offensive to eject Saddam Hussein from Kuwait. 'By any standard it was a superlative performance.'[48] This is not a widely shared view, with various commentators remarking on Bush's failure to make clear what was at stake and what would be gained by going to war against Iraq.[49] In November 1990 Jim Hoagland of the *Washington Post* wrote of the 'need for a clear and ideally inspirational statement to the nation to explain the goals of the potentially bloody conflict we may be approaching.'[50]

A review of the 'road to war' in late January 1991 noted that Bush on 10 November, baffled by declining support in the polls asked close advisers 'What am I doing wrong', only to be told that 'he had to get out every day and explain why he was there. He said he had made his case over and over.'[51] The fact that the Gulf War, in the short term at least, was seen as a fabulous success for the Administration should not obscure the fact that Bush's chronic inability to articulate his purposes, his failure to make good use of the bully pulpit, was a major disadvantage in this crisis as it was in others.

SUMMARY OF BUSH'S LEADERSHIP DURING THE CRISIS

To summarize this discussion of Bush's leadership during the Gulf crisis. Valuable though Woodward's book is as source, it has perhaps been relied on too heavily by others who have written about these events. As several have emphasized, Woodward's picture is incomplete and his perspective is largely that of the Pentagon. In this analysis, I have attempted to give an airing to rather different recollections from within the White House.

The notion that Mrs Thatcher gave Bush a backbone 'transplant' at the beginning has been shown to be without foundation. The complaints about the President's tendency to

personalize this conflict need to be set against Scowcroft's explanation, particularly the fact that Bush, in the end, did not seek
Saddam's removal from office.

The allegations that decision-making was unstructured and
lacking in rationality, that the President made policy on the
run and sprang surprises on the military is contested by NSC
sources. They insist that decision-making was orderly and
rational, that many meetings took place and contentious
issues were vigorously debated. There is no disagreement
with the claim that the crucial policy decisions were made by
an inner circle of largely like-minded individuals, but this is
not seen to be a source of weakness. The advice of outside
Middle East experts was sought and multiple advocacy, we are
told, did occur. It is also reliably reported that ample opportunities were available to those who dissented from the
developing consensus.

Briefly stated, that consensus embraced an early agreement
that the invasion of Kuwait could not be allowed to stand, but
before that objective could be pursued steps had to be taken
to ensure that Saddam Hussein did not move into Saudi Arabia.
Once the defence of Saudi Arabia had been assured by the
arrival of sufficient troop numbers and sanctions had been
brought into play, it was deemed essential to increase substantially the number of troops in order to keep open the option
of freeing Kuwait by force, while continuing to explore the
possibility of a diplomatic solution.

The consensus began to fray somewhat over the question of
when to resort to force, with a majority convinced that sanctions were only plausible as a basis for policy for a few months
given the fragility of the allied coalition. As Richard Haass put
it to me, there were 'legitimate differences about how long to
let sanctions work, but the purpose of a decision-making system
is not to eliminate those differences, it is simply to resolve
them. That is what Bush did.' Colin Powell's reservations
were evident, but the President finally had to decide: 'That is
what political leaders do. [They] ought to be making the big
decisions. The president sets general policy after deliberation
with his principal advisers.'[52]

Powell, it should be noted, has said much the same himself:
'There was no disagreement . . . We hoped sanctions would
work.' As time passed, however, doubts grew within the inner

circle of decision-makers as to whether sanctions would actually work and, as the Chairman of the Joint Chiefs saw it, it was his responsibility to ensure 'that we knew what the military component was for whatever policy choice [the President] made . . . what military strategy and force structure associated with the continuing sanctions would be and what military and force structure associated with going on the offensive would be. And we talked about it. We talked about the pros and cons. And we talked about at what point we should shift the strategy.'[53]

This hardly supports the suggestion that the military were shut out of the crucial decision to move to a resolution of the crisis by the use of force. Better than some of the critics, Powell had a good understanding of what his role should be: 'It was clear to me by late December that the sanctions were not working, . . . [but] What I said was: How long sanctions should be allowed to go is essentially a political question, whether it be six, twelve, eighteen, twenty-four months. It's a policy and political judgment . . .'[54] In other words, the Chairman gave his advice and made his recommendations, but the critical decisions about whether and when to go to war finally rested with the President.

THE WAR POWERS DEBATE

As we have seen, there was some modest recognition from within the White House that consultation with Congress could have been better handled. On the other hand, there is much evidence to support the conclusion that Bush himself was quite prepared to go to war without congressional approval if that should prove necessary.[55] On this, as on other occasions where his constitutional authority was at stake, Bush was a tough and uncompromising president determined to defend his prerogatives. His doubling of US forces in the Gulf in the fall of 1990 without consulting Congress, not surprisingly alarmed members of the legislature concerned that an irreversible momentum towards military action was building up which placed in jeopardy the congressional war power.

The President, however, supported as always on such issues by his chief legal adviser C. Boyden Gray, remained utterly convinced that he, as Commander in Chief and repository of the executive power of the government, had the constitutional right to take whatever action he thought necessary to defend the vital interests of the United States. More than once Bush made it clear that if forced into it he would embark on military action, even in the face of unanimous congressional opposition and hostile public opinion: 'If I have to go, it's not going to matter to me if there isn't one congressman who supports this, or what happens to public opinion. If it's right, it's gotta be done.'[56] Despite such statements George Bush worried about the political consequences of going to war without Congress behind him. As Scowcroft explained, while the President had no doubt about his right to take military action without congressional approval, he was conscious of Lyndon Johnson's desperate difficulties during the Vietnam war and recognized the value of having Congress 'on board'.[57] Vice President Quayle confirms that while Bush was glad to get congressional authorization for the use of force, 'I am convinced [he] would still have made war against Saddam Hussein without it.'[58]

The question of whether the President should seek congressional authorization for the use of force became a hotly debated issue within the Administration. According to Gray, several members of the inner circle, including Cheney, Baker, Scowcroft and Sununu, were against going to Congress because they feared Bush would lose such a vote: 'There were three people who felt differently and the only one who mattered, of course, was Bush, but Bush, Vice President Quayle and I were the three people who felt that he had to go and get authority from Congress . . . that it would be a disaster without it.'[59]

In light of his recent background as Minority Whip in the House, Richard Cheney's membership of the group willing to resort to force without first obtaining congressional agreement is particularly noteworthy. He explained his position after the war:

The concern was that if we went to Congress and asked for a vote and they voted no, that would weaken our position. We always believed that the President had the constitutional authority to go forward and to send the troops into combat and liberate Kuwait and that we did not need an

additional vote from Congress. You had the Truman precedent. In 1950 Harry Truman committed forces to Korea,
to liberate Korea after the North had attacked; he did so
under the UN Charter which was a treaty ratified by the
US Senate. The President had all the authority he needed
to act in this case . . . There was no legal requirement for
us to go to Congress.[60]

Despite this highly controversial view, anathema to many of
his former colleagues in the legislature, Cheney joined with
other senior figures in the Administration in a lobbying blitz
in support of a congressional resolution authorizing the use
of force. This passed, but only by small margins with voting
taking place largely on party lines. In the Senate, all but two
Republicans voted yea, while on the Democratic side 45 voted
no, with 10 voting yea; this made possible a vote of 52–47 in
favour. In the House, only three Republicans voted no while
164 voted yea. The Democrats split 86 in favour and 179 against
and the overall vote was 250–183 in favour of the resolution.[61]
While Bush got the resolution he asked for from Congress
supporting his use of force he had no intention of conceding
the constitutional point, as he explained in a signing statement: 'As I made clear to congressional leaders at the outset,
my request for congressional support did not, and my signing
this resolution does not constitute any change in the long
standing positions of the executive branch on either the
President's constitutional authority to use the Armed Forces
to defend vital US interests or the constitutionality of the War
Powers Resolution.'[62]
The implications of this statement were, of course, unacceptable to many members of Congress, 56 of whom, as we
saw earlier, had attempted to get the Supreme Court to prohibit
the President from going to war without a declaration of war
from the legislature. Most scholars side with Congress in such
disputes over the meaning of the Constitution, although the
pros and cons of this never-ending debate are evenly balanced
and coming down on one side or another tends to follow
partisan affiliation.
While understanding the enormous symbolic significance
of the Constitution itself and acknowledging the great wisdom
of those who drew it up, it is surely the case that distant histor-

ical precedents and literal interpretations of a document drawn up more than two centuries ago have only a limited relevance to modern situations. There is no doubt that the Founding Fathers intended to give the war power to Congress; however, when they, rather briefly, considered these matters at Philadelphia they conceded that it was necessary to allow the President the 'power to repel sudden attacks'.[63] In those days, protecting the nation's vital interests was a relatively straight-forward matter; it primarily entailed securing the country's borders against imperialist predators, dependent on sailing ships. Yet if those who drew up the Constitution had been able to envisage the future place of the United States in a complicated, interdependent, highly technological world, they might well have modified their position even further.

Antique definitions of the nation's vital interests are hardly appropriate now and there was some logic to Bush's claim on 15 August 1990 when he said: 'Our jobs, our way of life, our own freedom and the freedom of friendly countries around the world would suffer if control of the world's great oil resources fell into the hands of Saddam Hussein.'[64] Moreover, despite the dangers, it cannot be denied that presidents are normally in a better position than legislators to judge when the national security is threatened, although this is, of course, no guarantee of that their judgements will be wise.

It is also the case that there have now been many instances where presidents have successfully claimed the right to commit American forces without meaningful consultation with Congress. The list is long and encompasses some of the greatest names in the history of the United States – Lincoln, Theodore Roosevelt, Wilson, FDR, Truman, Kennedy, Johnson, Nixon, Carter, Ford, Reagan, Bush and Clinton. When considering this roll call, members of Congress and scholars alike are prone to be selective – to approve, or at least to acquiesce in, some violations of the Constitution and to disapprove of others.

The basis upon which such distinctions are made often has little to do with constitutional law and everything to do with partisan affiliation. Much also turns on whether the military conflcit in question is crowned by success. In the euphoria of victory, constitutional concerns tend to be forgotten, a pheno-menon that, in itself, points to the limited relevance of such considerations when the national security is deemed to be under threat.

Having said all that it is nevertheless the case that Bush and his advisers pushed to the very outer limits, and beyond, the case for presidential primacy in war-making. They placed far more weight on the Commander-in-Chief clause in the Constitution than it could reasonably bear and argued spuriously that UN resolutions superseded congressional constitutional responsibilities. Furthermore, this crisis could hardly be said to fall within the President's constitutional right to 'repel sudden attacks'. The situation was not comparable to, say, the Cuban Missile Crisis where swift decision-making was, arguably, imperative. The war with Iraq did not begin until four and a half months after the invasion of Kuwait and there had, therefore, been ample time for extensive consultation with Congress. The Administration rode roughshod over the rights of Congress and it is highly questionable whether the assault on Kuwait really represented the large threat to American interests claimed by the President and his spokesmen. In these matters, Bush was quite unlike that other guardian president Dwight Eisenhower, who was, by comparison, a meticulous constitutionalist.

STATECRAFT AND GOOD FORTUNE

Initially, George Bush was the beneficiary of much post-war euphoria. He was rapturously received when he addressed a joint session of Congress at the end of the war, while among the public, those approving of his conduct of the presidency soared to 92 per cent in one poll, the highest figure ever recorded.[65] As an exercise in leadership Bush's performance in response to the Gulf crisis was, in many respects, undeniably impressive. The contrasts with the last occasion when the US had despatched massive military force abroad – the war in Vietnam – could hardly have been more striking. Lyndon Johnson's lack of experience in international affairs had been a grave disadvantage and the Vietnam conflict turned into a long drawn-out affair bedevilled by uncertain objectives, bringing heavy US casualties and conducted in the face of widespread international opprobrium. Rather than immediately committing large forces to Vietnam, Johnson had begun by sending relatively small numbers which were subsequently surreptitiously escalated over several years until they reached half a million plus. Johnson had also made the mistake of immersing himself in the detail of military planning.

George Bush and his advisers were keenly aware of Johnson's mistakes as well as those made by President Carter during the Iranian hostage crisis of 1979–81. They also assumed that, particularly after the trauma of Vietnam, the American people lacked the stomach for a long drawn-out conflict. If there was to be a war, it needed to be short and sharp and, to accomplish that, a whole-hearted commitment of troops on a massive scale was required. Saddam Hussein made a most plausible enemy and, as a short-term objective, the intention of ejecting him from Kuwait was undeniably clear-cut. The UN threw its support behind the United States from the start and President Bush was able to draw on his experience in putting together a vast, disparate anti-Saddam alliance. The President made no attempt to micro manage the war, which, in any case, lasted for only a few weeks and incurred few American casualties.[66]

Even the most severe critics of the Bush Administration's conduct of the Gulf War have been obliged to concede that the diplomatic skills of the President and his Secretary of State played a vital part in securing what was ultimately an impressive victory.[67] The contacts with leaders overseas that Bush had built up over the years and his mastery of telephone diplomacy now proved to be formidable assets enabling him to fashion an extraordinary international coalition.[68]

The intimate knowledge of world leaders and world politics that he had acquired during his years as ambassador to the UN, envoy to Beijing and CIA director helped him forge an unprecedented international alliance. Throughout, Bush ... displayed an exquisite sensitivity to diplomatic nuance and the need for subtle compromise – and sometimes outright bribes – required to bring together such mutually suspicious bedfellows as Syria, Israel, Iran and the Soviet Union. His performance went beyond competence to sheer mastery.[69]

Any assessment of Bush's leadership during this crisis, however, needs to include recognition that his achievements were much dependent on the fortuitous conjunction of circumstances that existed in 1990. The UN, for instance, was now in a position to play a part in pressurizing Saddam Hussein and in cementing the international coalition that made possible his ejection from Kuwait. It had, however, only recently become possible for the UN to take on such a role. For the previous four decades it had been racked by ideological division with the Soviet Union routinely using its veto in the Security Council to defeat Western initiatives, and vice versa. The General Assembly, meanwhile, had, by the 1970s, become a bastion of Third World and other powers generally hostile to the United States. As a consequence, many Americans, particularly conservatives, remained deeply sceptical of the value of the United Nations. One who held these views in the late 1980s was Vice President George Bush, as he made clear in his autobiography: 'Clearly, the United Nations has much to be said for it, but it still has a long way to go before it can ever achieve its early promise as "the world's best hope for peace".'[70] By 1990, however, the Cold War was at an end, the Warsaw Pact had disintegrated and Soviet–American relations had never been more amicable. In these new circumstances the Bush Administration was able to utilize the UN fully in its efforts to drive Iraq out of Kuwait.

In the past the Middle East had been a region of intense superpower rivalry and any move made by presidents from Truman to Reagan had to take careful account of how the USSR might respond. No such difficulty attended the Gulf crisis. Notwithstanding the Soviet Union's earlier support for Iraq it now gave US policy-makers a free hand. This new posture can hardly be explained as simply a result of Bush's diplomacy and the efforts of his Secretary of State – it arose in large part from the fortuitous accession of Gorbachev and the internal and external weakness of the Soviet Union, all developments which pre-dated the Bush presidency. The end of the Cold War furthermore, made it possible for the Administration to respond to General Schwarzkopf's insistence that if Saddam Hussein was to be driven from Kuwait, he would need the VII Corps, the centrepiece of US ground defence in

Europe. This was an extraordinary request that could not possibly have been met only a year previously.[71]

President Bush was also fortunate to face a crass and incompetent foe in Saddam Hussein. The Iraqi invasion was instantly the subject of condemnation throughout the world and there must be doubts about the competence of a national leader who causes his country to become such a pariah in the international community. Even Nazi Germany was never as isolated as Iraq became in 1990–91 with overwhelming votes against it not only in the Security Council, but also in the General Assembly where, for example, it was condemned by a vote of 132–1 on 3 December 1990 and by 144–1 on 18 December 1990.[72]

Bush and his advisers knew that it was important that the United States not become bogged down in a long Vietnam-type war with heavy casualties. However, contrary to the pre-war hype regarding the might and prowess of the Iraqi army, it soon became apparent that Bush and his allies had the good fortune to be facing military forces much smaller than anticipated and singularly lacking in the will to fight. Various sources have suggested that far from 'a million man army', as Secretary of Defense Cheney and others maintained, Saddam may have had less than 200 000 troops in the field facing coalition forces in excess of 550 000 and in possession of vast technological superiority. When the war got under way the ill-equipped, demoralized, ramshackle army of an impoverished Third World country was, not surprisingly, no match for the overwhelming weight of the American-led coalition.[73]

It is evident from the above that President Bush enjoyed a considerable amount of luck during this crisis. In addition, any complete assessment of his leadership must go beyond the sequence of events that extended from the invasion at the beginning of August to the cessation of hostilities at the end of the following February. It has, for instance, been argued that the Bush Administration failed to heed many warning signs of a crisis developing throughout the first half of 1990 and even gave Saddam Hussein reason to believe that the US would not intervene if he attacked Kuwait.[74] Such an attack had been a possibility for some time. Although the two countries were temporarily allied during the Iraq/Iran war there were longstanding areas of dispute between them.[75] The mutual border was arbitrarily, and none too precisely, drawn by the British in the 1920s and, in particular, two islands, Warba and Bubiyan, controlling Iraq's access to the sea had been given to Kuwait. For years this had rankled with the Iraqis and after the Iraq/Iran war ended relations with Kuwait deteriorated even further. In May 1990, Saddam Hussein complained bitterly that Kuwait, by grossly exceeding its OPEC oil production quota, had severely depressed the price of oil with disastrous consequences for Iraq: 'You are wrecking our means of sustenance,' Saddam told the Kuwaitis, 'and if you cut people's means of sustenance, it is equivalent to cutting their neck and killing them.'[76]

Aggrieved by longstanding border disputes and the violation of OPEC rules Saddam, in 1990, made numerous belligerent statements, but the Bush Administration, preoccupied with events elsewhere in the world, gave mixed signals in response. Thus eight days before the Iraqi invasion Ambassador April Glaspie, in a meeting with Saddam, assured him that the United States wanted better relations with Iraq and went on: 'We have no opinion on the Arab–Arab conflicts, like your border disagreement with Kuwait.'[77] Ms Glaspie later claimed that she also said that the US would protect its interests in the area and that Saddam had asked her to assure President Bush that he had no intention of attacking Kuwait.[78] Nevertheless, the comments of Glaspie and other Administration spokespeople at this time suggested that the US would not interfere if Iraq seized Kuwait. It is arguable, in other words, that a more alert Administration might have taken steps to prevent the invasion before it occurred, thereby preventing a conflict which, while it ended in success for the US and its allies, had disastrous consequences for the Iraqi people, including an enormous loss of life.

With the advantage of hindsight it is easy to be critical of Bush's management of the Persian Gulf crisis: to question the validity of the decision-making process, to emphasize the elements of good fortune while downplaying the hazards that had to be negotiated and the desperately difficult choices that the President alone was ultimately responsible for. Nevertheless during this, the greatest challenge of his presidency, Bush appears to have been strong, resolute and decisive. He stated his objective in early August: 'This will not stand this aggression against Kuwait' and drove unflinchingly towards it, declining to be deflected by those who looked for compromise, wanted more time for sanctions to work, or shrank from the probability of large-scale bloodshed. In this instance at least Bush was, within limits, a highly effective leader. Irrespective of the merits of the policy that he and his advisers developed, the President was, without doubt, successful in imposing his priorities and in moving the nation in the direction in which he sought to take it. Having said that it is the case that this was a narrowly focused demonstration of statecraft which, to be seen in its best light, has to be isolated from what went before and what has happened since.

9 Conclusions

It has been argued throughout this book that presidents are entitled to be judged on their own terms rather than on those preferred by their political opponents, media pundits or academics. As a guardian president Bush expressed boundless faith in the American political and economic system.[1] Furthermore, in contrast to reforming presidents of the past like Wilson, the two Roosevelts and Johnson, he regarded extensions of the role of government without enthusiasm. He shared Eisenhower's belief that presidents had a responsibility 'to restrain and limit government, not to force it to fulfil any great mission or obligation.'[2]

In the early weeks of his presidency Bush was reported to have installed a portrait of Theodore Roosevelt in the Cabinet Room and to have told a visitor: 'I'm an Oyster Bay kind of guy . . . Maybe I'll turn out to be a Teddy Roosevelt.'[3] This was never more than a fanciful suggestion for while not unlike TR in his origins, Bush's style in office was far removed from that of his aggressively proactive predecessor. The first Roosevelt was a combative, creative leader and is remembered particularly for his mastery of the bully pulpit; in domestic policy he was anything but an unambitious near-passive leader, abjuring rhetorical appeals and responding to problems as they arose on a case-by-case basis, in the manner of guardians like Eisenhower, Ford and Bush. The parallels between Roosevelt and Bush are somewhat more meaningful in foreign policy where both vigorously asserted presidential prerogatives and compiled records of achievement.

RECORD OF ACHIEVEMENT

It seems likely that Bush's place in history will be determined almost entirely by his accomplishments in foreign policy. As we saw in Chapter 7, US policy in Central America had been a disaster area for the Reagan Administration and the Iran Contra affair had damaged severely executive relations with the legislature. James Baker as Bush's Secretary of State

202

skilfully mended fences with Congress and developed a bipartisan policy that relied on diplomacy in contrast to the military emphasis of the previous administration. In early 1990 this approach was apparently vindicated by the electoral defeat in Nicaragua of the governing Sandinistas and the election as president of Violeta Chamorro.[4] Further success for the Bush Administration in Central America came with the eventual invasion of Panama and the removal from the area of the troublesome Manuel Noriega.

Earlier, in reviewing Bush's contribution to the end of the Cold War, I indicated that this would remain a matter of some dispute for a long time to come. Nevertheless, for the moment, it is interesting to consider the early verdicts of some specialists in this field who could in no way be described as political allies of the President. Michael Mandelbaum, for instance, observed that Bush was gifted the 'greatest geopolitical windfall in the history of American foreign policy' when the communist regimes of Eastern Europe fell apart; however, the President is praised for his handling of the situation, for ensuring that the United States stayed on the sidelines while these extraordinary events occurred. The President's restraint 'served America's interests well . . . the qualities most characteristic of [his Administration] – caution, modest public pronouncements and a fondness for private communications – were admirably suited to the moment.' There was nothing inevitable about the relatively smooth ending of communism in Europe; there were many hazards and possible disasters, but Bush is credited with managing to avoid them all.[5]

Michael Elliott, the diplomatic editor of *Newsweek*, applauds in particular Bush's commitment to a unified Germany in the face of resistance from Mrs Thatcher and François Mitterrand. He commends also his refusal to engage in triumphalism at Gorbachev's expense, thereby ensuring that the new Germany would stay within NATO.[6] Two other students of these matters, Michael Beschloss and Strobe Talbott, who later became Deputy Secretary of State in the Clinton Administration, while questioning Bush's extravagant representation of himself at the 1992 Republican convention as some sort of hero in the struggle to end communism, are willing to concede that he 'made an indispensable contribution to the Cold War's end. From January 1989 through December 1991, he coaxed the Soviet

Union toward worldwide surrender. He did so largely by exercising restraint and refraining from pushing the Soviet government too hard, thus never giving Moscow a pretext to reverse course.'⁷

Bush's leadership during the crisis created by Saddam Hussein's invasion of Kuwait will obviously be central to any consideration of his historical significance. Leaving aside the alleged inadequacies of American foreign policy that arguably helped to bring this crisis about, George Bush's conduct during these most testing moments of his presidency is not easy to fault. It is, however, the case that in the Gulf War, as with the ending of the Cold War, Bush's strength was in managing change rather than in charting a new course. He made his contribution by dealing skilfully with problems on an *ad hoc* basis, in engaging in transactional rather than transformational leadership, a style of leadership particularly appropriate to the situations he faced.⁸

The North American Free Trade Agreement finally adopted by Congress in 1993 can also be counted among President Bush's foreign policy achievements. The idea of such an agreement first emerged during the Reagan years when it was seen as a natural outgrowth of the free trade agreement negotiated in 1987 between the US and Canada. In September 1990, Bush informed Congress of his intention to negotiate a free trade pact with Mexico and announced in Febuary 1991 that Canada would join the talks. Under the terms of the 1988 Trade Act the President was given authority for three months to negotiate a trade agreement that would then be submitted for congressional approval under 'fast-track' procedures. These gave Congress 90 days to act once an agreement was concluded and protected it from amendments.

An extension of the President's negotiating authority for two years became the subject of intense political debate in 1991 with opponents of a free trade agreement in both houses of Congress seeking to pass resolutions disapproving an extension. If either of these had passed the effect would have been to terminate the fast-track process and to wreck the negotiations. The Bush Administration fought vigorously and successfully against the resolutions, thereby making it possible for the negotiations to proceed and leading eventually to the signing of NAFTA in December 1992.⁹

Far more comfortable with foreign policy-making and instinctively doubtful of the efficacy of governmental action in domestic policy, Bush, as we saw in Chapter 4, nevertheless felt obliged to have an agenda at home. Asked by journalists, late in his term, to identify the most significant domestic initiatives that he had 'originated, promoted and seen through to fruition' the President referred to education, child care, the Americans with Disabilities Act, revision of the Clean Air Act and appointments to the federal bench.[10]

During the 1988 campaign Bush had vowed to be 'the education president' and in September 1989 he followed this up by holding an education summit with state governors where a number of educational goals were agreed. In the first Congress of his presidency, however, Bush failed to secure passage of legislation that would have provided some first steps towards the fulfilment of those goals.[11] In 1991 the Administration initiated 'America 2000', an education reform programme including voluntary national testing; merit pay for teachers; reductions in regulations; and the establishment of innovative schools financed by business and the federal government. A voucher scheme for low and middle income families was subsequently added to this list of proposals, but none of these various initiatives became law and there is little hard evidence to support Bush's inclusion of education as an area of significant achievement.[12]

In 1990, Bush signed into law major child care legislation and he had campaigned on the issue in 1988. On the other hand, important though his commitment was, Bush was by no means alone in pressing the case for this measure. According to the *Congressional Quarterly*, the $22.5 billion package eventually passed represented the culmination of a 'three year effort by a coalition of child care advocacy groups, organized labor and educators.'[13] Similarly, as I argued earlier, while Bush was undoubtedly an enthusiastic supporter of the ADA there were many others involved in that cause and it might well have passed without the President's help. The 1990 Clean Air Act also had a complex legislative history, but Bush's claim to a significant role in its fashioning is less open to dispute than it is in the cases of the ADA and child care legislation.

For Bush's many critics on the right of his own party the clean air and aid for the disabled bills were, in any case, distinctly dubious accomplishments for a president supposedly dedicated to deregulation. As Vice President, Bush had been chairman of Reagan's Task Force on Regulatory Relief and had been notably successful in reducing the burden of government regulations. With Bush in the White House the situation appeared to change radically with regulation substantially increasing.[14] The pages of new regulations in the *Federal Register* had totalled 50 997 in the final year of Reagan's first term and 53 376 in the last year of his presidency whereas in the concluding year of Bush's term the figure rose to 67 716.[15] Moreover, after adjustment for inflation, 'the amount that the government [spent] on its regulatory activities [was] 22% higher in fiscal 1991 than in Carter's last year.'[16] Conservatives outraged by the increase in regulation during the Bush years were much inclined to hold the ADA and the clean air legislation especially responsible.[17]

None of this helped Bush's chances of re-election, but, aside from that, it can hardly be denied that his legislative record was thin. I discussed the unprecedented paucity of his presidential success scores in Chapter 5, although I also drew attention to the inadequacy of such measures when applied to guardian presidents. While the latter are obliged to labour in an activist ethos they take very seriously indeed their responsibility, in Hamilton's words, for 'preventing bad laws' and, as we saw, Bush deftly wielded the veto power and signing statements to shape or to prevent the passage of laws he found wanting.

It was not unreasonable for George Bush to place his judicial appointments among his most noteworthy domestic policy accomplishments. His predecessor had shown that by careful screening of nominations to the federal courts it was possible to exercise a crucial influence in policy areas of particular importance to conservative presidents such as abortion, affirmative action, religious freedom and the rights of criminal defendants.[18] In the Bush administration the conservative C. Boyden Gray, Counsel to the President and one of his closest allies, took charge of the judicial selection process and institutionalized the elaborate arrangements for screening candidates begun under Reagan.[19] Out of this process emerged a preponderance of relatively young, white males 'true to the key tenets of the conservative agenda'.[20]

During the course of his presidency Bush appointed 185 federal district and circuit court judges, nearly a quarter of the federal bench.[21] He also had the opportunity to appoint two US Supreme Court justices, David Souter and Clarence Thomas. Little was known of Souter's views when he was appointed in 1990, but, to the chagrin of right-wing Republicans, he has joined with Sandra Day O'Connor and Anthony Kennedy to form an alliance of moderate conservative justices 'responsible for preventing a reversal of the court's long-held positions on abortion, school prayer and, in one key case, prisoners' rights.'[22] Thomas, on the other hand, has consistently voted with the hardline conservatives Antonin Scalia and Chief Justice William H. Rehnquist.[23] Overall, while Bush has been fiercely criticized by conservatives in his party for other reasons, his efforts to carry on Reagan's mission of moving the federal bench to the right have met with approval; in July 1992 it was reported that in this regard at least: 'The conservative community is extremely pleased.'[24]

C. BOYDEN GRAY

The fact that Bush's judicial appointments largely satisfied conservatives owed much to the efforts of C. Boyden Gray, without question one of the most influential members of the White House staff. The role of the president's Counsel, or legal adviser, has varied from one adminstration to another, but Gray, with good reason, came to be indentified as Bush's *éminence grise*.[25] The two men had not met before Gray was interviewed in 1981 for the post of Counsel to the Vice President. However, their backgrounds gave them much in common. Both were from wealthy Eastern establishment families and were educated at private schools and elite universities, Yale in Bush's case and Harvard in Gray's. The President's father, Prescott Bush, had been a United States Senator from 1953 until 1962 and was a friend of Gray's father, Gordon Gray, Army Secretary in the Truman Administration and National Security Adviser to President Eisenhower. Both fathers and sons became members of the Alibi Club, one of the most exclusive clubs in Washington.[26]

After eight years on Vice President Bush's staff, C. Boyden

Gray became Counsel to the President in 1989 with special responsibility for monitoring ethical standards among admin-istration officials, overseeing the judicial nomination process and protecting the constitutional prerogatives of the presi-dency.[27] Gray's closeness to the President, his unquestionable loyalty, his intellect and his forceful personality allowed him to emerge as a major player in the upper reaches of the Bush Administration, someone able to 'go in and talk to the President on any issue he chooses.'[28] Involved not only in judicial selec-tions, but in all nominations, Gray also had a role in policy formulation and was one of the prime movers behind both the clean air legislation and the ADA. Beyond that, Gray advised the President on his exercise of the veto and was the principal architect of the strategy of using signing statements to defend presidential prerogatives, most notably in the realm of foreign policy. Gray was clearly a figure of some weight in the Bush White House and his influence was particularly evident on those occasions when the President displayed some mettle in his dealings with Congress.

LEGISLATIVE LEADERSHIP

The acid test of presidential leadership is widely believed to be a chief executive's capacity to fashion a productive rela-tionship with Congress. For activist presidents this is obviously imperative, and while it is less essential for guardians, given their limited agendas, they also require cooperation from the legislature. I referred in Chapter 2 to Bush's initial adoption of a conciliatory approach towards Congress. Some conserv-atives were troubled by this stance from the beginning, but Roger Porter, Assistant to the President for Economic and Domestic Policy, felt that Bush had little option to do other-wise in light of the configuration of party strength in the legislature. Porter also vigorously rebutted the suggestion that Bush's record of achievement in domestic policy was weak and emphasized the successes of his veto strategy.[29]

Gray, while recognizing that the President's violation of his no new taxes pledge 'will dog him through the rest of time' thought 'he did rather well with a hostile Congress.' Despite the machinations of the Democratic leader in the Senate,

George Mitchell, Bush had 'revolutionized' the enforcement of environmental controls, 'triggered educational reform', 'cleaned up the savings and loan mess', obtained passage of the ADA and left behind an economy 'as good as any left to anybody in American history'. As Porter did, Gray laid great stress on the fact that Bush had to deal with a Congress controlled by the Democrats by large margins. Reagan, the yardstick against which Bush was so often measured, had enjoyed a Senate controlled by the Republicans for six of his eight years. Consequently, the Senate was like an echo chamber for Reagan. He would make pronouncements and present policies which would then be sympathetically heard whereas Bush's initiatives were promptly subject to partisan mutilation, a disadvantage the importance of which 'could not be emphasized too much.'[30]

Despite these rationalizations it surely is the case that Bush's early strategy of conciliation towards the legislature was ill-judged. As he said himself towards the end, he 'held out the hand of friendship ... and these old mossbacks bit it off.'[31] That this would happen was entirely predictable. At the best of times, Congress is packed with ruthless adversaries who revel in creating difficulties for the man in the White House and they were unlikely to be much impressed, in the long term, by honeyed words and gestures of friendship.

As several observers noted in reflecting on Bush's approach, presidents cannot afford to be unduly accommodating in their dealings with legislators. A veteran of the Reagan White House said: 'Presidents do well when the people on the Hill have a healthy regard for them – verging on fear.'[32] A House Democratic leadership aide made the same point when he noted that Bush 'did not generate the raw political fear that Mr Reagan had in his glory years ... there isn't any cost to crossing him.'[33] Authoritative confirmation of the inadvisability of Bush's 'kinder gentler' style was provided later by one the most experienced and hard-headed members of his Administration, Clayton Yeutter: 'Bush was never sufficiently aggressive with the Congress. He just didn't want to do it that way. He never realized that those folks were doing him in. He had so many good friends over there, and, on a one-on-one basis, they all loved George Bush and he loved them and it was marvellous. But he was never able to separate the personal relationships with the Congress from the political relationships. He couldn't comprehend that those who were great friends of his were doing him in politically every day of the week.'[34]

GOING PUBLIC

As Bobbie Kilberg, among other members of the Communications division of the White House staff, discovered, Bush had neither the capacity nor the inclination for 'going public', for appealing to the American people over the heads of his old friends in Congress.[35] He was not, in short, a particularly good mass communicator and saw no need to become one. This was surely one of the gravest weaknesses in Bush's style of leadership, providing a key to an understanding of why his presidency ultimately failed, on the domestic front at least.

In 1988 he had campaigned on the strength of his CV, boasting of being 'Ready from day one to be a great president', but, in truth, he was not fully qualified to meet the demands of the US presidency in the late twentieth century. As Samuel Kernell has demonstrated, the American political system has undergone change in recent decades. As recently as the 1960s, in the circumstances of 'institutional pluralism', it had been appropriate to focus on bargaining as the principal means whereby coalitions were formed and policies were agreed. In Congress there had been party and committee leaders of consequence allowing presidents to cut deals, largely behind the scenes, to advance their programmes. In such conditions, insiders thrived and the influence of public opinion was relatively limited in normal circumstances. By the 1980s, however, institutional pluralism had decayed and been replaced by 'individualized pluralism'. Parties had weakened and centrifugal tendencies in Congress had intensified; there were now hardly any leaders of significance in the legislature with whom a president could negotiate and the ethos of 'To get along, go along' had been replaced by rampant individualism.[36] Success in the White House now increasingly required a capacity the part of chief executives for going public, for 'forcing compliance from fellow Washingtonians by going over their heads to appeal to their constituents'.[37]

The various activities associated with going public – making trips around the country, visits overseas, prime-time addresses, televised news conferences and ceremonial occasions – all made for situations where Bush did not perform particularly well. His fractured syntax, his unwillingness to take direction from media advisers, his 'hot' rather than 'cool' persona, his obvious discomfort in front of television cameras and his oratorical limitations combined to make him a less than effective communicator. As one presidential scholar, Thomas Cronin, said of the President: 'He is rhetorically and oratorically a handicapped man.'[38] The President's 'tone deafness' was remarked on by another critic, the conservative commentator, Robert Novak, who went on to say: 'Of all successful politicians Bush has the least feel for language . . . [he] lacks an essential weapon of politics: the ability to stir the nation with words.'[39]

Even more telling was the rueful awareness among Bush's senior staff of his weakness as a communicator. Andrew Card, Deputy Chief of Staff and later Secretary for Transportation, declared that Bush was 'a great President' and 'a great leader for the world' and yet he was not 'a great communicator [and] he was not good on television.'[40] According to James Ciccone, Bush singularly lacked Reagan's 'quite extraordinary' talent for communicating with the public. Not only did he 'distrust the power of rhetoric' he also displayed a 'lack of comfort in front of the media.'[41]

Even the ultra-loyalist C. Boyden Gray, who in the course of two long interviews hardly let a word critical of the President pass, accepted that as a communicator Bush was not in the same league as his predecessor: 'Reagan had a capacity to exploit the bully pulpit; he was a masterful public speaker [whereas] Bush just did not have that very awesome talent.' The no less loyal Gregg Petersmeyer spoke of Bush being 'not particularly warm with the camera lens' and, in contrast to Reagan 'he never thought about the presidency in wholesale terms versus retail terms.' In other words, while Bush was a master of retail politics, in dealing with people one on one, he had no feel for 'projecting to large numbers of people'.[42]

Several members of Bush's staff drew my attention to the President's often impressive performances at press conferences in contrast to Reagan's inadequacies in that setting. Bush, moreover, held far more press conferences than his predecessor.

However, Terry Eastland has written perceptively about the limitations of press conferences, as compared to set speeches, as techniques for marshalling support behind policy proposals:

> [P]ress conferences are a poor means of presenting a legislative policy and offering a coherent argument on its behalf. The President must share time with reporters who ask questions that can bounce from one subject to another or who wish to 'pin' him down on a matter he would not care, or is not prepared, to talk about . . . a President who so prefers press conferences that he neglects the public argument he can make through well-considered speeches is underemploying the presidential office.[43]

In the late twentieth century, effective communication with the American public, largely through the medium of television, has become an essential prerequisite for success in the White House. Behind the scenes leadership and bargaining skills are not enough in the present age and, in that sense, Bush was less well qualified for the presidency than he and others recognized. None of the jobs he had held in the past had prepared him for the demands of going public, and he lacked both the talent and the inclination for mass communication – major handicaps in an era of individualized pluralism.

Outside of those brief periods when he was in what he described as his 'campaign mode', Bush seemed to have an aversion to selling himself and the policies he espoused. Several of his senior staff expressed their frustration at his failure to understand that it was not sufficient for him to work hard and to pursue the correct policies. The President's naivety in these matters bemused John Keller, the Director of Advance, and a devoted Bush admirer. 'He thought that you should be able to just work your ass off and people would love you. You really do get into some genuine innocence if he really thought that, but he did!'[44] Similarly, Nicholas Calio believed that Bush was mistaken in believing that 'you didn't need to communicate through sound bites or creating perception.' This was to ignore the fact that if the people 'don't understand what you're doing, you're going to have a problem accomplishing what you want to achieve', whereas Bush erroneously 'assumed that the American public would understand perfectly well what he was doing.' It was also matter of regret for Calio, as a legislative liaison chief, that Bush's disinclination to go public, as a means of framing the debate on contentious issues, often resulted in his being upstaged by the Democrats in Congress. In this regard, there were two exceptions :the fight to obtain fast-track authority for the North American Free Trade Agreement and the Persian Gulf war. 'In both [of those] cases he went very public, got right behind it, communicated specific messages and brought the public along. That normally didn't happen.'[45]

Few would question that foreign policy was an area of achievement for President Bush, but whatever success he enjoyed in that realm turned primarily on personal diplomacy. Here too he often appeared to believe that as long as his policies were sound the public would understand, an attitude that exasperated Scowcroft's aide Richard Haass, who was of the view that the administration should have:

> gone public more in arguing why it was we were doing things the way we were and not doing things the way some of our critics wanted . . . it isn't enough just to do the right things and have them turn out right, you have to go out and sell and explain policy. I think Bush's sense of stewardship was 'I will do the right things and they will turn out well and the people will see that and they will reward me for it.' And that is just inadequate.[46]

AN ABSENCE OF VISION

George Bush's weakness as a communicator bears on his alleged lack of vision. Presidents who have vision are blessed with a clear sense of direction, and they come into office with a master plan, or blueprint, that can be readily communicated to the people. No one ever accused Ronald Reagan of being without vision and he famously entered office with a preconceived plan. For years he had been traipsing around the country exalting the advantages of lower taxes, less government and stronger defence – stark and simple aims that were relatively easy to communicate, that clearly differentiated him from his political opponents and that ultimately gave coherence and direction to his presidency. The constant insistence by critics on the right that he too exhibit vision baffled George Bush. In his autobiography he reluctantly addressed the complaint by wheeling out a few vapid references to freedom, justice, opportunity, minimal government and economic freedom before saying: 'My "vision" – it was all there in everything I'd said as a candidate and done in nearly twenty years of public life.'[47]

This dismissive comment is particularly revealing; those who wished to find out what Bush stood for could be left to work it out for themselves by examining his record. Such things were to be divined rather than articulated by the man himself who was 'not comfortable with rhetoric for rhetoric's sake'.[48] There is an elitist ring to Bush's persistent insistence that he should not have to explain himself and it is at odds with Reagan's more populist approach. For the latter, the establishment of a dialogue with the people, explaining what he was trying to do, and why, was a matter of the first priority.

While Bush himself remained unconvinced of the need for vision, for any sort of master plan, this could not be said of some of his senior staff. One of those closest to him, Gregg Petersmeyer, regretted his 'failure to project a vision for America . . . people expect of leaders just two things: they expect to be told where we are going and how we are going to get there,' but Bush had been found wanting on both counts.[49] Sununu's executive assistant, Ed Rogers, put it differently; as he saw it the problem was that: 'Nobody knew if Bush was a dictator what he would do about anything. If he was a dictator, what would he do about our education problem, what would he do about our crime problem, what would he do about our economic problems?'[50]

In the same vein Constance Horner noted that in domestic policy:

> The big picture wan't there in the President's mind . . . He had good particulars that he was committed to, and in fact achieved through legislation, but there was no articulation of a grand design that would compel other people's attention. There was therefore, no basis for determining what was important from day to day in domestic policy . . . I think President Bush would view a grand design as a burden to be avoided, as a potential embarrassing conflict with what daily reality required.

As Ms Horner said, this was 'quite different from Reagan' and her analysis neatly distinguishes Bush as a reactive, pragmatic leader from the proactive, ideological president who preceded him.[51]

Given the nature of the American political system, there are clearly advantages to be derived from a chief executive working to a grand design. Such a strategy makes for coherence and gives direction to the administration in a polity marked by chronically weak political parties and a centrifugal structure of power. As Charles Kolb emphasized, Reagan's political appointees took up their posts with a clear sense of what they were expected to do, whereas the Bush Administration was encumbered by 'an aimless agenda nursed along by thousands of clueless appointees wondering what they were hired for.'[52]

Such scorn was to be expected from a conservative and a Reaganite like Kolb, yet Clayton Yeutter said something very similar: 'Reagan was very skilful in laying out the things that were fervently important to him. He did that better than any president in my lifetime . . . He did it year in and year out for 40 or 50 years [*sic*] . . . He had four or five major objectives and everybody in the United States understood them. That helped in governing too because people within his own administration understood what the priorities were . . . Bush was never that clear in what his presidential objectives were.'[53]

Yeutter understood that a president stood a better chance of being successful if he had some sense of direction. On the other hand he also appeared to recognize how unusual Reagan was in possessing vision, in having a master plan that gave coherence and direction to his presidency. Indeed, as I argued earlier, Bush's style of leadership was, in some respects, far more typical than Reagan's – visionless, non-ideological, pragmatic presidents have been the norm, historically.[54] Vision is synonymous with ideology loosely defined, but the political context in the United States has never encouraged ideological approaches to leadership. Furthermore, it is difficult to recall any president other than Reagan who could be said to have had vision. Certainly that infinitely influential, master of statecraft Franklin Roosevelt does not qualify. Far from being any sort of visionary, FDR was, in the words of Theodore Lowi: 'a broker, an eclectic, a pragmatist, an improviser, one who lived comfortably with great inconsistencies.'[55] Those activist presidents nursing the ambition to follow in Roosevelt's footsteps such as Truman, Kennedy, Johnson, Carter and Clinton may have had far more extensive agendas than guardians like Eisenhower, Ford and Bush, but it is questionable whether their lists of proposals have been bound together by intellectual coherence sufficiently to merit use of the term vision.

While there are obvious advantages in a president having some sort of grand design there is also a downside. At its worst, it demands simple-mindedness rather than sophistication in decision-making. Charles Kolb, one of those within the White House most severely critical of Bush's lack of an overall plan, made much in conversation with me of the fact that what Reagan stood for could be summarized in six words, a test that his successor certainly could not meet.[56] Unquestionably it was one of the strengths of Reagan's presidency that what he was trying to accomplish could be stated so briefly: 'lower taxes, less government, stronger defense.'[57] Yet, as I noted earlier, simple clear-cut goals, while beneficial for communication purposes, may not do justice to the complexity of the issues.[58]

Environmental protectionism was one such issue. In accepting the Republican nomination in 1988 Bush committed himself to improving the environment: 'We must clean the air. We must reduce the harm done by acid rain.' Those who worried about such matters were subsequently encouraged by the appointment of a conservationist, William Reilly, to head the Environmental Protection Agency and by the Administration's crucial role in the passage of the 1990 Clean Air Act, discussed in more detail in Chapter 4 above. Late in Bush's term, however, he came under attack from environmentalists for failing to implement clean air legislation with sufficient resolution.[59] At the same time, conservatives complained bitterly about the mounting regulatory burdens being placed on industry by the Administration-sponsored Clean Air Act and the Americans with Disabilities Act.

As Bush prepared to face the voters in 1992 it appeared that he favoured both deregulation and environmental protection, a posture which his critics derided as symptomatic of the absence of vision: 'It is a real dichotomy. On one hand, he is too "green"; on the other hand he is not "green" enough. It all goes back to the idea of leadership and vision. We don't know what his vision really is. He wants the best of two conflicting worlds – to be green and to deregulate.'[60] Bush's straddling of both positions moreover was reflected in conflict within his Administration, with Reilly finding himself engaged in a constant struggle with prominent conservatives in the White House like John Sununu and Dan Quayle, who did not share his concerns.

For the purposes of communication, unity within the Administration and effective leadership in general, it would have been far better if Bush had set aside the complexities and come down firmly on one side or the other of the issue – if he had committed himself firmly to environmental protection or deregulation; there had, of course, been no such ambiguity about Reagan's position – he had consistently resisted clean air proposals.

A charitable interpretation of Bush's stance, however, requires some recognition of the fact that environmental protectionism raises complex questions that are not susceptible to easy answers. There is surely a case for being simultaneously a green and an advocate of deregulation; the centrist position may well be sounder and more intellectually honest than either of the two extremes.[61] Much the same could also be said of other contentious issues that troubled Bush such as abortion, civil rights and management of the economy. None of this was likely to impress the President's many critics on the right who interpreted his ambiguities and uncertainties as nothing more than a lack of convictions 'as the incoherence that afflicts a public person operating without a public philosophy'.[62]

A LACK OF CONVICTIONS?

Throughout his presidency Bush was haunted by the widely held perception that he was a man without convictions; that he really did not believe in anything very much and sought office, at best, out of sense of duty to serve, or at worst, merely for 'the honor of it all'.[63] Some of Bush's staff indignantly rejected such allegations. As I recorded earlier, James Cicconi attributed noble motives to the President, claiming that he had 'an inner core of conviction that was rooted in doing what's right for the country regardless [of the consequences] ... there are many occasions when he stood up to the political heat because of that integral conviction'. [64] David Demarest was equally dismissive of the 'no convictions' charge seeing it as a cover for the argument 'he's not on our team 100%' and for the complaint that Bush was not 'really a true believer'. [65]

Despite such protestations, there is a lot of evidence tending to support the contention that Bush, to an unusual degree, lacked settled beliefs. He is, to put it another way, vulnerable to the charge of political opportunism, appearing, on a number of occasions, to shift his ground on the issues for reasons of political expediency. Thus my discussion of the 1990 budget crisis in Chapter 6 drew attention to Bush's, ultimately fatal, havering on economic policy. He denounced supply-side economics in the 1980 primaries as 'voodoo economics' but then swiftly became a 'born-again supply sider' once he had become Reagan's running mate.[66] When he ran for the presidency in his own right he repeatedly promised 'no new taxes', a pledge that seems to have been born out of electoral considerations, with Bush's advisers convincing him that such an undertaking was necessary to shore up conservative support and to exorcize the 'wimp' allegation.

His lack of serious commitment to the pledge was revealed by his cavalier reneging on it when it was deemed necessary; a manoeuvre executed with hardly a word of explanation or justification. Moreover, during the crisis that followed, Bush swung back and forth with dizzying speed on a central issue of economic policy – the question of whether he would agree to an increase in income tax in return for a reduction in capital gains tax. The President's several U-turns, within a few days, on this matter further damaged his collapsing credibility as economic policy manager.

Over a much longer time scale, Bush appeared to undergo a number of changes of position on one of the most vexed issues of domestic policy, civil rights, even though this was categorically denied by that most forcefully loyal member of his senior staff, C. Boyden Gray. When I referred to Bush's alleged inconsistencies in this area outlined in newspaper articles Gray retorted: 'I dont think that is true. They just don't understand what they are talking about.'[67] Nevertheless, there do seem to have been a number of shifts in Bush's position on these matters over the years.

In 1948 Bush's liberalism on the race issue was apparently reflected in his leadership of the United Negro College fund drive at Yale University.[68] Yet his first run for public office in 1964, when he sought a seat in the Senate, found him supporting Goldwater without reservation and inveighing against the legislation that would eventually become the Civil Rights Act of 1964.[69] Elected to the US House of Representatives in 1966, Bush shed the conservative position he had taken earlier to join the moderate wing of the Republican Party.

In 1968, Bush voted in favour of a civil rights bill, the Open Housing Act and, subsequently, at a meeting with constituents outraged by this vote, he cited Edmund Burke's theory of representation in his defence before going on to say: 'Sometimes it seems fundamental that a man should not have a door slammed in his face because he is a Negro or speaks with a Latin American accent.' Open housing, Congressman Bush declared, offered a ray of hope for minorities 'locked out by habit and discrimination'. The subject of catcalls initially, Bush was finally given a standing ovation and, in recalling the occasion in his autobiography, observed: 'More than twenty years later I can truthfully say that nothing I've experienced in public life, before or since, has measured up to the feeling I had when I went home that night.'[70]

As Ruth Marcus has shown, however, the background to this incident is revealing. In the first place Bush's electoral position was so safe that he was re-elected without opposition; secondly, in running for election in 1966 he had spoken out against open housing legislation; thirdly, the crucial vote on the bill in question was not on final passage, when Bush voted in favour, but on the procedural question of whether to send the bill back to the conference committee, a manoeuvre that would have almost certainly killed the bill off. This earlier critical vote found Bush siding with the forces hostile to civil rights.[71]

Nevertheless, between 1966 and 1980, Bush generally took liberal positions on civil rights, but as Reagan's Vice President he appeared to move to the right on this, as on other issues. He made no more than modest attempts to counter the anti civil rights thrust of the Reagan Administration and his record in this area was further tarnished in 1988 by the racial undertones of the infamous Willie Horton advertisement. In office Bush, despite having spoken out in favour of quotas twenty years earlier, found it necessary to veto the 1990 civil rights bill on the grounds that it would lead to quotas.[72]

The 1990 bill arose from concern among congressional Democrats at the consequences of a number of decisions by the US Supreme Court, most notably *Wards Cove Packing Company* v. *Antonio* (1989). This overruled the precedent set by *Griggs* v. *Duke Power Company* (1971) when the Court ruled that employment practices that led to discrimination were unacceptable even if there was no discriminatory intent. Under the *Griggs* ruling, moreover, the statistical underrepresentation of minorities in the workforce of a company could, in itself, be the source of litigation, with the onus of proof placed on the employer to show that the employment practices being used were not discriminatory.[73] *Wards Cove* reversed the *Griggs* decision with the Court now arguing that statistical evidence of underrepresentation was not enough to justify proceeding with a prima facie case against an employer, while also shifting the burden of proof from the employer to the worker. 'Instead of employers having to show that a legitimate business necessity existed for challenged practices workers were required to prove that there was not.'[74]

Conservatives, appalled by *Griggs* because they believed that it obliged employers to use quotas, enthusiastically welcomed *Wards Cove*, whereas it horrified Senator Edward Kennedy and Congressman August Hawkins who co-sponsored the 1990 civil rights bill designed to reinstate the essence of the *Griggs* judgment. In vetoing the bill, Bush confusingly indicated his wish to sign a civil rights bill and, in 1991, he duly signed a bill which most observers regarded as an only slightly modified version of that which he had vetoed the year before.[75] In explaining why Bush was willing to sign the 1991 bill, commentators were quick to point to the furores created by the nomination of Clarence Thomas to the Supreme Court and the candidacy of the former Klansman David Duke for the governorship of Louisiana. Political expediency, in other words, supposedly led Bush to sign.[76] But whatever the reasons it had become difficult to say where Bush stood on quotas; he favoured them in 1970, denounced them in 1990 but, a year later seemed willing to accept them.

Bush's position on another of the great contemporary issues, abortion, was similarly marked by inconsistency. Jefferson Morley has carefully documented Bush's enthusiastic support for family planning as a congressman in the late 1960s. During this period he became the chairman of a House Republican Task Force on Earth Resources and Population Planning which recommended revising abortion laws 'to eradicate the increasing number of unlicensed and unqualified practitioners who jeopardize the health and safety' of women seeking abortions.[77] For the next decade Bush remained pro-choice and, as late as the spring of 1980, was prepared to express publicly his support for *Roe* v. *Wade*, the abortion rights decision.[78]

A few months later he became Reagan's running mate and quietly abandoned his pro-choice stance; by the time he was ready to compile his autobiography Bush found it possible to say, without a word of explanation of his dramatic change of mind: '*Abortion*. I oppose abortion, except in cases of rape, incest, or when the life of the mother is at stake. Reagan and I both disapproved of the Supreme Court ruling in *Roe* v. *Wade*; we agreed that some form of constitutional amendment was needed to overturn the decision.'[79]

When challenged on his U-turn on abortion Bush argued that the enormous increase in abortions had caused him to reconsider. He also replied tartly to one questioner: 'Have you ever changed your mind? That's one thing about intellectual honesty.'[80] These were perfectly reasonable responses; the number of abortions did increase massively between the 1960s and the 1980s. On both sides of the abortion question there are those who take the view that the answers are self-evident and clear-cut with no place for refinement, doubt or reconsideration. However, such dogmatic certainty on complicated matters is of dubious merit and there is something to be said for politicians being willing to change their minds in the light of further thought and new circumstances.

Having said that, there are two considerations that add weight to the charges of political opportunism laid against George Bush. The first of these concerns the timing of his shifts in his positions on the issues – time and again he seemed to move at moments when it was politically expedient to do so. The second relates to his tendency, on occasion, to be extraordinarily transparent and naive in explaining his inconsistencies.

Thus, in defence of the pro-Goldwater stance he had taken in running for the Senate in 1964 he told the minister of his church: 'You know, John, I took some of the far right positions to get elected. I hope I never do it again. I regret it.'[81] This was a remarkably frank admission of tailoring political views to meet the needs of campaigning for office.

As I noted in Chapter 6 Bush was still blurting out the unthinkable in the closing months of his political career. In 1990 he had abandoned his 'no new taxes' pledge and insisted that the budget deal including a tax increase was essential to American prosperity, but then in early March 1992 he declared the budget compromise to be the worst mistake of his presidency: 'Listen, if I had to do that over, I wouldn't do it. Look at all the flak it's taking.' In explaining why this had been such a terrible mistake the President focused not on considerations of economic policy, but on the adverse consequences for his chances of re-election – Republican voters were 'just overwhelmed by the fact that I went for a tax increase' and were giving him 'political grief' as a result.[82] As one commentator remarked, this was to virtually admit 'that cynical political calculations had dictated the latest U-turn.'[83]

A few weeks later Bush laid himself open to the charge of rampant political opportunism all over again when he was asked why he was now making much of welfare reform when he had ignored the issue for the previous three years. The President replied: 'The politics drives some things . . . a lot of the issues we're talking about . . . they get much more clearly in focus every four years, and then you go ahead and try to follow through and do something about them.'[84] This was yet another statement of astonishing frankness with the President, in effect, confessing that his domestic policy was driven by political expediency.

FINALE

The most conclusive evidence of Bush's failure as President is to be seen in the result of the 1992 election. In 1988 Bush had defeated Dukakis 53 per cent to 45 per cent in the popular vote, whereas after the votes were counted in 1992 the President with 38 per cent was 15 per cent down on his 1988 total; Clinton secured victory with 43 per cent and Perot obtained 19 per cent.[85] In accounting for this result it is first necessary to acknowledge that the timing was to the incumbent's considerable disadvantage; it is inconceivable that Clinton, with his record of avoiding the draft and protesting against the Vietnam war, could have beaten Bush prior to 1992. In other words, the ending of the Cold War, which, of course, Bush had helped to bring about, was crucial to his defeat.[86]

Foreign policy was, without question, Bush's strongest suit in the 1992 campaign, but unfortunately for him, this was not an issue area concerning many American voters at that moment. A *Time*/CNN poll at the end of August 1992 asked: 'Which of these is the main problem the candidates should be addressing?' and of the suggested answers 2 per cent opted for foreign policy while 60 per cent indicated the economy.[87] Later, exit polls, used to determine which issues mattered most to voters in deciding whom to vote for, found that only 8 per cent mentioned foreign policy with 87 per cent of those voting for Bush, 8 per cent for Clinton and 5 per cent for Perot.[88]

Strong on the major issue that mattered least, Bush was weak on many of the concerns troubling voters the most, in particular the weakness of the economy. For much of the Bush presidency the economy was in the doldrums, and it remained 'sluggish throughout 1991 and the first half of 1992'.[89] As the voters went to the polls in November 1992 the economy was recovering rapidly, but this came too late to influence the result.

Seymour Martin Lipset in commenting on the failure of Raymond Fair's economic model to predict the result of the 1992 election noted that, comparatively speaking, the state of the economy was not all that bad during the Bush years: 'The 1991–92 downturn was more moderate than the Reagan 1981–82 recession, or the Carter 1977 decline, while the misery index – unemployment plus the inflation rate – was much worse in 1979–80.' However, Bush's problem was that the American people thought that the economy was much worse than it actually was and 'perception is more important than reality.'[90]

Senior White House staff attributed popular misconceptions about the health of the economy to media bias: 'To hear the press talk about 1992 it was the worst year since the Great Depression.'[91] While there may be some justification for such complaints it is also surely the case that Bush's credibility suffered badly from his obvious lack of interest in domestic policy, and his unwillingness to act in response to the widely held belief that the economy was in trouble. As we saw in Chapter 1, Bush, as a guardian president was instinctively resistant to intervention in the economy, believing that recessions arose from business cycles and that there was little the government could do to control them.[92] Public concern at the state of the economy, coupled with the President's disinclination to attempt corrective action, helps to account for Gallup poll figures in 1992 where 80 per cent disapproved of Bush's handling of the economy.[93]

The outcome of the 1992 presidential election can, in part, be explained by the weakness of the Republican campaign. Confirmation of just how inadequate it was has been provided by some authoritative sources including Dan Quayle and Ed Rollins, the Republican strategist, who presided over the Reagan landslide in 1984. In his memoirs, the former Vice President remarks: 'This was the most poorly planned and executed incumbent presidential campaign in this century.'[94] Meanwhile Rollins went further, declaring on a number of occasions that this was 'the worst campaign ever seen'.[95]

The gross inadequacies of the 1992 campaign had much to do with the personality and leadership style of the candidate himself. There is more than a little evidence from within the White House that Bush found campaigning distasteful; that he regarded it as an activity that he was obliged to participate in from time to time, but which he regarded as an unwelcome, unseemly distraction from the really important work of governance. Paul Bateman commented on the President's dislike for campaigning and his belief that it was undignified.[96] The Secretary to the Cabinet, Edie Holiday, observed that Bush 'much preferred governing to campaigning . . . and felt that was what he was elected to do was to govern, not to be out campaigning.' She referred also to the President's resistance to advisers trying to get him to turn his attention to campaigning for re-election, even as early as the Gulf War.[97]

Clayton Yeutter, at the time Chairman of the Republican National Committee, was firmly of the view that Bush erred in not getting his campaign under way earlier than he did. He recalled writing to the President in July 1991 to urge him to decide who would be on his campaign staff: 'When you head out to Kennebunkport in August put your feet up on your desk . . . figure out who's going to do what and announce them right after Labor Day.' But as Yeutter records, while 'that would have been the ideal scenario . . . he wouldn't buy it; he thought that was too early.'

The same vastly experienced member of the President's staff put his finger on the underlying cause of Bush's aversion to campaigning:

What he was saying to the American public was 'I have just done a heck of a good job as President of this country; I deserve a second term and I shouldn't have to go through all this hassle to get there. The American public ought to be able to perceive that I have done a fine job . . .' He just didn't feel that he should be compelled to go and present his case before the American public in a campaign setting. It was almost as if it was belittling at this stage in his life and at this stage in his distinguished career. He felt that his track record accumulated over several decades was there for everybody to behold.[98]

Yeutter's revealing insights bring us back to that major flaw in Bush's makeup, his shortcomings as a communicator. He not only lacked any feel for words, he seemed unable to grasp that effective communication with the people is indispensable to presidential leadership – necessary not just for winning elections, but for governance itself. The need to explain himself or to marshall public support for his policies appears to have escaped George Bush. Those who doubted whether he had vision could be left to examine his record, and it was not necessary for him to explain in any detail his policy reversals on 'no new taxes', abortion or anything else. And when it came to re-election, the American public ought to be able to see for themselves what a fine job he had done without him having to suffer the grubby processess of campaigning. Meanwhile, he would get on with the business of government, reacting to problems, parleying with other leaders and making decisions, and not engaging in 'rhetoric for rhetoric's sake'.

According to Lipset, Bush made the mistake of not adhering to the Franklin Roosevelt model of governance: 'The Roosevelt approach is the way to run the presidency, i.e. as a continuing campaign. Some like Jimmy Carter and George Bush never understood this. Ronald Reagan did, as he noted when he said repeatedly that he modelled himself on Roosevelt.'[99] In some respects such analysis runs counter to mine. As I have argued throughout this book, presidents are entitled to be judged on their own terms. At no point did Bush aspire to be another FDR, he was not even trying to be another Reagan.

As a guardian in the White House, Bush was not attempting to advance a large programme of reform legislation, nor was he bent on fundamental change. It makes little sense therefore to judge him according to standards set by predecessors with quite different aims. Nevertheless, however modest a chief executive's ambitions may be, he cannot avoid having some sort of agenda. Furthermore, even a guardian president's success in office will, to some extent, turn on his capacity for speaking to the American people, a skill that George Bush singularly lacked and was never disposed to acquire.

Notes

INTRODUCTION

1. See, for example, Stephen Graubard, *Mr Bush's War: Adventures in the Politics of Illusion* (London: I.B. Tauris, 1992) and Jean Edward Smith George Bush's War (New York: Henry Holt, 1992).
2. Theodore Sorensen, *Decision-Making in the White House* (New York: Columbia University Press, 1963), p. xii.
3. For example, Richard Nixon, *In the Arena* (New York: Pocket Books, 1990), pp. 80–81 and Edwin Meese, *With Reagan: The Inside Story* (Washington DC: Regnery Gateway, 1992), p. 332.
4. 'Politics of the Professoriate' *The American Enterprise*, Vol. 2, No. 5, July/August, 1991 pp. 86–87.
5. Christopher J. Bosso, 'Congressional and Presidential Scholars: Some Basic Traits', (PS: *Political Science and Politics*, December, 1989, pp. 839–848.
6. Walter B. Roettger and Hugh Winebrenner, 'Politics and Political Scientists', *Public Opinion*, September/October, 1986, pp. 41–44.
7. Robert Murray and Tim Blessing, *Greatness in the White House: Rating the Presidents* (University Park, Penn. The Pennsylvania State University Press, 1994), p. 164.
8. I have developed this argument elsewhere – see David Mervin, *Ronald Reagan and the American Presidency* (London and New York: Longman, 1990) and David Mervin, 'Ronald Reagan's Place in History', *Journal of American Studies*, Vol. 23, No. 2, 1989, pp. 269–286.
9. Murray and Blessing, op. cit., pp. 141, 142, 144, 145, 147, and 149. As *Time* magazine sharply commented when the results of the Murray/Blessing poll were first made public, 'Such a harsh and inclusive indictment will raise further questions about the partisanship and competence of the historians as well as about Reagan' (International edition, 15 April 1991, p. 39. See David Mervin, 'Political Science and the Study of the Presidency', *Presidential Studies Quarterly* (forthcoming).
10. William Leuchtenburg, *In the Shadow of FDR* (New York: Cornell University Press, 1983), p. x.
11. Richard Neustadt, *Presidential Power and the Modern Presidents* (New York: John Wiley and Sons, 1960). In subsequent editions Neustadt has done very little backtracking from his earlier harshness towards Eisenhower. In the 1976 edition he wrote somewhat defensively: 'To write in Eisenhower's time after serving under Truman was to writhe with impatience at the President's concern for his extraordinary public standing, his hero's prestige, hoarding not risking it, being not doing. Especially during his second term, Eisenhower's quietude seemed more conservative in terms of policy than I, for one, deemed prudent. So I still think it was. We paid a price for damming up

reform until the flood of the mid-sixties. Still, it also was conservative in institutional terms, identifying man and office to the office's advantage. Looking back after Nixon, that seems a more impressive contribution than it did before.' *Presidential Power and the Modern Presidents* (New York: The Free Press, 1990), pp. 190–191. This offsets very slightly some of the earlier criticism although Eisenhower is also condemned all over again for failing to adopt the presidential style of a liberal Democrat, for not being another Roosevelt. See also ibid, pp. 295–301 for another modest rethinking of Eisenhower's presidency.

12. Fred J. Greenstein is the most notable of the revisionists: see *The Hidden-Hand Presidency: Eisenhower as Leader* (New York: Basic Books, 1982.

13. Michael Oakeshott, *Rationalism in Politics* (London: Methuen, 1962), p. 191.

14. Richard Rose, 'Evaluating Presidents', in George Edwards, John Kessel and Bert Rockman (eds), *Researching the Presidency* (Pittsburgh: University of Pittsburgh Press, 1993,) p. 473. Murray and Blessing, op. cit., p. 57.

15. Charles O. Jones, *The Presidency in a Separated System* (Washington DC: The Brookings Institution, 1994), p. 11.

16. Federalist No. 73, Clinton Rossiter (ed.) *The Federalist Papers* (New York: New American Library, 1961), p. 444.

17. Margaret Coit (ed.), *John C. Calhoun* (New Jersey: Prentice Hall, 1970), p. 21.

18. Terry Eastland, *Energy in the Executive: The Case for the Strong Presidency*, (New York: The Free Press, 1992), p. 31.

19. Nixon, op. cit., p. 42 and p. 132.

20. Alonzo Hamby, essay on Truman, in Fred Greenstein (ed.), *Leadership in the Modern Presidency* (Cambridge: Harvard University Press, 1988), p. 43.

21. Ibid.

22. Robert Ferrell (ed.), *The Eisenhower Diaries* (New York: W.W. Norton, 1981), pp. 246–247.

23. Michael Duffy and Dan Goodgame, *Marching in Place: The Status Quo Presidency of George Bush* (New York: Simon & Schuster, 1992), p. 65.

24. For the guardian concept of presidential leadership see Rose, op. cit., p. 473–80. Also Richard Rose, *The Postmodern President* (Chatham, New Jersey: Chatham House, 1991), pp. 48–49 and pp. 307–309.

25. Oakeshott, op. cit., p. 184.

26. Emmet Hughes, *The Ordeal of Power* (London: Macmillan, 1963), p. 58.

27. Rose, *The Postmodern President*, op. cit, p. 46.

28. Bert Rockman, *The Leadership Question: The Presidency and the American System* (New York: Praeger, 1984), p. 12. A similar emphasis on effectiveness as the hallmark of presidential leadership is to be found in Barbara Kellerman's *The Political Presidency* (New York: Oxford University Press 1984), p. x, who writes: 'When I speak of an effective presidency, or effective presidential leadership, I am speaking

here in terms of functional criteria only. I am not asking if the leadership was, for example, courageous, wise or moral, or if it led the
country down the proper path. I am asking only if it was effective in
the sense that the president was able to accomplish what he wanted
to accomplish.' Similarly, Aaron Wildavsky portrays Ronald Reagan
as 'a superb political strategist' successful in the sense of effectively
moving the nation in the directions in which he chose to take it, but
who goes on to say: 'Nothing is implied about the desirability of the
directions chosen, for then (such) politicians could be (successful) strategists only by being in accord with the preferences of the analyst.
Society, May/June 1987, pp. 56–62.

29. John Hart, *The Presidential Branch* (New York: Pergamon Press, 1987),
p. 127.
30. Ibid, p. 104.
31. Lyn Ragsdale, *Presidential Politics* (Boston: Houghton Mifflin, 1993),
p. 225.
32. Charles Kolb. *White House Daze: The Unmaking of Domestic Policy in the
Bush Years* (New York: The Free Press, 1994), p. xii.

CHAPTER 1 THE MAKING OF A GUARDIAN PRESIDENT

1. Robert Shogan, *The Riddle of Power: Presidential Leadership from Truman
to Bush* (New York: Dutton, 1991), p. 259.
2. Michael Oakeshott, *Rationalism in Politics* (London: Methuen, 1962),
p. 184.
3. George Bush (with Victor Gold), *Looking Forward* (London: The Bodley
Head, 1988), p. 81.
4. Ibid, pp. 39–40.
5. Ibid, p. 44.
6. Ibid.
7. Fitzhugh Green, *George Bush: An Intimate Portrait* (New York:
Hippocrene Books, 1991), p. 78.
8. Shogan, op. cit., p. 270.
9. Donnie Radcliffe, 'The Bush in the Background', *Washington Post
National Weekly Edition*, 13–19 June 1988, pp. 10–11.
10. Bush, op. cit., p. 25.
11. See Donald Matthews, *US Senators and their World* (New York: Vintage
Books, 1960).
12. Green, op. cit., p. 9.
13. Kerry Mullins and Aaron Wildavsky, 'The Procedural Presidency of
George Bush', *Political Science Quarterly*, Vol. 107, No. 1, 1992,
pp. 31–62.
14. David Hoffman, 'Patrician with a Common Touch', *Washington Post
National Weekly Edition*, 14–20 November, 1988, pp. 6–7.
15. Bush, op. cit., p. 46.
16. Green, op. cit., pp. 63–64.

17. Michael Barone, 'George Bush: Not So Much a Preppie as a Pioneer', *Washington Post National Weekly Edition*, 4–10 July, 1988, p. 29.

18. See Shogan, op. cit., pp. 259–268.

19. John Newhouse, 'Profiles: The Tactician', *New Yorker*, 7 May, 1990, pp. 50–82.

20. Nicholas King, *George Bush: A Biography* (New York: Dodd Mead, 1980), p. 53.

21. See Barbara Kellerman, *The Political Presidency: Practice of Leadership From Kennedy Through Reagan* (New York: Oxford University Press, 1984), p. 38.

22. See Fred Greenstein, 'Ronald Reagan's Presidential Leadership', in Ellis Sandoz and Cecil Crabb (eds), *Election 84: Landslide Without a Mandate?* (New York: New American Library, 1985), p. 78.

23. See William Adams, 'Recent Fables About Ronald Reagan', *Public Opinion*, Vol. VII, No. 5, October/November 1984.

24. Interview with James Cicconi, 8 November 1993.

25. Interview with John Keller, 18 November 1993.

26. Interview with Gregg Petersmeyer, 16 November 1993.

27. Interview with Gail Wilensky, 14 November 1993.

28. Peggy Noonan, *What I Saw at the Revolution: A Political Life in the Reagan Era* (New York: Ivy Books, 1990), p. 313.

29. Interview with C. Boyden Gray, 10 November 1993.

30. Interview with Andrew Card, 15 November 1993.

31. Interview with David Demarest, 12 November 1993. See also Kristin Clark Taylor, *The First to Speak* (New York: Doubleday, 1993), *passim*.

32. For a different perspective on Bush's 'niceness' see Michael Kinsley, 'Is Bush Nice? A Contrarian View', *Time* (International edition),16 July, 1990.

33. David Hoffman, 'George Bush and the Power of the Thankyou Note', *Washington Post National Weekly Edition*, 21–27 August, 1989, pp. 22–23.

34. Ruth Shalit, 'What I Saw at the Devolution', *Reason*, 9 March, 1993, pp. 27–33.

35. Interview with Gregg Petersmeyer, op. cit.

36. Hoffman, 'Patrician with the Common Touch', op. cit.

37. Richard Brookhiser, 'A Visit with George Bush', *Atlantic Monthly*, August 1992, pp. 22–28.

38. *Time* (International edition), 20 March, 1989, p. 38.

39. Mullins and Wildavsky, op. cit. p. 31 and Charles Kolb, *White House Daze: The Unmaking of Domestic Policy in the Bush Years* (New York: Free Press, 1994, p. 314.

40. See Bush, op. cit., pp. 94–95.

41. Ronald Elving, 'House Service Set Course for New President', *Congressional Quarterly Weekly Report*, 14 January, 1989, pp. 55–57.

42. When he first ran for the presidency in 1979, Bush 'referred to his House service with an ironic joke, implying that it had been too brief to be a liability.' Ibid.

43. Walter Pincus and Bob Woodward, 'The Bumpy Years of Bush, From UN Ambassador to CIA Head', *Washington Post National Weekly Edition*, 29 August–4 September, 1988, p. 12.

44. Ibid. and Green, op. cit., pp. 119–120.
45. Ibid, p. 141.
46. Ibid, p. 153.
47. Pincus and Woodward, op. cit.
48. Apparently a sanitized version of what Garner actually said.
49. Jules Witcover, *Crapshoot: Rolling the Dice on the Vice Presidency* (New York: Crown, 1992), p. 59.
50. See H.R. Haldeman, *The Haldeman Diaries* (New York: G.P. Putnam's Sons, 1994), pp. 52–53 and 106.
51. Joseph Pika, 'A New Vice Presidency', in Michael Nelson (ed.), *The Presidency and the Political System*, 2nd edn. (Washington DC: The Congressional Quarterly Press, 1988).
52. C. Boyden Gray, 'The Coordinating Role of the Vice Presidency' in James Pfiffner and Gordon Hoxie (eds) *The Presidency in Transition* (New York: Center for the Study of the Presidency, 1989), pp. 427–428.
53. Bush, op. cit., p. 234.
54. Gray, op. cit., p. 426. See also Pika, op. cit., p. 475 for details of significant foreign travel by Bush as Vice President.
55. Witcover ,op. cit., p. 327.
56. Arthur Schlesinger Jr, *The Cycles of American History* (London: André Deutsch, 1986), pp. 363 and 365.
57. Gail Sheehy, *Character: America's Search for Leadership*, revised edition (New York: Bantam Books, 1990), p. 198.
58. Witcover, op. cit., p. 319 and David Stockman, *The Triumph of Politics: Why the Reagan Revolution Failed* (New York: Harper & Row, 1986), p. 86.
59. Michael Duffy and Dan Goodgame, *Marching in Place: The Status Quo Presidency of George Bush* (New York: Simon & Schuster, 1992), pp. 38–39 and Michael Barone, 'The Vice President's Problem', *Washington Post National Weekly Edition*, 1622 June 1988, p. 28.
60. David Hoffman, 'George Bush Takes Up the Baton', *Washington Post National Weekly Edition*, 16–22 January 1989, pp. 6-8.
61. For the Vice President's conviction that he was amply qualified see Bush, op. cit., pp. 192–193.
62. Duffy and Goodgame, op. cit., p. 21, Kolb, op. cit., pp. 5–6; and John Podhoretz, *Hell of a Ride: Backstage at the White House Follies 1989–1993*, (New York: Simon & Schuster, 1993), p. 129.
63. George Will, 'A National Embarrassment', *Washington Post National Weekly Edition*, 3–9 October 1988, p. 33.
64. Theodore Lowi, 'Ronald Reagan – Revolutionary?', in Lester Salamon and Michael Lund (eds) *The Reagan Presidency and the Governing of America* (Washington DC, The Urban Institute Press, 1984).
65. Hoffman, 'Patrician With a Common Touch', op. cit.
66. Nomination acceptance speech, Republican National Convention, New Orleans, 18 August 1988.
67. Emmet Hughes, *The Ordeal of Power* (London: Macmillan, 1963), p. 60.
68. See James Cicconi as quoted in Kolb, op. cit., p. 95.

69. Duffy and Goodgame, op. cit., p. 56.
70. Interview with William Kristol, 23 March 1994.
71. See especially Richard Neustadt, *Presidential Power and the Modern Presidents* (New York: Free Press, 1990).
72. Stephen Ambrose, *Nixon, Volume Two: The Triumph of a Politician 1962–1972* (New York: Simon & Schuster, 1989), p. 26.
73. Richard Nixon, *In the Arena* (New York: Pocket Books, 1990), p. 43.
74. David Broder, 'The Chief Myth-Maker', *Washington Post National Weekly Edition*, 27 May–2 June 1991, p. 4.
75. Mullins and Wildavsky, op. cit., p. 47. See also Bush, op. cit., p. 193 for his faith in the American system.
76. Quoted in John Yang, 'Who is George Bush?', *Washington Post National Weekly Edition*, 24 Febuary–1 March 1991, pp. 9–10.
77. Inaugural address.
78. See Fred Greenstein, *The Hidden-Hand Presidency: Eisenhower as Leader* (New York: Basic Books, 1982).
79. Interview with Edward Rogers, 3rd November 1993.
80. Duffy and Goodgame, op. cit., p. 65.
81. Ann Devroy, 'The Reluctant Activist; Domestically, Bush Tries to Recast Himself', Washington Post National Weekly Edition, 17 August 1992.
82. Joseph Califano, *A Presidential Nation* (New York: W.W. Norton, 1975), p. 20.
83. Broder, op. cit.
84. Inaugural address.
85. Duffy and Goodgame, op. cit., p. 283.
86. Michael Beschloss and Strobe Talbott, *At the Highest Levels: The Inside Story of the End of the Cold War* (Boston: Little Brown, 1993), p. 21. 87. ibid. p. 205.
88. Devroy, op. cit.
89. Interview with Bobbie Kilberg, 19 November 1993.
90. Devroy, op. cit.
91. Interview with James Cicconi, op. cit.
92. See David Hoffman, 'Zip My Lips: George Bush's Penchant for Secret Decisions', *Washington Post National Weekly Edition*, 15–21 January 1990, p. 23.
93. Quoted in Ann Devroy, 'There's No Homecoming For Bush', *Washington Post National Weekly Edition*, 17–23 June 1991, p. 12.
94. For others sharing this view see Kolb, op. cit., pp. 187–88.

CHAPTER 2 STRATEGIES OF LEADERSHIP

1. Martin Anderson, *Revolution* (New York: Harcourt Brace Jovanovich, 1988) p. 204.
2. Edwin Meese, *With Reagan: The Inside Story* (Washington DC: Regnery Gateway, 1992), pp. 87–88.
3. Hedrick Smith, *The Power Game* (New York: Random House, 1988), pp. 475–476.

4. David Hoffman, 'At Last, a President Who Ran as an Insider, Not an Outsider', *Washington Post National Weekly Edition*, 26 December–1 January 1989, p. 31.

5. Burt Solomon, 'Bush's Lack of Ambitious Policies . . . Makes His Plans Seem Thin Gruel', *National Journal*, 6 May 1989, No. 18, p. 1102.

6. James Pfiffner *The Managerial Presidency* (Pacific Grove, Calif. Brooks/Cole, 1991), p.12.

7. 'Establishing the Bush Presidency', *Public Administration Review*, January/Febuary 1990, pp. 64–72.

8. Interview with Constance Horner, 10 November 1993.

9. Richard Ben Cramer, *What It Takes* (New York: Random House, 1992), p. 153. See also David Hoffman, 'George Bush and the Power of the Thankyou Note', *Washington Post National Weekly Edition*, 21–27 August 1989, pp. 22–23.

10. Maureen Dowd, 'Bush's Fierce Loyalty Raises Debate On Whether It Hinders His Judgment', *New York Times*, 10 March 1989, B6.

11. Kenneth Thompson, *Presidential Transitions: The Reagan to Bush Experience* (Lanham,MD: University Press of America), p. 95.

12. Pfiffner, 'Establishing the Bush Presidency', op. cit.

13. Interview with Ronald Kaufman, 19 November 1993.

14. Ibid.

15. Ibid.

16. 'With 115 Nominations Awaiting Votes, Fingers Point Fast and Furious', *New York Times*, 28 August 1989, p. A13.

17. Interview with Constance Horner, op. cit.

18. Maureen Dowd, 'Transformation of Bush: His Own Man', *New York Times*, 21 January 1989, p.1.

19. Bob Woodward and Walter Pincus, *Washington Post National Weekly Edition*, 15–21 August 1988, p. 8.

20. Kerry Mullins and Aaron Wildavsky, 'The Procedural Presidency of George Bush', *Political Science Quarterly*, Vol. 107, No. 1, 1992, pp. 31–62 and Michael Duffy and Dan Goodgame, *Marching in Place: The Status Quo Presidency of George Bush* (New York: Simon & Schuster, 1992), p. 51.

21. Maureen Dowd, 'Kindness is Foundation as Bush Builds Bridges', *New York Times*, 6 Febuary 1989, p. A13.

22. Bradley Patterson, *The Ring of Power: The White House Staff and Its Expanding Role in Government* (New York: Basic Books, 1988), p. 210.

23. Interview with Bobbie Kilberg, 19 November 1993.

24. Charles Kolb, *White House Daze: The Unmaking of Domestic Policy in the Bush Years* (New York: Free Press, 1994), p. 5.

25. Interview with Bobbie Kilberg, op. cit.

26. Ibid.

27. Interview with William Kristol, 23 March 1994.

28. See Chapter 5 below.

29. See Samuel Kernell, *Going Public* (Washington DC: Congressional Quarterly Press, 1986), *passim*. Also William Kerr Muir, *The Bully Pulpit: The Presidential Leadership of Ronald Reagan* (San Francisco: Institute for Contemporary Studies, 1992) and David Mervin, 'The Bully Pulpit', *Presidential Studies Quarterly*, Vol. XXV, 1995, pp. 19–23.

30. Interview with Clayton Yeutter, 22 March 1994.
31. Interview with C. Boyden Gray, 10 November 1993.
32. Interview with Gregg Petersmeyer, 16h November 1993.
33. Interview with Constance Horner, 10 November 1993.
34. Interview with James Cicconi, 8 November 1993.
35. Interview with John Keller, 18 November 1993.
36. Interview with Betsey Anderson of the Bush Office of Policy Development, 28 March 1994.
37. Interview with Bobbie Kilberg, 19 November 1993.
38. Interview with Clayton Yeutter, 22 March 1994.
39. Interview with William Kristol, op. cit.
40. Interview with David Demarest, 12 November 1993.
41. Ibid.
42. Peggy Noonan, *What I Saw at the Revolution: A Political Life in the Reagan Era* (New York: Ivy Books, 1990), p. 356.
43. Eleanor Randolph, 'The Newly Polite Press', *Washington Post National Weekly Review*, 20–26 March 1989, pp. 14-15.
44. Maureen Dowd, 'Basking in Power's Glow: Bush's Year as President', *New York Times*, 31 December 1989, p. A1
45. David Hoffman, 'What Bush Lacks in Style He Makes Up for in Method', *Washington Post National Weekly Edition*, 2–8 April 1990, p. 24; David Ignatius, 'After Reagan, the Media Miss Being Manipulated', *Washington Post National Weekly Edition*, 15–21 May 1989, p. 23–24; and John Cassidy, 'America Loves Its Inaction Man', *Sunday Times* (London), 16 April 1989, p. B7.
46. Maureen Dowd, 'Journalists Debate the Risks as President Woos the Press', *New York Times*, 2 April 1989, p. A1.
47. Edwin Diamond, Adrian Marin and Robert Silverman, 'Bush's First Year: Mr Nice Guy Meets The Press', *Washington Journalism Review*, Vol. XII, 1990, pp. 42–44.
48. Interview with John Keller, op. cit.
49. Interview with C. Boyden Gray, op. cit.
50. Interview with David Demarest, op. cit.
51. Interview with Gail Wilensky, 14 November 1993
52. Noonan, op. cit., p. 148
53. Ignatius, op. cit.
54. Andrew Rosenthal, 'President Seeks a Way to Adapt His Cool Persona to a Hot Medium', *New York Times*, 22 November 1989, p. B6.
55. Interview with Nicholas Calio, 19 November 1993.
56. Interview with John Keller, op. cit.
57. See, for example, Peter Goldman and Tom Mathews, *The Quest for the Presidency: The 1988 Campaign* (New York: Simon & Schuster, 1989), pp. 190–196.
58. 'What Bush Lacks in Style He Makes Up for in Method', *Washington Post National Weekly Edition*, 2–8 April 1990, p. 24.
59. Interview with Barbara Kilberg, op. cit.
60. Cramer, op. cit., p. 27.
61. Green, op. cit., p. 79.
62. Ibid.

63. Duffy and Goodgame, op. cit., pp. 44-45. For the fractured syntax see especially Maureen Dowd, 'The Language Thing', *New York Times Magazine*, 29 July 1990, pp. 32 and 48.
64. Green, op. cit., p. 16.
65. Green, op. cit., pp. 26–27.
66. Duffy and Goodgame, op. cit., p. 46.

CHAPTER 3 ORGANIZING THE PRESIDENCY

1. Richard Neustadt, *Presidential Power and the Modern Presidents* (New York: Free Press, 1990), p. xx.
2. John Ehrlichman, *Witness to Power* (New York: Pocket Books, 1982).
3. John Hart, *The Presidential Branch* (New York: Pergamon Press, 1987), p. 125.
4. Ibid.
5. Fred Greenstein, *The Hidden Hand Presidency: Eisenhower As Leader* (New York: Basic Books, 1982), p. 115.
6. James Pfiffner, *The Modern Presidency* (New York: St. Martin's Press, 1994), p. 116. See also Bradley Patterson, *The Ring of Power* (New York: Basic Books, 1988), p. 29.
7. According to Pfiffner, ibid., 'President Bush was one of the few modern presidents who did not promise cabinet government in campaigning for the Presidency.' One source did suggest that Bush was 'seeking to use the concept of Cabinet government to run his administration.' Gerald Boyd, 'On Bush's Team, Key Word in Assistant to the President Will Be Assistant', *New York Times*, 20 January 1989, Section A10, p 10.
8. Interview with David Bates, 17 November 1993. The words quoted are from an interview with Edith Holiday, 11 November 1993.
9. Ibid. Eliot Richardson and James Pfiffner noted that Bush would hear at Cabinet meetings 'what all recent Presidents have heard: a briefing on the budget, a Vice Presidential travelogue or a review of pending legislation. Big issues are seldom debated, much less decided.' 'Our Cabinet System Is a Charade', *New York Times*, 28 May, 1989, Section IV, p. 15.
10. Dan Quayle, *Standing Firm* (New York: Harper Collins, 1994), pp. 99–100.
11. Interview with Edith Holiday, op. cit.
12. Colin Campbell and Bert Rockman (eds), *The Bush Presidency: First Appraisals* (Chatham, New Jersey: Chatham House, 1991), p. 211 and Burt Solomon, 'In Bush's Image', *National Journal*, 7 July 1990, p. 1642.
13. Pfiffner, *The Modern Presidency*, op. cit., p. 116.
14. James Pfiffner, 'Establishing the Bush Presidency', *Public Administration Review*, January/Febuary 1990, pp. 64–72.
15. Bernard Weinraub, 'White House: The President has a Cabinet that is (a) runaway (b) powerful. (Choose one.)', *New York Times*, 19 May 1989, p. A14.

16. David Hoffman and Ann Devroy, 'The Open Oval Office Door', *Washington Post National Weekly Edition*, 14–20 August 1989, pp. 6–7.

17. Burt Solomon 'When the Bush Cabinet Convenes . . . Its a Gathering of Presidential Pals', *National Journal*, 1 July 1989, No. 26, pp. 1704–1705. Also Solomon, 'In Bush's Image' op. cit., and Ann Reilly Dowd, 'How Bush Manages the Presidency', *Fortune* 27 August 1990, pp. 38–43.

18. The title of an article by Burt Solomon, *National Journal*, 10 June 1989, pp. 1402–1403.

19. Interview with Edward Rogers, 3 November 1993.

20. Interview with Edith Holiday, op. cit.

21. Ibid.

22. Interview with Andrew Card, 15 November 1993.

23. Interview with James Pinkerton, 8 November 1993.

24. *United States Government Manual* (Washington DC: US Government Printing Office, 1990). p. 83.

25. Patterson, op. cit., labels one of his chapters 'Crisis Management: Command Center at 1600 Pennsylvania Avenue'.

26. Interview with Nicholas Calio, 19 November 1993.

27. Interview with James Cicconi, 8 November 1993.

28. Patterson, op. cit., p. 85.

29. Lyn Ragsdale, *Presidential Politics* (Boston: Houghton Mifflin, 1993), p. 223.

30. 'Panetta goes in goal', *The Economist*, 2 July 1994, p. 44. For Rockman quotation see Juan Williams, 'John Sununu, The White House Chief of Gaffe', *Washington Post National Weekly Edition*, 2–8 December 1991, pp. 22–23. For other negative views of Sununu's tenure see Michael Duffy and Dan Goodgame, *Marching in Place* (New York: Simon & Schuster, 1992), Ch. 5, Pfiffner, *The Modern Presidency*, op. cit., Chapter 3, and 'The President's Chief of Staff: Lessons Learned', *Presidential Studies Quarterly*, Vol. XXIII, No. 1, 1993, pp. 77–102.

31. Peter Goldman, *The Quest for the Presidency: The 1988 Campaign* (New York: Simon & Schuster, 1989), pp. 258–262.

32. Kristin Clark Taylor, *The First to Speak* (New York: Doubleday, 1993), p. 190.

33. Kolb, op. cit., p. 183, and interview with John Keller, 18 November 1993.

34. Interview with C. Boyden Gray, 10 November 1993.

35. Interview with Andrew Card, 15 November 1993.

36. Interview with Nicholas Calio, 19 November 1993.

37. Interview with James Cicconi, op. cit.

38. At an early stage Sununu said rather revealingly to a journalist: 'The staff is beginning to realize that they don't have to prepare a 15 page memo for me. They can wander in and raise an issue and I can give them a decision by the President either at 4.45 or the next morning. You get rapid feedback.' Bernard Weinraub, 'Sununu, the Staff Chief, Is Learning the Ropes the Hard Way', *New York Times*, 6 February 1989, p. A12.

39. Interview with Roger Porter, 23 November 1993.

40. Maureen Dowd, 'The "Impossible" Happens to Bush: He is Isolated, Associates Say', *International Herald Tribune*, 30 October 990, p. 1.
41. David Hoffman and Ann Devroy, 'The White House Tough Guy', *Washington Post National Weekly Edition*, 5–11 Febuary 1990, pp. 6–7.
42. According to some sources Bush's original preference for the post was Frederic Malek, a former Nixon Administration official with a reputation for toughness. Ibid.
43. See p. 68 above.
44. Dan Goodgame, 'Bush's Big Bad Cop', *Time* (International Edition), 28 May 1990, p. 42.
45. For the lightning rod concept see Greenstein, op. cit., pp. 238–239.
46. Hoffman and Devroy, 'The White House Tough Guy', op. cit.
47. Interview with Constance Horner, 10 November 1993.
48. Williams, op. cit.
49. Interview with Ed Rogers, op. cit.
50. Interview with James Pinkerton, op. cit.
51. Hoffman and Devroy, 'The White House Tough Guy', op. cit.
52. Interview with Ed Rogers, op. cit.
53. Interviews with Bobbie Kilberg, 19 November 1993, and Clayton Yeutter, 22 March 1994.
54. Hoffman and Devroy, 'The White House Tough Guy', op. cit.
55. Eleanor Randolph, 'The Man Washington Loves to Hate', *The Washington Post National Weekly Edition*, 17–23 December 1990, pp. 6–7.
56. R.W. Apple, 'Emotions in Check, Intellect Not, Sununu Wins Reluctant Respect in Capital', *The New York Times*, 13 September 1989, p. A18.
57. Hoffman and Devroy, 'The White House Tough Guy', op. cit.
58. Randolph, op. cit.
59. Duffy and Goodgame, op. cit. p. 120.
60. Interview with Bobbie Kilberg, op. cit.
61. Interview with Ed Rogers, op. cit.
62. On the 'Air Sununu' matter see, for example, Edwin Yoder Jr., 'Puritan in Babylon', *The Washington Post National Weekly Edition*, 29 April–5 May 1991, p. 28.
63. Burt Solomon, 'George Bush's Congressional Crew Has an Oar or Two Out of Sync', *National Journal*, 24 June 1989, pp. 1650–1657.
64. Boyd, op. cit.
65. Solomon, 'George Bush's Congressional Crew . . .' , op. cit.
66. Bernard Weinraub, 'White House Staff Makes Series of Tactical Errors', *New York Times*, 1 March 1989, IV, p. 4.
67. Calio interview, op. cit.
68. Sununu made the comment to a Conservative Leadership Conference meeting in Washington on 9 November 1990. Duffy and Goodgame, op. cit., p. 82.
69. See p. 34 above.
70. Interview with Nicholas Calio, op. cit.
71. Interview with David Demarest, 12 November 1993.
72. See Patterson, op. cit., p. 87 and *passim*.
73. Interview with David Demarest, op. cit.

74.   See, for example, John Podhoretz, *Hell of a Ride: Backstage at the White House Follies 1989–1993* (New York: Simon & Schuster, 1993), pp. 81–82 and Charles Kolb, *White House Daze: The Unmaking of Domestic Policy in the Bush Years* (New York: The Free Press, 1994), p. 5.

75.   Interview with David Demarest, op. cit.

76.   See Patterson, op. cit., pp. 209–210.

77.   Interview with Bobbie Kilberg, op. cit.

78.   Podhoretz, op. cit. p. 94.

79.   Interview with Bobbie Kilberg, op. cit.

80.   On 8 August 1991 the paid staff of the Office of Public Liaison was 16, eleven of whom were women. Source White House document kindly provided by Bobbie Kilberg in the author's possession.

81.   Interview with Bobbie Kilberg, op. cit.

82.   For example, interviews with Edie Holiday, Clayton Yeutter and Betsy Anderson, all op. cit.

83.   Interview with Bobbie Kilberg, op. cit.

84.   Quoted in Bernard Weinraub, 'How the President lost his tongue, or, the Bush speechwriters leave a mess', *New York Times*, 7 April 1989, p. A14.

85.   Interview with Clayton Yeutter, op. cit.

86.   David Broder described Skinner as 'one of the best people President Bush has brought to Washington – an energetic, intelligent, politically skillful manager committed to doing a job, not just filling an office.' 'The Man, the Plan, the Pothole', *The Washington Post National Weekly Edition*, 19–25 March 1990, p. 4.

87.   Interview with Nicholas Calio, op. cit.

88.   Interview with Bobbie Kilberg, op. cit.

89.   Interview with John Keller, op. cit.

90.   Interview with Edith Holiday, op. cit.

91.   Interview 3.5.

92.   Don Phillips and Bob Woodward, 'An Ambitious Pragmatist Takes Over', *The Washington Post National Weekly Edition*, 9–15 December 1991, p. 9.

93.   Marjorie Williams, 'An Eagle Scout Gets His Wings Clipped', *The Washington Post National Weekly Edition*, 15–21 June 1992, pp. 6-9.

94.   Interview 3.5.

CHAPTER 4 A GUARDIAN'S AGENDA

1.   Stephen Hess, *Organizing the Presidency*, 2nd edn. (Washington DC: The Brookings Institution, 1988), p. 55.

2.   David Hoffman, 'One Hundred Days of Solicitude', *Washington Post National Weekly Edition*, 8–14 May 1989, p. 13.

3.   Acceptance speech, Republican Convention, New Orleans, 1988.

4.   Ibid.

5.   Marshall Ingwersen, 'Bush Lags at Setting Agenda!', *Christian Science Monitor*, 25–31 May 1989 pp. 1–2.

6. David Hoffman, 'Setting the Pace for the Bush Presidency', *Washington Post National Weekly Edition*, 23–29 January 1989, p. 11.

7. Roger Davidson and Walter Oleszek, *Congress and Its Members*, 4th edn. (Washington DC: Congressional Quarterly Press, 1994), p. 457.

8. Acceptance speech.

9. *Roosevelt: The Lion and the Fox* (New York: Harcourt Brace and World, 1957), p. 186.

10. *Congress and the Nation*, Vol. VIII, 1989–1992 (Washington DC: Congressional Quarterly Press, 1993), p. 339.

11. George Church, 'Is This Goodbye?', *Time* (International edition), 6 March 1989, pp. 10–14.

12. Ibid.

13. *Congress and the Nation*, op. cit., p. 340.

14. Charles O. Jones, *The Presidency In A Separated System* (Washington DC: The Brookings Institution, 1994), p. 11.

15. Gerald Boyd, 'Bush Aides Play Him Up As 100-Day Mark Nears', New York Times, 22 April 1989, p. 1.

16. See, for example, Chuck Alston, 'Rules of Political Navigation Altered by Bush Centrism, *Congressional Quarterly Weekly Report*, 6 May 1989, pp. 1017–1019.

17. Editorial, 'President Bush's Hundred Days', *New York Times*, 23 April 1989, Section V, p. 22.

18. Janet Hook, 'Bush Inspired Frail Support For First-Year President', *Congressional Quarterly Weekly Report*, 30 December 1989, pp. 3540–3545. Helen Dewar and Tom Kenworthy, 'Putting Off Till Tomorrow What They Could Have Done Today', *Washington Post National Weekly Edition*, 4–10 December 1989, p. 13.

19. 'The Can't Do Government', *Time,* (International Edition) 23 October 1989, p. 22–25.

20. Interviews with Edie Holiday, C. Boyden Gray, Katharine Super, Roger Porter, Nicholas Calio, et al.

21. *Congress and the Nation*, op. cit., p. 474.

22. Michael Weisskopf, 'Environmental Impact', *Washington Post National Edition*, 17–23 October 1988.

23. Editorial, 'The President's Clean Air Plan', *Washington Post National Weekly Edition*, 19–25 June 1989, p.26.

24. *Congressional Quarterly Almanac, 1990* (Washington DC: Congressional Quarterly Press, 1991), p. 232.

25. Ibid., pp. 236–237.

26. Ibid., pp. 242–243 and 279.

27. Ibid. Interview with C. Boyden Gray, 10 November 1993.

28. Ibid.

29. Michael Duffy and Dan Goodgame, *Marching in Place: The Status Quo Presidency of George Bush* (New York: Simon & Schuster, 1992), p. 88.

30. *Congressional Quarterly Almanac*, op. cit., p. 278.

31. Interview with Nicholas Calio, 19 November 1993.

32. 'Domestic Policy: Divided Government and Cooperative Presidential Leadership' in Colin Campbell and Bert Rockman, *The Bush Presidency: First Appraisals* (Chatham, NJ: Chatham House, 1991), pp. 69–91.

33. Michael Barone and Grant Ujifusa, *The Almanac of American Politics 1994* (Washington DC: National Journal, 1993), p. 584.
34. *Congressional Quarterly Almanac*, op. cit., p. 448.
35. Stephen Percy, *Disability, Civil Rights and Public Policy* (Tuscaloosa: University of Alabama Press, 1992) p. xi.
36. 'The Disabilities Act', *CQ Researcher*, 27 December 1991, Vol. I, No.32 pp. 993–1016.
37. *Congressional Quarterly Almanac*, op. cit., p. 447.
38. Jonathan Rauch, 'The Regulatory President', *National Journal*, 30 November 1991, Vol. XXIII, pp. 2902–2906.
39. Charles Kolb, *White House Daze: The Unmaking of Domestic Policy in the Bush Years* (New York: The Free Press, 1994), p. 70.
40. Interviews with C. Boyden Gray, 10 November 1993 and 21 March 1994.
41. Percy, op. cit., p. 8.
42. 'The Disabilities Act', op. cit.
43. Interview with C. Boyden Gray, 21 March 1994.
44. Ibid.
45. Interview with C. Boyden Gray, 30 March 1994.
46. Interview with C. Boyden Gray, 21 March 1994.
47. William Kerr Muir, *The Bully Pulpit: The Presidential Leadership of Ronald Reagan* (San Francisco: Institute for Contemporary Studies, 1992), pp. 61–63.
48. Duffy and Goodgame, op. cit., pp. 209–12.
49. Remarks at a Celebration of the Points of Light, The White House, 14 January 1993, in *Public Papers of the Presidents of the United States, 1992–1993* (Washington DC: Government Printing Office, 1993), Book II, p. 2251.
50. See Peggy Noonan, *What I Saw at the Revolution* (New York: Ivy Books, 1990), Chapter 17.
51. Acceptance speech, 1988 Republican Convention.
52. Inaugural address.
53. Remarks in New York City, 22 June 1989, in *Public Papers of the Presidents of the United States, 1989* (Washington DC: Government Printing Office, 1990), Book I, p. 785.
54. '"Thousand Points" as a Cottage Industry', *The New York Times*, 29 May 1991 p. 1.
55. Interview with Gregg Petersmeyer, 16 November 1993.
56. Ibid.
57. Ibid.
58. *The Points of Light Movement: The President's Report to the Nation*, January 1993, in the author's possession, p. 7.
59. Ibid., p. 9.
60. Ibid., p. 48.
61. Ibid., p. 11.
62. Interview.
63. *The Points of Light Movement*, op. cit., pp. 10–11.
64. Statement on Signing the National and Community Service Act of 1990, 16 November 1990 in *Public Papers of the Presidents of the United*

States, 1990 (Washington DC: Government Printing Office, 1991), Book II, p. 1613.

65. *The Points of Light Movement,* op. cit., p. 3.
66. Interview with Gregg Petersmeyer, op. cit.
67. J. Pederzane, 'As Society's Need Increases, So Does Volunteerism', *New York Times,* 6 January 1992, p. A1.
68. Ibid.
69. Pierre Kim, 'From Carter to Reagan to Bush', *Policy Review,* Winter 1993, pp. 18–19.
70. Rauch, op. cit.

CHAPTER 5 'PREVENTING BAD LAWS'

1. *Congressional Quarterly Almanac,1992* (Washington DC: Congressional Quarterly Press, 1993), p. 9B.
2. Ibid., p. 3B.
3. Ibid., p. 4B.
4. See especially George Edwards, 'Measuring Presidential Success in Congress: Alternative Approaches', *Journal of Politics,* Vol. 47, 1985, pp. 667–685.
5. Janet Hook, 'Bush Inspired Frail Support For First Year President', *Congressional Quarterly Weekly Report,* 30 December 1989, pp. 3540–3545.
6. Anthony King, 'A Mile and a Half Is a Long Way', in Anthony King, *Both Ends of the Avenue: The Presidency, the Executive Branch and Congress in the 1980s* (Washington DC: American Enterprise Institute, 1983), pp. 246–273.
7. Edwards, op. cit.
8. *Congressional Quarterly Almanac,* op. cit., p. 5B.
9. Richard Rose, *The Postmodern President,* 2nd edn (Chatham, NJ: Chatham House, 1991), p. 313.
10. 'Presidential Vetoes, 1989–1992', *Congress and the Nation, Vol. VIII, 1989–1992* (Washington DC: Congressional Quarterly Press, 1993), pp. 1181–1182.
11. Richard Watson, *Presidential Vetoes and Public Policy* (Lawrence: University of Kansas Press, 1993), p. 146.
12. Interview with Nicholas Calio, 19 November 1993.
13. Federalist Papers, Number 73, *The Federalist Papers* (New York: New American Library, 1961), pp. 443 and 446.
14. Max Farrand (ed.), *The Records of the Federal Convention of 1787* (New Haven, Conn.: Yale University Press, 1937), Vol. II, p. 76.
15. Ibid., p. 78.
16. Interview with Roger Porter, 23 November 1993.
17. Kenneth Walsh, 'Bush's Veto Strategy', *U.S. News and World Report,* 2 July 1990, pp. 18-20.
18. Robert Spitzer, *The Presidential Veto: Touchstone of the American Presidency* (Albany: State University of New York Press, 1988), p. 85.
19. Paul Light, *The President's Agenda* (Baltimore, Md.: Johns Hopkins University Press, 1982), p. 113.

20. Janet Hook, 'President's Mastery of Veto Perplexes Hill Democrats', *Congressional Quarterly Weekly Report*, 27 July 1991, pp. 2041–2045.

21. Michael Duffy and Dan Goodgame, *Marching in Place: The Status Quo Presidency of George Bush* (New York: Simon & Schuster, 1992), p. 78.

22. Terry Eastland, *Energy in the Executive: The Case for the Strong Presidency* (New York: The Free Press, 1992), p. 73.

23. David Stockman, *The Triumph of Politics* (New York: Harper & Row, 1986), pp. 234, also 157 and 337.

24. Hook, 'President's Mastery . . .' op. cit.

25. Ibid.

26. Eastland, op. cit., p. 71, discusses and rejects Charles Black's insistence that the veto should be used only rarely and not as a means of policy control.

27. Federalist Papers, Number 73, op. cit., p. 443.

28. Farrand, op. cit., Vol. II, p. 74.

29. *Congress and the Nation*, op. cit., p. 355.

30. US House of Representatives, 101st Congress, *Congress and Foreign Policy, 1989* (Washington DC: US Government Printing Office, 1990), p. 9.

31. US House of Representatives, 101st *Congress, Congress and Foreign Policy, 1990* (Washington DC: US Government Printing Office, 1991), pp. 17–19.

32. *Congress and the Nation*, op. cit., pp. 1181–1182.

33. Ibid., p. 598.

34. See Spitzer, op. cit., on the value of veto threats, pp. 100–103.

35. Charles Kolb, *White House Daze; The Unmaking of Domestic Policy in the Bush Years* (New York: The Free Press, 1993), p. 11.

36. Interview with Nicholas Calio, op. cit.

37. Interview with David Demarest, 12 November 1993.

38. Interview with James Cicconi, 8 November 1993.

39. Hook, 'President's Mastery . . . , op. cit.

40. *Congress and the Nation*, op. cit., pp. 1181–1182.

41. Robert Spitzer, 'Presidential Prerogative Power: The Case of the Bush Administration and Legislative Power', *PS: Political Science and Politics*, March 1991, pp. 38–42.

42. *Congress and the Nation*, op. cit., p. 721.

43. Hook, 'President's Mastery . . op. cit.

44. Walsh, op. cit.

45. Interview with Charles Kolb, 29 March 1994.

46. Stockman, op. cit., p. 371

47. 'Excerpts From Interview With Bush on First Term and Future', *New York Times*, 25 June 1992, p. A24.

48. Hook, 'President's Mastery . . . , op. cit.

49. Duffy and Goodgame, op. cit., pp. 79–80.

50. Edwards, op. cit.

51. Watson, op. cit.

52. Ibid., pp. 167–168, Spitzer, op. cit., p. 139; and Louis Fisher, *Constitutional Conflicts Between Congress and the President* (Princeton, NJ: Princeton University Press, 1985), pp. 154–162.

53. Charles Tiefer, *The Semi-Sovereign Presidency: The Bush Administration's Strategy For Governing Without Congress*, (Boulder, Colo.: Westview Press, 1994), p. xi.

54. Statement on signing the National and Community Service Act of 1990, 16 November 1990 in *Public Papers of the Presidents of the United States, 1990* (Washington DC: US Goverment Printing Office, 1991) Book II, p. 1613.

55. US House of Representatives, 102nd Congress, *Congress and Foreign Policy, 1991* (Washington DC: US Government Printing Office, 1992), p. 17.

56. See Tiefer, op. cit., pp. 153–158.

57. Ibid., *passim*.

58. Theodore Sorensen, *Decision-Making in the White House* (New York: Columbia University Press, 1963), pp. 83–84.

59. See Federalist Papers, Number 73.

60. Thomas Geoghegan, 'Bust the Filibuster', *Washington Post National Weekly Edition*, 12–18 September 1994, p. 25.

61. See Charles O. Jones, The Presidency in a Separated System (Washington DC: Brookings, 1994).

62. Farrand, op cit. ,Vol II, pp. 74 and 76.

63. Federalist Papers, Number 73, p. 442.

64. Dean Acheson, *Present at the Creation* (New York: W.W. Norton, 1987), p. 415.

65. Sorenson, op. cit., p. 84.

66. The phrase quoted is from Barbara Sinclair, 'Governing Unheroically (and Sometimes Unappetizingly): Bush and the 101st Congress', in Colin Campbell and Bert Rockman (eds), *The Bush Presidency: First Appraisals* (Chatham, NJ: Chatham House, 1991).

67. See Eastland, op. cit., *passim*, for a conservative commentator's criticisms of Reagan's failure to make good use of the veto.

CHAPTER 6 THE 1990 BUDGET CRISIS

1. Bob Woodward, 'Origin of the Tax Pledge; In '88, Bush Camp Was Split on "Read My Lips" Vow', *Washington Post*, 4 October 1992, pp. A1, A22.

2. Bob Woodward, 'Primary Heat Turned Deal Into a "Mistake"; Disappointed Darman Offered to Resign', *Washington Post*, 6 October 1992, pp. A1, A14–A15.

3. Woodward, 'Origin of the Tax Pledge . . . op. cit.

4. Charles Kolb, *White House Daze: The Unmaking of Domestic Policy in the Bush Years* (New York: The Free Press, 1994), p. 57.

5. Peggy Noonan, *What I Saw at the Revolution* (New York: Ivy Books, 1990), p. 319.

6. Bob Woodward, 'No-Tax Vow Scuttled Anti-Deficit Mission', *Washington Post*, 5 October 1992, pp. A1, A8–A9.

7. Interview with James Cicconi, 8 November 1993.

8. Kolb, op. cit., p. 56.

9. Interview with James Pinkerton, 8 November 1993.
10. Interviews with David Demarest., 12 November 1993, and C. Boyden Gray, 10 November 1993.
11. Interview with Andrew Card, 15 November 1993.
12. Interview with Clayton Yeutter, 22 March 1994.
13. Interview with Bobbie Kilberg, 19 November 1993. For Darman's influence over both Sununu and Bush see Dan Quayle, *Standing Firm* (New York: Harper Collins, 1994) p. 107.
14. Interview with Bobbie Kilberg, op. cit.
15. Burt Solomon, 'In Bush's Image', *National Journal*, 7 July 1990, pp. 1642–1647.
16. George Church, 'Ignore My Lips', *Time* (International Edition), 21 May 1990, pp. 44–46.
17. Woodward, 'Primary Heat . . . op. cit.
18. *New York Times*, 27 June 1990, Section B, p. 6.
19. *Congress and the Nation*, Vol. VIII, 1989–1992 (Washington DC: Congressional Quarterly Press, 1993), p. 55.
20. Woodward, 'Primary Heat . . . op. cit.
21. *New York Times*, 3 October 1990, Section A, p. 1.
22. See articles by George Hager, Pamela Fessler, John Cranford and Janet Hook, *Congressional Quarterly Weekly Report*, 6 October 1990, pp. 3189–3195.
23. John Yang and Steven Mufson, 'The End of Self-Delusion: Congress makes a modest beginning at paring the deficit', *Washington Post National Weekly Edition* 5–11 November 1990, pp. 6–7.
24. James Pfiffner, 'The President and the Postreform Congress', in Roger Davidson (ed.), *The Postreform Congress* (New York: St. Martin's Press, 1992).
25. *Congress and the Nation*, op. cit., pp. 58–59.
26. Ibid., p. 57.
27. See, for example, Richard Lacayo, 'Dose of Reality', *Time* (International edition), 5 November 1990, pp. 30–32 and Yang and Mufson op. cit.
28. Janet Hook, 'Budget Ordeal Poses Question: Why Can't Congress Be Led?' *Congressional Quarterly Weekly Report*, 20 October 1990, pp. 3471–3473.
29. John Yang, 'Is George Bush Casting Fiscal Stones From A Glass House', *Washington Post National Weekly Edition*, 27 August–2 September 1990, p. 13.
30. David Broder, 'Take It From Those Who Know Best: Congress is a Wreck', *Washington Post National Weekly Edition*, 14–20 January 1991, p. 24.
31. See, for example, Thomas Mann and Norman Ornstein (eds) *The New Congress* (Washington DC: American Enterprise Institute, 1981); Hedrick Smith, *The Power Game* (New York: Random House, 1988); and Davidson, op. cit.
32. Broder, op. cit.
33. Hook, op. cit.
34. Janet Hook, 'Anatomy of a Budget Showdown: The Limits of Leaders' Clout', *Congressional Quarterly Weekly Report*, 6 October 1990,

pp. 3189–3191.
35. As quoted in *Congressional Quarterly Weekly Report*, 29 September 1990, p. 3096.
36. Interview with Edith Holiday, 17 November 1993.
37. Interview with David Demarest, 12 November 1993.
38. Dan Goodgame, 'Read My Hips', *Time* (International Edition) 22 October 1990, pp. 54–56.
39. Interview with John Keller, 18 November 1993.
40. Interview with Clayton Yeutter, op. cit..
41. Interview with Andrew Card, op. cit.
42. Interview with Constance Horner, 10 November 1993.
43. Kolb, op. cit., p. 95.
44. Interview with William Kristol, 23 March 1994.
45. Interview with James Pinkerton, 8 November 1993.
46. Interview with David Demarest, op. cit.
47. Interview with James Cicconi, op. cit.
48. Interview with John Keller, op. cit.
49. Interview with Nicholas Calio, 19 November 1993.
50. Ibid.
51. Interview 3.5.
52. As quoted in *Congressional Quarterly Weekly Report*, 13 October 1990, p. 3447.
53. As quoted in Terry Eastland, *Energy in the Executive* (New York: The Free Press, 1992), pp. 56–57.
54. *Congressional Quarterly Weekly Report*, 29 September 1990, p. 3094.
55. Ibid. 20 October 1990, p. 3472.
56. Bill Whalen, 'For Republicans, a House Divided', *Insight*, 12 November 1990, pp. 8–13.
57. Laurence Barrett, '1,000 Points of Spite', *Time* (International Edition), 15 October 1990, p. 24.
58. Whalen, op. cit.
59. *Congressional Quarterly Weekly Report*, 6 October 1990, p. 3189.
60. Interview with Bobbie Kilberg, op. cit.
61. Interview with James Cicconi, op. cit.
62. Interview with Edith Holiday, op. cit.
63. Interview with Bobbie Kilberg, op. cit.
64. Ibid. See also Goodgame, op. cit.
65. Interview with Bobbie Kilberg, op. cit.
66. Dan Balz and Ann Devroy, 'Sununu and Darman Give the Hill the Screaming Meanies', *Washington Post National Weekly Edition*, 15–20 October 1990, pp. 7–8.
67. See, for example, interviews with Bobbie Kilberg and Edie Holiday, both op. cit. Also Quayle, op. cit., pp. 94–95.
68. Interview 3.5.
69. Bert Rockman, 'The Leadership Style of George Bush', in Colin Campbell and Bert Rockman, *The Bush Presidency: First Appraisals* (Chatham, NJ: Chatham House, 1991), p. 18.
70. Interview with James Cicconi, op. cit.
71. *Congress and the Nation*, op. cit., p. 1189.

72. As reported in *Congressional Quarterly Weekly Report*, 13 October 1990, p. 3447.

73. George Hager, 'Parties Angle For Advantage As White House Falters', *Congressional Quarterly Weekly Report*, 13 October 1990, pp. 3389–3398.

74. Goodgame, op. cit.

75. Hager, op. cit.

76. Ibid.

77. Interview with Edie Holiday, op. cit.

78. Stuart Eizenstat, 'What Bush Should Do About Taxes', *Washington Post National Weekly Edition*, 25 June–1 July 1990, p. 29.

79. Hook, op. cit.

80. Interviews. Also interviews with Nicholas Calio, Roger Porter and Clayton Yeutter.

81. Smith, op. cit., p. 476.

82. *Miller Center Report*, Vol. 6, No. 4, Winter 1990.

83. As quoted in Whalen, op. cit.

84. Quayle, op. cit., p. 203.

85. Interviews with Bobbie Kilberg.

86. Kolb, op. cit., p. 95.

87. Interview with Nicholas Calio, op. cit., and Quayle, op. cit, p.202.

88. Goodgame, op. cit.

89. Richard Neustadt, *Presidential Power and the Modern Presidents* (New York: The Free Press, 1990), p. 50.

90. Thomas Edsall, 'The Gridlock of Government', *Washington Post National Weekly Edition*, 15–21 October 1990, p. 6.

91. Interviews.

92. Martin Walker and Simon Tisdall, 'Bush Says Sorry for Tax U turn', *Guardian* (London) 4 March 1992, p. 1.

93. Quoted in Dan Balz, 'Hussein Made Him Break the Tax Pledge – Yeah, That's It', *Washington Post National Weekly Edition*, 3–9 August 1992, p. 15. *Note*: Balz effectively disposes of the claim raised, more than once, by Vice President Quayle that the tax increase in 1990 was forced upon the President by the crisis created by the Iraqi invasion of Kuwait. As Balz points out, and Quayle concedes in his memoirs, Bush broke the tax pledge well before the invasion took place. See Quayle, op. cit., pp. 195–196.

94. Interview 3.5.

95. Interviews.

96. Michael Nelson (ed.), *The Elections of 1992* (Washington DC: CQ Press, 1993) p. 81. *Note:* On the other hand, as James Pfiffner pointed out to me without the budget deal the deficit would have been larger and the health of the economy probably even worse than it was in fact.

CHAPTER 7 GUARDIANSHIP AND FOREIGN POLICY

1. Richard Rose, *The Postmodern President*, 2nd edn (Chatham, NJ: Chatham House, 1991), p. 308.

2. K. Thompson (ed.), *Presidential Transitions: The Reagan to Bush Experience* (Lanham, MD: University Press of America, 1993), p. 19.

3. Michael Beschloss and Strobe Talbott, *At the Highest Levels: The Inside Story of the End of the Cold War* (Boston: Little Brown, 1993), pp. 7071.

4. 13 January 1993, Official Text, USIS, US Embassy, London.

5. David Hoffman, 'The Politics of Timidity', *Washington Post National Weekly Edition*, 23–29 October 1989, p. 67.

6. John Newhouse, 'Profiles: The Tactician', *New Yorker*, 7 May 1990, pp. 5082.

7. Henry Allen, 'The Quintessential Establishmentarian', *Washington Post National Weekly Edition*, 9–15 January 1989.

8. The first quotation is from John Yang, 'Who is George Bush?', *Washington Post National Weekly Edition*, 24 Febuary–1 March 1991, pp. 910; the second quotation is from Newhouse, op. cit.

9. Don Oberdorfer, 'It Helps to Have a Buddy in the White House', *Washington Post National Weekly Edition*, 14–20 November 1988, p. 15.

10. Christopher Ogden, 'Vision Problems at State . . . *Time* (International Edition), 25 September 1989 p. 36.

11. Richard Lacayo, *Time* (International Edition, 9) March 1992 pp. 34–35.

12. George Bush, *Looking Forward* (London: The Bodley Head, 1987), p. 174. See also Bradley Patterson, *The Ring of Power* (New York: Basic Books, 1988), Chapter 7, for the various functions of the Assistant to the President for National Security Affairs.

13. Tower Commission Report (New York: Bantam Books, 1987).

14. Interview with Brent Scowcroft, 28 March 1994.

15. Christopher Madison, 'No Sharp Elbows', *National Journal*, 26 May 1990, pp. 1277–1281, and Andrew Rosenthal, 'National Security Adviser Redefines the Role, Drawing Barrage of Criticism', *New York Times*, 3 November 1989 p. A16.

16. Hoffman, op. cit.

17. Roger Porter, *Presidential Decision Making: The Economic Policy Board* (New York: Cambridge University Press, 1980), p. 216.

18. Interview with Richard Haass, 24 March 1994.

19. Ogden, op. cit.

20. Newhouse, op. cit.

21. Ogden, op. cit.

22. David Hoffman, 'James Baker's Determination To Put the New World in Order,' *Washington Post National Weekly Edition*, 24–30 August 1992, p. 31.

23. US House of Representatives, 101st Congress, *Congress and Foreign Policy 1989* (Washington DC: Government Printing Office, 1990), p. 58.

24. Don Oberdorfer, 'Behind a Bipartisan Announcement, a Long Trail of Secret Meetings', *Washington Post National Weekly Edition*, 3–9 April 1989, p. 14.

25. Rochelle Stanfield, 'Cutting Deals', *National Journal*, 8 April 1989 p. 889.

26. Robert Pear, 'Unease Is Voiced On Contra Accord', *New York Times*, 26 March 1989, p. 1.

27. Jeremy Rabkin, 'At the President's Side: The Role of the White House Counsel in Constitutional Policy', *Law and Contemporary Problems*, Vol. 56, No. 4, Autumn 1993, pp. 63–98.

28. Bernard Weinraub, 'White House Rebukes Counsel on Pact', *New York Times*, 28 March 1989, p. A6.

29. Pear, op. cit.

30. *Congress and Foreign Policy 1989*, op. cit., p. 76.

31. Hoffman, 'The Politics of Timidity' . . . op. cit.

32. Bob Woodward, *The Commanders* (New York: Simon & Schuster, 1991), p. 164.

33. *Congress and Foreign Policy 1989*, op. cit., p. 86.

34. Bush's already high standing in the polls – 68 per cent approval according to Gallup – rose to 80 per cent after the invasion and the surrender of Noriega. Paul Brace and Barbara Hinckley, *Follow the Leader: Opinion Polls and the Modern Presidents* (New York: Basic Books, 1992), p. 110.

35. *Congress and Foreign Policy 1989*, op. cit., p. 85.

36. George McGovern, 'A Betrayal of American Principles', *Washington Post National Weekly Edition*,22–28 January 1990, p. 29.

37. David Hoffman and Bob Woodward, 'This Guy Is Not Going to Lay Off', *Washington Post National Weekly Edition*, 25–31 December 1989, p. 6.

38. *Congress and Foreign Policy 1989*, op. cit., p. 86.

39. For example, Lyndon Johnson's massive escalation in Vietnam and Nixon's incursion into Cambodia.

40. David Hoffman, 'The President's New Stand Towards Gorbachev: No More Wait and See', *Washington Post National Weekly Edition*, 19–25 March 1990, p. 11.

41. Lou Cannon, 'Reagan Is Concerned About Bush's Indecision', *Washington Post National Weekly Edition*, 15–21 May 1989, p. 28.

42. Don Oberdorfer, *The Turn: From the Cold War to a New Era* (New York: Simon & Schuster, 1992), p. 346.

43. Editorial, *Christian Science Monitor*, 'What's Bush's Vision?', 11–17 May 1989, p. 20.

44. Interview with Brent Scowcroft, op. cit.

45. Beschloss and Talbott, op. cit., p. 86.

46. Ibid., p. 92.

47. Oberdorfer, *The Turn* . . ., op. cit., p. 364, and Beschloss and Talbott, op. cit., p. 135.

48. Ibid.

49. Interview with Andrew Card, 15 November 1993.

50. Oberdorfer, The Turn . . ., op. cit., p. 367.

51. Interview with Brent Scowcroft, op. cit.

52. Beschloss and Talbott, op. cit., p. 163–164.

53. Ibid., p. 165.

54. Dan Quayle, Standing Firm (New York: Harper Collins, 1994) p. 175.

55. Interview with Brent Scowcroft, op. cit.

56. Beschloss and Talbott, op. cit. p. 205.

57. Kim Holmes, 'In Search of a Strategy', *Policy Review*, Winter 1991, pp. 72–75.
58. Interview with Brent Scowcroft, op. cit.
59. Interview with James Cicconi, 8 November 1993.
60. Interview with Brent Scowcroft, op. cit.
61. Interview with James Ciconni, op. cit.
62. See, for example, Michael Mandelbaum, 'The Bush Foreign Policy', *Foreign Affairs*, Spring 1991, Vol. 70 pp. 5–22.

CHAPTER 8 THE WAR IN THE GULF

1. *The Gulf Crisis: A Chronology, July 1990–July 1991*, USIS, US Embassy, London, 1991, p. 2. Subsequently cited as Chronology.
2. Dilop Hiro, *Desert Shield to Desert Storm: The Second Gulf War* (London: Harper Collins, 1992), Appendix 1.
3. Bob Woodward, *The Commanders* (New York: Simon & Schuster, 1991), pp. 225 and 231.
4. *The Washington Version*, television documentary on the Gulf crisis decision-making process made by the American Enterprise Institute and the BBC, 1991. Commended to the author as 'a pretty good primary source' by one of those close to these events. Interview with Richard Haass, 24 March 1994.
5. *Chronology*, p. 3.
6. Woodward, op. cit., p. 285.
7. *Chronology*, pp. 15 and 18.
8. Ibid., p.21.
9. *Congress and the Nation*, Vol. VIII, 1989–1992 (Washington DC: Congressional Quarterly Press, 1993), pp. 309 and 1061.
10. Ibid., p. 315.
11. Dan Balz and Ann Devroy, 'Bush Became a Leader When It Mattered Most', *Washington Post National Weekly Edition*, 11–17 March 1991, p. 9. Dan Goodgame, 'What if we do nothing?', *Time* (International Edition) 7 January 1991, pp. 14–15.
12. For example, Jean Edward Smith, *George Bush's War* (New York: Henry Holt, 1992); Alex Roberto Hybel (foreword by James Rosenau), *Power Over Rationality: The Bush Administration and the Gulf Crisis* (Albany: State University of New York Press, 1993); Roger Hilsman, *George Bush Versus Saddam Hussein* (Novato, CA: Presidio Press, 1992); James Pfiffner, 'Presidential Policy-Making and the Gulf War', in Marcia Lynn Whicker, James Pffifner and Raymond Moore, *The Presidency and the Persian Gulf War* (Westport, Conn.: Praeger, 1993).
13. Ibid. p. 20.
14. Interview with Brent Scowcroft, 28 March 1994.
15. Interview 3.8.
16. 'In DOD We Trust', *New Republic*, 17 June 1991, pp. 29–35.
17. See especially Smith, op. cit., Chapter 2.
18. Interview with Brent Scowcroft, op. cit.
19. Smith, op. cit., p. 68. See also Hilsman, op. cit., p. 45.

20. *Washington Version*, op. cit.
21. Interview with Richard Haass.
22. *Washington Version*, op. cit.
23. Ibid.
24. Ibid.
25. Margaret Thatcher, *The Downing Street Years* (London: Harper Collins, 1993), p. 821.
26. *Washington Version*, op. cit.
27. See, for example, Smith and Hilsman, both op. cit. Also Stephen Graubard, Mr Bush's War: Adventures in the Politics of Illusion (New York: I.B. Tauris, 1992).
28. Interview with Brent Scowcroft, op. cit.
29. Ibid.
30. Woodward, op. cit., p. 234.
31. Ibid., p. 261.
32. Interview with Brent Scowcroft, op. cit.
33. Interview with Richard Haass.
34. The first source is Hybel, op. cit., p. 8; the second is Smith, op. cit., p. 255.
35. Interview with Brent Scowcroft, op. cit.
36. Smith, Hybel and Pfiffner, all op. cit. Also Elizabeth Drew, 'Letter From Washington', *New Yorker*, 4 Febuary 1991, pp. 82–90.
37. Interview with Brent Scowcroft, op. cit.
38. Interview with Richard Haass.
39. Alexander George, 'The Case for Multiple Advocacy in Making Foreign Policy', *American Political Science Review*, Vol. 66, September 1972, pp. 751–785. Irving Janis, *Victims of Groupthink* (Boston: Houghton Mifflin, 1972).
40. Interview with Richard Haass.
41. See Pfiffner and Drew, both op. cit.
42. Interview with Brent Scowcroft, op. cit.
43. For example, Hybel, op. cit., p. 8.
44. Interview with Brent Scowcroft, op. cit.
45. *Washington Version*, op. cit.
46. Ibid.
47. Interviews with Brent Scowcroft, op. cit., and Richard Haass.
48. Smith, op. cit., p. 161.
49. See Terry Eastland, *Energy in the Executive* (New York: The Free Press, 1992), p. 133.
50. Jim Hoagland, 'Wanted: A Clear Statement Of Purpose', *Washington Post National Weekly Edition*, 12–18 November 1990, p. 23.
51. Tom Mathews, 'The Road to War', *Newsweek*, 28 January 1991, p. 34–45.
52. Interview with Richard Haass.
53. David Roth, *Sacred Honor: Colin Powell* (New York: Harper Collins, 1993), p. 262.
54. Ibid., p. 263.
55. For some of the objections to the constitutionality of this position see especially Louis Fisher, 'The Power of Commander in Chief', in

Whicker, Pfiffner and Moore, op. cit. Also Michael Glennon, 'The Gulf War and the Constitution', *Foreign Affairs*, Spring 1991, Vol. 70, pp. 84–101.

56. Matthews, op. cit.
57. Interview with Brent Scowcroft, op. cit.
58. *Standing Firm*, op. cit., p. 227.
59. Interview with Boyden Gray, 21 March 1994.
60. *Washington Version*, op. cit.
61. *Congress and the Nation*, op. cit., p. 310.
62. US House of Representatives, 102nd Congress, *Congress and Foreign Policy 1991* (Washington DC: US Government Printing Office, 1992), p. 17.
63. Max Farrand (ed.), *The Records of the Federal Convention of 1787* (New Haven, Conn.: Yale University Press, 1937), Volume II, p. 318.
64. Hilsman, op. cit., p. 48. For other Administration justifications of the US intervention see Colin Campbell and Bert Rockman (eds) *The Bush Presidency: First Appraisals* (Chatham, NJ: Chatham House, 1991), p. 117.
65. Richard Marin, 'George Bush Could Set A Record', *Washington Post National Weekly Edition*, 16–22 March 1990, p. 37.
66. Roth, op. cit., p. 231.
67. On Baker's role see David Hoffman, 'Jim Baker: Global Dealmaker', *Washington Post National Weekly Edition*, 19–25 November 1990, pp. 6–7.
68. According to one source between 2 August 1990 and Febuary 1991 the President made 231 phone calls to other heads of state. David Lauter and James Gerstenzag, 'The Clutch President', *Los Angeles Times Magazine*, 14 July 1991, p. 12.
69. Goodgame, op. cit.
70. George Bush, *Looking Forward* (London: The Bodley Head, 1988), p. 120.
71. Woodward, op. cit., p. 310.
72. *Chronology*, pp. 19 and 23.
73. Theodore Draper, 'The True History of the Gulf War', *New York Review of Books*, 30 January 1992, pp. 38–45.
74. Don Oberdorfer, 'The War No One Saw Coming', *Washington Post National Weekly Edition*, 18–24 March 1991, pp. 6–10.
75. Theodore Draper, 'The Gulf War Reconsidered', *New York Review of Books*, 16 January 1992, pp. 46–53.
76. Oberdorfer, 'The War No One ... op. cit.
77. Draper, 'The Gulf War ... op. cit.
78. For a robust response to the allegation that the Bush Administration 'coddled' Saddam Hussein see Brent Scowcroft, 'We Didn't "Coddle" Hussein', *Washington Post National Weekly Edition*, 19–25 October 1992, p. 29.
79. Terry Diebel, 'Bush's Foreign Policy: Mastery and Inaction', *Foreign Policy*, No. 84, Fall 1991, pp. 3–23.

CHAPTER 9 CONCLUSIONS

1. See, for example, George Bush, *Looking Forward* (London: The Bodley Head, 1988), p. 193.
2. Alan Brinkley, as quoted in Robert J. Samuelson, 'There's Good Reason To Like Ike,' *Washington Post National Weekly Edition*, 22–28 October 1990, p. 31.
3. R.W. Apple, 'In the Capital', *New York Times*, 29 March 1989, p. A16.
4. *Congress and the Nation*, Vol. VIII, 1989–1992 (Washington DC: Congressional Quarterly Press, 1993), pp. 218–219.
5. Michael Mandelbaum, 'The Bush Foreign Policy', *Foreign Policy*, Spring 1991, Vol. 70, pp. 5–22.
6. Michael Elliott, 'The Gipper vs the Evil Empire', *Washington Post National Weekly Edition*, 22–28 August 1994, p. 35.
7. Michael Beschloss and Strobe Talbott, *At the Highest Levels: The Inside Story of the End of the Cold War* (Boston: Little Brown, 1993), p. 469.
8. See James MacGregor Burns, *The Power to Lead* (New York: Simon & Schuster, 1984), p. 16.
9. Committee on Foreign Affairs, US House of Representatives, 102nd Congress, *Congress and Foreign Policy 1991* (Washington DC: US Government Printing Office, 1992), pp. 103–117.
10. 'Excerpts From Interview With Bush on First Term And Future', *New York Times*, 25 June 1992, p. A24.
11. *Congress and the Nation* . . ., op. cit. p. 657.
12. See ibid., pp. 643–658. It is the case however, that spending for the Head Start programme went up by 22 per cent a year during the Bush presidency and federal expenditures on elementary and secondary education increased by 11 per cent per year. Robert Pear 'Social Programs Grow, But Largely By Neglect', *New York Times*, 2 August 1992, p. 1.
13. *Congress and the Nation* . . ., op. cit., p. 611.
14. See Jonathan Rauch, 'The Regulatory President', *National Journal*, 30 November 1991, pp. 2902–2906 and Matthew P. Weinstock, 'Running On His Record', *Occupational Hazards*, October 1992, Vol. 54, pp. 75–79.
15. Pierre Kim, 'From Carter to Reagan to Bush', *Policy Review*, No. 63, Winter 1993, pp. 18–19.
16. Rauch, op. cit.
17. See Charles Kolb, *White House Daze: The Unmaking of Domestic Policy in the Bush Years* (New York: The Free Press, 1994), p. 73, and John Podhoretz, *Hell of a Ride: Backstage at the White House Follies 1989–1993* (New York: Simon & Schuster, 1993), p. 227.
18. See David O'Brien, 'The Reagan Judges: His Most Enduring Legacy', in Charles O. Jones, *The Reagan Legacy* (Chatham NJ: Chatham House, 1988).
19. Interview with C. Boyden Gray.
20. Neil A. Lewis, 'Selection of Conservative Judges Insures a Presidential Legacy', *New York Times*, 1 July 1992.
21. *Congress and the Nation* . . ., op. cit., p. 776.
22. Joan Biskupic, 'The Reagan-Bush Court Is Back To Keep The Nation

Guessing', *Washington Post National Weekly Edition*, 12–18 October 1992, p. 32.

23. Ruth Marcus, 'It's All in the Interpretation for Justices Souter and Thomas', *Washington Post National Weekly Edition*, 13–19 July 1992, p. 31.

24. Lewis, op. cit.

25. Jeremy Rabkin, 'At the President's Side: The Role of the White House Counsel in Constitutional Policy', *Law and Contemporary Problems*, Vol. 56, No. 4, Autumn 1993, pp. 63–98. John E. Yang and Sharon Lafraniere, 'George Bush's Eminence Grise', *Washington Post National Weekly Edition*, 2–8 December 1991, p. 14.

26. Charles Tiefer, *The Semi-Sovereign Presidency* (Boulder, Colo.: Westview Press, 1994), p. 34.

27. Ibid., p. 35.

28. Neil Lewis, 'Turning Loyalty and Service to Bush Into Power as Presidential Counsel', *New York Times*, 12 December 1990, p. B12.

29. Interview with Roger Porter, 23 November 1993.

30. Interview with C. Boyden Gray.

31. David Broder, 'Getting Government Moving Again', *Washington Post National Weekly Edition*, 7–13 September 1992, p. 4.

32. David Broder, 'Bush Showed He Can Fight, but Does He Know How to Lead', Washington Post National Weekly Edition, 20–26 March 1989, p. 23.

33. Robin Toner, 'For Bush and Congress, Some Spirited Battles But No Full Scale War', *New York Times*, 9 August 1989, p. B6.

34. Interview with Clayton Yeutter, 22 March 1994.

35. See p.158 above.

36. Samuel Kernell, *Going Public: New Strategies of Presidential Leadership* (Washington DC: CQ Press, 1986), Chapter 2 *passim*.

37. Ibid., p. 1.

38. Quoted in Andrew Rosenthal, 'Bush in a World Remade', *New York Times*, 25 June 1992, p. A1.

39. Robert Novak, 'How George Bush May Snatch Defeat From the Jaws of Victory', *Washington Post National Weekly Edition*, 24–30 August 1992, p. 23.

40. Interview with Andrew Card, 15 November 1993.

41. Interview with James Cicconi, 8th November 1993.

42. Interviews with C. Boyden Gray and Gregg Petersmeyer.

43. Terry Eastland, *Energy in the Executive* (New York: The Free Press, 1992), pp. 53–54.

44. Interview with John Keller, 18 November 1993.

45. Interview with Nicholas Calio, 19 Novemer 1993.

46. Interview with Richard Haass.

47. Bush, *Looking Forward*, op. cit., p. 204.

48. Ibid., p. 205.

49. Interview with Gregg Petersmeyer, 16 November 1993.

50. Interview with Ed Rogers, 3 November 1993.

51. Interview with Constance Horner.

52. Kolb, *White House Daze*, op. cit., p. 242.

53. Interview with Clayton Yeutter, op. cit.
54. See Chapter 1.
55. Theodore Lowi, *The Personal Presidency* (Ithaca, NY: Cornell University Press, 1985), p.59.
56. Interview with Charles Kolb, 29 March 1994.
57. For the advantages of simplicity in political rhetoric see John Lewis Gaddis, *The United States and the End of the Cold War* (Oxford: Oxford University Press, 1992), p. 131.
58. See Chapter 2.
59. Keith Schneider 'Bush on the Environment: A Record of Contradictions', *New York Times*, 4 July 1992, p. A1.
60. Weinstock, op. cit.
61. For some of the arguments in favour of balance in such matters see C. Boyden Gray and David B. Rivkin, 'A "No Regrets" Environmental Policy', *Foreign Policy*, No. 83, Summer 1991, pp. 47–65.
62. George Will, 'A Figure of Genuine Pathos', *Washington Post National Weekly Edition*, 3–9 August 1992, p. 29.
63. Michael Duffy and Dan Goodgame, *Marching in Place: The Status Quo Presidency of George Bush* (New York: Simon & Schuster, 1992), Chapter 1.
64. Interview with James Cicconi, op. cit.
65. Interview with David Demarest, 12 November 1993.
66. Gail Sheehy, *Character: America's Search for Leadership* (New York: Bantam Books, 1990), p. 198.
67. Interview with C. Boyden Gray. The articles in question were Ruth Marcus, 'What Does Bush Really Believe?; Civil Rights Record Illustrates Shifts', *The Washington Post*, 18 August 1992, p. A1, and Jefferson Morley, 'Bush and the Blacks: An Unknown Story', *New York Review of Books*, 16 January 1992, pp. 19–26.
68. Bush, Looking Forward, op. cit., p. 91.
69. Morley, op. cit.
70. Bush, *Looking Forward*, op. cit., pp. 92–93.
71. Marcus, 'What Does Bush Really Believe?', op. cit.
72. See Morley, op. cit., on Bush's advocacy of quotas in 1970. In fairness it should be said that Bush is by no means the only prominent public figure to change his mind about the desirability of quotas.
73. Kolb, op. cit., pp. 248–249.
74. *Congress and the Nation*, op. cit., p. 78.
75. Dan Goodgame, 'Trumpeting Victory in Retreat', *Time* (International Edition), 2 December 1991, pp. 68–69. William Raspberry, 'Bush's Missing Drummer', *Washington Post National Weekly Edition*, 2–8 December 1991, p. 29. Kolb, op. cit., p. 258. For the opposite view that the Democrats 'beat a total retreat on quotas' see C. Boyden Gray, 'Civil Rights: We Won, They Capitulated', *Washington Post National Weekly Edition*, 18–24 November 1991, p. 29.
76. Raspberry, op. cit., and Kolb, op. cit., p. 257.
77. Morley, op. cit.
78. Duffy and Goodgame, op. cit., p. 282.
79. Bush, *Looking Forward*, op. cit., p. 207.
80. Duffy and Goodgame, op. cit., p. 91.

81. Robert Shogan, *The Riddle of Power: Presidential Leadership From Truman to Bush* (New York: Dutton, 1991), p. 264.

82. Quoted in Martin Walker and Simon Tisdall, 'Bush Says Sorry For Tax U-turn', *The Guardian* (London), 4 March 1992, p. 1.

83. Michael Duffy, 'Is Bush Getting a Free Ride', *Time* (International Edition), 27 April 1992, pp. 43–45.

84. 'The Other Character Question', Editorial, *Washington Post National Weekly Edition*, 27 April–3 May 1992, p. 26.

85. Seymour Martin Lipset, 'The Significance of the 1992 Election', *PS: Political Science and Politics*, March 1993, pp 7–16.

86. See Joshua Muravchik 'Why the Democrats Finally Won', *Commentary*, Vol. 95, January 1993, pp. 17–22.

87. John Mueller, *Policy and Opinion in the Gulf War* (Chicago: University of Chicago Press, 1994), p 336.

88. Michael Nelson (ed.), *The Elections of 1992* (Washington DC: CQ Press, 1993), p. 81.

89. Ibid., p. 61.

90. Lipset, op. cit.

91. Interview with C. Boyden Gray, 10 November 1993.

92. See p. 34 above.

93. Mueller, op. cit., p. 185.

94. Dan Qyale, *Standing Firm* (New York: Harper Collins, 1994), p. 355.

95. Maureen Dowd, 'A Presidency Lost: Bush and Campaign Were Out of Touch', *International Herald Tribune*, 6 November 1992, p. 1.

96. Interview with Paul Bateman, 15 November 1993.

97. Interview with Edith Holiday, 17 November 1993.

98. Interview with Clayton Yeutter, op. cit.

99. Lipset, op. cit.

Bibliography

Dean Acheson, *Present at the Creation* (New York: W.W. Norton, 1987).

Chuck Alston, 'Rules of Political Navigation Altered by Bush Centrism, *Congressional Quarterly Weekly Report*, 6 May 1989, pp. 1017–1019.

Stephen Ambrose, *Nixon, Volume Two: The Triumph of a Politician 1962–1972* (New York: Simon & Schuster, 1989).

Martin Anderson, *Revolution* (New York: Harcourt Brace Jovanovich, 1988).

Michael Barone and Grant Ujifusa, *The Almanac of American Politics 1994* (Washington DC: National Journal, 1994).

Michael Beschloss and Strobe Talbott, *At the Highest Levels: The Inside Story of the End of Cold War* (Boston: Little Brown, 1993).

Christopher Bosso, 'Congressional and Presidential Scholars: Some Basic Traits', *PS: Political Science and Politics*, December 1989, pp. 839–848.

James MacGregor Burns, *The Power to Lead* (New York: Simon & Schuster, 1984).

James MacGregor Burns, *Roosevelt: The Lion and the Fox* (New York: Harcourt Brace and World, 1957).

George Bush (with Victor Gold), *Looking Forward* (London: The Bodley Head, 1988).

Joseph Califano, *A Presidential Nation* (New York: W.W. Norton, 1975).

Colin Campbell and Bert Rockman (eds), *The Bush Presidency: First Appraisals* (Chatham, New Jersey: Chatham House, 1991).

Margaret Coit (ed.), *John C. Calhoun* (New Jersey: Prentice Hall, 1970).

Committee on Foreign Affairs, US House of Representatives, 101st Congress, *Congress and Foreign Policy, 1989* (Washington DC: US Government Printing Office, 1990).

Committee on Foreign Affairs, US House of Representatives, 102nd Congress, *Congress and Foreign Policy, 1991* (Washington DC: US Government Printing Office, 1992).

Congress and the Nation, Vol. VIII, 1989–1992 (Washington DC: Congressional Quarterly Press, 1993).

Congressional Quarterly Almanac, 1990 (Washington DC: Congressional Quarterly Press, 1991).

Congressional Quarterly Almanac, 1992 (Washington DC: Congressional Quarterly Press, 1993).

Richard Ben Cramer, *What It Takes* (New York: Random House, 1992).

Roger Davidson (ed.), *The Postreform Congress* (New York: St. Martin's Press, 1992).

Roger Davidson and Walter Oleszek, *Congress and Its Members*, 4th edn (Washington DC: Congressional Quarterly Press 1994).

Terry Diebel, 'Bush's Foreign Policy: Mastery and Inaction', *Foreign Policy*, No. 84, Fall 1991, pp. 3–23

'The Disabilities Act', *CQ Researcher*, 27 December 1991, Vol. I, No. 32, pp. 993–1016.

Ann Reilly Dowd, 'How Bush Manages the Presidency', *Fortune*, 27 August 1990, pp. 38–43.

Theodore Draper, 'The Gulf War Reconsidered', *New York Review of Books*, 16 January 1992, pp. 46–53.

Theodore Draper, 'The True History of the Gulf War', *New York Review of Books*, 30 January 1992, pp. 38–45.

Elizabeth Drew, 'Letter from Washington', *New Yorker*, 4 February 1991, pp. 82–90.

Michael Duffy and Dan Goodgame, *Marching in Place: The Status Quo Presidency of George Bush* (New York: Simon & Schuster, 1992).

Terry Eastland, *Energy in the Executive: The Case for the Strong Presidency* (New York: The Free Press, 1992).

George Edwards, 'Measuring Presidential Success in Congress: Alternative Approaches', *Journal of Politics*, Vol. 47, 1985, pp. 667–685.

George Edwards, John Kessel and Bert Rockman (eds) *Researching the Presidency* (Pittsburgh: University of Pittsburgh Press, 1993).

John Ehrlichman, *Witness to Power* (New York: Pocket Books, 1982).

Ronald Elving, 'House Service Set Course for New President', *Congressional Quarterly Weekly Report*, 14 January 1989, pp. 55–57.

Max Farrand (ed.), *The Records of the Federal Convention of 1787* (New Haven, Conn.: Yale University Press, 1937), 3 vols.

Louis Fisher, *Constitutional Conflicts Between Congress and the President* (Princeton: Princeton University Press, 1985).

Louis Fisher, 'The Power of Commander in Chief', in Marcia Whicker, James Pfiffner and Raymond Moore, *The Presidency and the Gulf War* (Westport, Conn.: Praeger, 1993).

John Lewis Gaddis, *The United States and the End of the Cold War* (Oxford: Oxford University Press, 1992).

Alexander George, 'The Case for Multiple Advocacy in Making Foreign Policy', *American Political Science Review*, Vol. 66, September 1972, pp. 751–785.

Michael Glennon, 'The Gulf War and the Constitution', *Foreign Affairs*, Spring 1991, Vol. 70, pp. 84–101.

Peter Goldman and Tom Mathews, *The Quest for the Presidency: The 1988 Campaign* (New York: Simon & Schuster, 1989).

Stephen Graubard, *Mr Bush's War: Adventures in the Politics of Illusion* (New York: I.B. Tauris, 1992).

C. Boyden Gray, 'The Coordinating Role of the Vice Presidency', in James Pfiffner and Gordon Hoxie (eds) *The Presidency in Transition* (New York: Center for the Study of the Presidency, 1989).

C. Boyden Gray and David B. Rivkin, 'A "No Regrets" Environmental Policy', *Foreign Policy*, No. 83, Summer 1991, pp. 47–65.

Fitzhugh Green, *George Bush: An Intimate Portrait* (New York: Hippocrene Books, 1991).

Fred Greenstein, *The Hidden-Hand Presidency: Eisenhower as Leader* (New York: Basic Books, 1982).

Fred Greenstein, 'Ronald Reagan's Presidential Leadership', in Ellis Sandoz and Cecil Crabb (eds), *Electon 84: Landslide Without a Mandate?* (New York: New American Library, 1985).

The Gulf Crisis: A Chronology, July 1990–July 1991, USIS, US Embassy, London, 1991.

George Hager, 'Parties Angle For Advantage As White House Falters', *Congressional Quarterly Weekly Report*, 13 October 1990, pp. 3389–3398.

H.R. Haldeman, *The Haldeman Diaries* (New York: G.P. Putnam's Sons, 1994).

John Hart, *The Presidential Branch* (New York: Pergamon Press, 1987).

Stephen Hess, *Organizing the Presidency*, 2nd edn (Washington DC: The Brookings Institution, 1988).

Dilys Hill and Phil Williams (eds), *The Bush Presidency: Triumphs and Adversities* (London: Macmillan, 1994).

Roger Hilsman, *George Bush Versus Saddam Hussein* (Novato, Calif: Presidio Press, 1992).

Dilop Hiro, *Desert Shield to Desert Storm: The Second Gulf War* (London: HarperCollins, 1992).

Kim Holmes, 'In Search of a Strategy', *Policy Review*, Winter 1991, pp. 72–75.

Janet Hook, 'Bush Inspired Frail Support For First-Year President', *Congressional Quarterly Weekly Report*, 30 December 1989, pp. 3540–3545.

Janet Hook, 'Anatomy of a Budget Showdown: The Limits of Leaders' Clout', *Congressional Quarterly Weekly Report*, 6 October 1990, pp. 3189–3191.

Janet Hook, 'Budget Ordeal Poses Question: Why Can't Congress Be Led?', *Congressional Quarterly Weekly Report*, 27 July 1991, pp. 2041–2045.

Emmet Hughes, *The Ordeal of Power* (London: Macmillan, 1963).

Alex Roberto Hybel (foreword by James Rosenau), *Power Over Rationality: The Bush Administration and the Gulf Crisis* (Albany: State University of New York Press, 1993).

Irving Janis, *Victims of Groupthink* (Boston: Houghton Mifflin, 1972).

Charles O. Jones, *The Presidency In A Separated System* (Washington DC: The Brookings Institution, 1994).

Barbara Kellerman, *The Political Presidency: Practice of Leadership From Kennedy Through Reagan* (New York: Oxford University Press, 1984).

Samuel Kernell, *Going Public: Strategies of Presidential Leadership*, (Washington DC: Congressional Quarterly Press, 1986).

Pierre Kim, 'From Carter to Reagan to Bush', *Policy Review*, No. 63, Winter 1993, pp. 18–19.

Anthony King, 'A Mile and a Half Is a Long Way', in Anthony King, *Both Ends of the Avenue: The Presidency, the Executive Branch and Congress in the 1980s* (Washington DC: American Enterprise Institute, 1983).

Charles Kolb, *White House Daze: The Unmaking of Domestic Policy in the Bush Years* (New York, The Free Press, 1994).

William Leuchtenburg, *In the Shadow of FDR* (Ithaca, NY: Cornell University Press, 1993).

Paul Light, *The President's Agenda* (Baltimore: Johns Hopkins University Press, 1982).

Seymour Martin Lipset, 'The Significance of the 1992 Election', *PS: Political Science and Politics*, March 1993, pp. 7–16.

Theodore Lowi, *The Personal Presidency* (Ithaca, NY: Cornell University Press, 1985).

David McKay, 'Presidential Strategy and the Veto Power: A Reappraisal', *Political Science Quarterly*, Vol. 104, no. 3, Fall 1989, pp. 447–461.

Christopher Madison, "No Sharp Elbows', *National Journal*, 26 May 1990, pp. 1277–1281.

Michael Mandelbaum, 'The Bush Foreign Policy', *Foreign Affairs*, Spring 1991, Vol. 70, pp. 5–22.

Thomas Mann and Norman Ornstein (eds), *The New Congress* (Washington DC: American Enterprise Institute, 1981).

Donald Matthews, *US Senators and their World* (New York: Vintage Books, 1960).

David Mayhew, *Divided We Govern: Party Control, Lawmaking and Investigations, 1946–1990* (New Haven, Conn.: Yale University Press, 1991).

Edwin Meese, *With Reagan: The Inside Story* (Washington DC: Regnery Gateway, 1992).

David Mervin, *Ronald Reagan and the American Presidency* (London and New York, Longman, 1990).

David Mervin, 'Ronald Reagan's Place in History', *Journal of American Studies*, Vol. 23, No. 2, August 1989, pp. 269–286.

David Mervin, 'The Bully Pulpit', *Presidential Studies Quarterly*, Vol. XXV, 1995, pp. 19–23.

Jefferson Morley, 'Bush and the Blacks: An Unknown Story', *New York Review of Books*, 16 January 1992, pp. 1–26.

John Mueller, *Policy and Opinion in the Gulf War* (Chicago: University of Chicago Press, 1994).

William Kerr Muir, *The Bully Pulpit: The Presidential Leadership of Ronald Reagan* (San Francisco: Institute for Contemporary Studies, 1992).

Kerry Mullins and Aaron Wildavsky, 'The Procedural Presidency of George Bush', *Political Science Quarterly*, Vol. 107, No. 1, 1992, pp. 31–62.

Joshua Muravchik, 'Why the Democrats Finally Won', *Commentary*, Vol. 95, January 1993, pp. 17–22.

Robert Murray and Tim Blessing, *Greatness in the White House: Rating the Presidents* (University Park, Penn.: The Pennsylvania State University Press, 1994).

Michael Nelson (ed.), *The Elections of 1992* (Washington DC: CQ Press, 1993).

John Newhouse, 'Profiles: The Tactician', *New Yorker*, 7 May 1990, pp. 50–82.

Richard Neustadt, *Presidential Power and the Modern Presidents* (New York: The Free Press, 1990).

Richard Nixon, *In the Arena* (New York: Pocket Books, 1990).

Peggy Noonan, *What I Saw at the Revolution: A Political Life in the Reagan Era* (New York: Ivy Books, 1990).

Michael Oakeshott, *Rationalism in Politics* (London: Methuen, 1962).

Don Oberdorfer, *The Turn: From the Cold War to a New Era* (New York: Simon & Schuster, 1992).

David O'Brien, 'The Reagan Judges: His Most Ensuring Legacy', in Charles O. Jones, *The Reagan Legacy* (Chatham, NJ: Chatham House, 1988).

Bradley Patterson, *The Ring of Power: The White House Staff and its Expanding Role in Government* (New York: Basic Books, 1988).

Stephen Percy, *Disability, Civil Rights and Public Policy* (Tuscaloosa: University of Alabama Press, 1992).

James Pfiffner, 'Establishing the Bush Presidency', *Public Administration Review*, January/February 1990, pp. 64–72.

James Pfiffner, *The Managerial Presidency* (Pacific Grove, Calif. Brooks/Cole, 1991).

James Pfiffner, 'The President and the Postreform Congress', in Roger Davidson (ed.), *The Postreform Congress* (New York: St. Martin's Press, 1992).

James Pfiffner 'The President's Chief of Staff: Lessons Learned', *Presidential Studies Quarterly*, Vol. XXIII, No. 1, 1993, pp. 77–102.

James Pfiffner, 'Presidential Policy-Making and the Gulf War', in Marcia Lynn Whicker, James Pfiffner and Raymond Moore, *The Presidency and the Persian Gulf War* (Westport, Conn.: Praeger, 1993).

James Pfiffner, *The Modern Presidency* (New York: St. Martin's Press, 1994).

James Pfiffner and Gordon Hoxie (eds), *The Presidency in Transition* (New York: Center for the Study of the Presidency, 1989).

Joseph Pika, 'A New Vice Presidency' in Michael Nelson (ed.), *The Presidency and the Political System*, 2nd edn (Washington DC: The Congressional Quarterly Press, 1988).

John Podhoretz, *Hell of a Ride: Backstage at the White House Follies 1989–1993* (New York: Simon & Schuster, 1993).

The Points of Light Movement: The President's Report to the Nation, January 1993, in the author's possession.

'Politics of the Professoriate', *The American Enterprise*, Vol. 2, No. 5, July/August 1991, pp. 86–87.

Roger Porter, *Presidential Decision Making: The Economic Policy Board* (New York: Cambridge University Press, 1980).

Dan Quayle, *Standing Firm* (New York: Harper Collins, 1994).

Jeremy Rabkin, 'At the President's Side: The Role of the White House Counsel in Constitutional Policy', *Law and Contemporary Problems*, Vol. 56, No. 4, Autumn 1993, pp. 63–98.

Lyn Ragsdale, *Presidential Politics* (Boston: Houghton Mifflin, 1993).

Jonathan Rauch, 'The Regulatory President', *National Journal*, 30 November 1991, pp. 2902–2906.

Bert Rockman, *The Leadership Question: The Presidency and the American System* (New York: Praeger, 1984).

Bert Rockman, 'The Leadership Style of George Bush', in Colin Campbell and Bert Rockman, *The Bush Presidency: First Appraisals* (Chatham, NJ: Chatham House, 1991).

Walter Roettger and Hugh Winebrenner, 'Politics and Political Scientists', *Public Opinion*, September/October 1986, pp. 41–44.

Richard Rose, *The Postmodern President*, 2nd edn (Chatman, NJ: Chatham House, 1991).

Richard Rose, 'Evaluating Presidents', in George Edwards, John Kessel and Bert Rockman (eds), *Researching the Presidency* (Pittsburgh: University of Pittsburgh Press, 1993).

Clinton Rossiter (ed.), *The Federalist Papers* (New York: New American Library, 1961).

David Roth, *Sacred Honor: Colin Powell* (New York: Harper Collins, 1993).

Arthur Schlesinger Jnr, *The Cycles of American History* (London: André Deutsch, 1986).

Gail Sheehy, *Character: American's Search for Leadership*, revised edition (New York: Bantam Books, 1990).

Robert Shogan, *The Riddle of Power: Presidential Leadership From Truman to Bush* (New York: Dutton, 1991).

Steven Shull, *A Kinder Gentler Racism? The Reagan-Bush Civil Rights Legacy*, (New York: M.E. Sharpe, 1993).

Barbara Sinclair, 'Governing Unheroically (and Sometimes Unappetizingly): Bush and the 101st Congress', in Colin Campbell and Bert Rockman (eds), *The Bush Presidency: First Appraisals* (Chatham, NJ: Chatham House, 1991).

Hedrick Smith, *The Power Game* (New York: Random House, 1988).

Burt Solomon, 'Bush's Lack of Ambitious Policies . . . Make His Plans Seem Thin Gruel', *National Journal*, 6 May 1989, No. 18. p. 1102.

Burt Solomon, 'George Bush's Congressional Crew Has an Oar or Two Out of Sync', *National Journal*, 24 June 1989, pp. 1650–1651.

Burt Solomon, 'When the Cabinet Convenes . . . It's Gathering of Presidential Pals', *National Journal*, 1 July 1989, No. 26, pp. 1704–1705.

Theodore Sorensen, *Decision-Making in the White House* (New York: Columbia University Press, 1963).

Robert Spitzer, *The Presidential Veto: Touchstone of the American Presidency* (Albany: State University of New York Press, 1988).

Robert Spitzer, 'Presidential Prerogative Power: The Case of the Bush Administration and Legislative Power', *PS: Political Science and Politics*, March 1991, pp. 38–42.

Rochelle Stanfield, 'Cutting Deals', *National Journal*, 8 April 1989, p. 889.

David Stockman, *The Triumph of Politics: Why the Reagan Revolution Failed* (New York: Harper & Row, 1986).

Kristin Clark Taylor, *The First to Speak* (New York: Doubleday, 1993).

Margaret Thatcher, *The Downing Street Years* (London: HarperCollins, 1993).

Kenneth Thompson, *Presidential Transitions: The Reagan to Bush Experience* (Lanham, Md.: University Press of America, 1994).

Charles Tiefer, *The Semi-sovereign Presidency: The Bush Administration's Strategy For Governing Without Congress* (Boulder, Colo.: Westview Press, 1994).

Tower Commission Report (New York: Bantam Books, 1987).

The Washington Version. Television documentary on the Gulf crisis made by the American Enterprise Institute and the BBC, 1991.

Richard Watson, *Presidential Vetoes and Public Policy* (Lawrence: University of Kansas Press, 1993).

Matthew P. Weinstock, 'Running On His Record', *Occupational Hazards*, October 1992, Vol. 54, pp. 75–79.

Marcia Lynn Whicker, James Pfiffner and Raymond Moore, *The Presidency and the Persian Gulf War* (Westport, Conn.: Praeger, 1993).

Jules Witcover, *Crapshoot: Rolling the Dice on the Vice Presidency* (New York: Crown, 1992).

Bob Woodward, *The Commanders* (New York: Simon & Schuster, 1991).

Index